The Study of
Violent Crime

Its Correlates and Concerns

The Study of
Violent Crime

Its Correlates and Concerns

Scott Mire and Cliff Roberson

CRC Press
Taylor & Francis Group
Boca Raton   London   New York

CRC Press is an imprint of the
Taylor & Francis Group, an **informa** business

CRC Press
Taylor & Francis Group
6000 Broken Sound Parkway NW, Suite 300
Boca Raton, FL 33487-2742

© 2011 by Taylor and Francis Group, LLC
CRC Press is an imprint of Taylor & Francis Group, an Informa business

No claim to original U.S. Government works

Printed in the United States of America on acid-free paper
10 9 8 7 6 5 4 3 2 1

International Standard Book Number: 978-1-4398-0747-7 (Hardback)

Library of Congress Cataloging-in-Publication Data

Mire, Scott.
   The study of violent crime : its correlates and concerns / Scott Mire and Cliff
Roberson.
      p. cm.
   Includes bibliographical references and index.
   ISBN 978-1-4398-0747-7
   1. Violent crimes--United States. 2. Violence--United States. 3. Crime--United States.
I. Roberson, Cliff, 1937- II. Title.

HV6791.M57 2011
364.150973--dc22   2010024390

Visit the Taylor & Francis Web site at
http://www.taylorandfrancis.com

and the CRC Press Web site at
http://www.crcpress.com

Contents

Preface: Is Violence as American as Apple Pie?

As the plan to write this book began to develop, a few central points became immediately apparent. First, the concept of violence represents a vast collection of behaviors and cognitions within a theoretical domain whose parameters are extremely ambiguous. Of course, there are distinctions between the types of violence and their nature, which can be clearly articulated, but the causal and correlational variables that contribute to the acts of violence are legion. As a result, it was quickly determined that an attempt to cover the entire domain of violence within a single book is futile and may even result in further confounding the already misunderstood concept of violence and its attendant characteristics that have such a profound impact on ideology and beliefs.

The latent theme of this book is to provide a current analysis of violence and violent crime perpetrated by adult offenders within the United States of America. The concept of *latent* is strategic and purposeful. The reason is that to understand adult violence in the United States one must explore historical trends in violence, including trends in other countries as a result of the United States as such a young populace. In addition, it is important to explore developmental processes, including some important facts related to juvenile violence, to understand adult violence.

Authors

Cliff Roberson LLM, Ph.D., is editor-in-chief of *Professional Issues in Criminal Justice Journal* and is academic chair for the Master of Science in Criminal Justice Program, Kaplan University. He is also an emeritus professor of criminal justice at Washburn University, Topeka, Kansas.

In 2009, a research study conducted by a group of professors from Sam Houston State University determined that Roberson was the leading criminal justice author in the United States based on his publications and their relevance to the profession [See *Southwest Journal of Criminal Justice*, Vol. 6, issue 1, 2009]. He has authored or coauthored more than 50 books and texts on legal subjects. His books include:

Cliff Roberson, Harvey Wallace, and Gilbert Stuckey (2009) *Procedures in the Justice* System, 9ᵗʰ ed. (Upper Saddle River, NJ: Pearson).

Cliff Roberson (2009) *Constitutional Law and Criminal Justice* (Boca Raton, FL: Taylor & Francis).

Harvey Wallace and Cliff Roberson (2008) *Principles of Criminal Law* 4ᵗʰ ed. (Boston: Allyn & Bacon).

Michael Birzer and Cliff Roberson (2008) *Police Field Operations: Theory meets Practice* (Boston: Pearson)

Cliff Roberson and Dilip Das (2008) *An Introduction to Comparative Legal Models of Criminal Justice* (Boca Raton, FL: Taylor & Francis)

Cliff Roberson and Scott Mire (2010, at printer) *Ethics and Criminal Justice* (Boca Raton, FL: Taylor & Francis)

Harvey Wallace and Cliff Roberson (in publication) *Family Violence* (Boston: Pearson).

His previous academic experiences include associate vice president for academic affairs at Arkansas Tech University; dean of arts and sciences, University of Houston, Victoria; director of programs for the National College of District Attorneys; professor of criminology and director of Justice Center, California State University, Fresno; and assistant professor of criminal justice, St. Edwards University.

Roberson's nonacademic experience includes U.S. Marine Corps service as an infantry officer, trial and defense counsel and military judge as a marine judge advocate; and serving as a director of the military law branch, U.S. Marine Corps. Other legal employment experiences include trial supervisor, Office of State Counsel for Offenders, Texas Board of Criminal Justice and judge pro-tem in the California courts. Roberson is admitted to practice before the U.S. Supreme Court, U.S. Court of Military Appeals, U.S. Tax Court, Federal Courts in California and Texas, Supreme Court of Texas and Supreme Court of California.

He earned his Ph.D. in human behavior at U.S. International University, his L.L.M. in criminal law, criminology, and psychiatry at George Washington University, his J.D. at American University, his B.A. in political science at the University of Missouri, and did one year of postgraduate study at the University of Virginia School of Law.

Dr. Scott Mire is currently an assistant professor of criminal justice at the University of Louisiana at Lafayette. He has held this position since August of 2005.

Before that, Dr. Mire spent several years in law enforcement. First, he served as a police officer and narcotics agent with the Lafayette, Louisiana Police Department.

Following his tenure with the Lafayette Police Department, Dr. Mire worked for the United States Border Patrol. He was assigned to the Laredo sector and was stationed in Laredo, Texas. As a Border Patrol agent, Dr. Mire carried out all relevant duties including tracking and apprehending illegal aliens as well as conducting in-depth investigations of alien smuggling. In that role, he was also responsible for conducting complex narcotics investigations that typically involved law enforcement officials of various countries.

Then Dr. Mire went to work for the Texas Police Corps as a training coordinator while pursuing a Ph.D. in criminal justice at Sam Houston State University. As a training coordinator he was responsible for all curriculum development in addition to providing training in all aspects of law enforcement.

More recently, Dr. Mire has authored or coauthored several journal articles and book chapters including two text books in the areas of correctional counseling and ethics in criminal justice.

Chapter 1

Introduction to the Study of Violence

Introduction

> Almost universally, historians agree that the United States has always been an extremely violent nation and that violence usually redounds to the ultimate advantage of those who control the levers of power.
>
> **Buenker, 1999, p. 314**

> We still kill each other at roughly three times the rate of most Western nations.
>
> **Brown, 1969, p. 243**

This chapter begins the examination of the concept of violence. As noted in the Preface, violence is as American as apple pie. An informal survey of local young people in urban neighborhoods found that nearly 80 percent have had family or friends wounded or killed by gun violence—a number that the report called "staggering." When asked for two ways to stop street violence, the largest proportion (18 percent) of the respondents to the survey cited banning or controlling guns. After that came more community activities, no solution, more police, staying off the streets, and jobs/education. Those suggestions (Kalson, 2010) are examined in the chapters of this book.

Chapter 1 starts the inquiry about this concept, and the following chapters explore all aspects of violence.

It is necessary to point out that much of what is contained in this chapter and the others is directly or indirectly supported by the work of the World Health Organization on violence. An immediate question may be why so much reliance would be placed on the work of an organization dedicated to improving conditions of the world and not just the United States. There are two primary reasons:

1. The variables associated with violence do not change or reconstrue themselves based on geographical boundaries. In other words, the underlying dynamics of violence are largely synonymous and are not dependent on a particular location.
2. The World Health Organization uses a public health approach to understanding and responding to violence. It is believed that this model is superior to any singular approach that relies solely on the criminal justice system to adequately deter violent actions.

Before getting into the specific objectives of this chapter, there is an important question that needs to be addressed: Why is it important to study violence and violent crime? After all, one would be hard-pressed to identify any period of time when violence was not present in some form or fashion (Krug, Dahlberg, Mercy, Zwi, and Lozano, 2002; Weiner, Zahn, and Sagi, 1990). The answer is really a basic one: We must continue to strive toward better understanding this phenomenon because the results of violent encounters are often damaging and severely destructive. Long after the physical wounds have healed, psychological and emotional damage is likely to persist, especially if appropriate treatment is not provided. In essence, violence is a phenomenon that is capable of significantly altering one's quality of life. And, this reduction of quality of life and the ability to experience happiness, joy, and pleasure do not occur in a vacuum. In other words, when one person is negatively affected by the consequences of violence, so are the person's family, community, and society in general. Having to constantly work to mitigate negative emotion and fear as a result of a violent experience greatly reduces one's ability to engage in meaningful activities, such as employment and interpersonal relationships.

Arguably, the most salient reason to study violence and violent crime is because both are preventable. It is possible to greatly reduce the amount of violence we currently experience in modern society. Society may not be ready to embrace some of the changes that would be necessary to prevent violence, but this should not be confused with the basic fact that violence can be prevented. First, however, we as a society would need to determine the extent to which we are willing to sacrifice. Consider the myriad cancerous diseases millions of people experience and die from each year. Furthermore, compare our current ability to successfully diagnose and treat cancer to that of 10, 20, or even 30 years ago. Today, we are much better equipped to save many of the lives that would certainly have been lost before because we as a society "put our money where our mouths are." We watched as many of our loved ones suffered excruciating pain and ultimately death, and we demanded that our medical profession become more effective and efficient in methods of treatment and intervention. Most important, however, we collectively proclaimed, "We don't care what it costs."

As is often the case in social sciences, the more research one does, the more questions that are generated. We began with a basic question: Why study violence? However, in exploring this question two additional questions were generated:

1. To what extent are we, as a society, willing to commit to preventing violence?
2. Who is most capable of engaging in interventions most able to prevent violence?

The answer to the first question is fairly straightforward. The extent to which we as a society are committed to preventing violence is portrayed in the extent to which we operationalize assets aimed at its reduction.

The answer to the second question is more involved. To begin, any serious attempt to reduce or prevent violence must be multimodal. As a society, we cannot afford simply to relegate the issue of violence to law enforcement and then sit back and relax as though the problem will now be addressed and solved. We have taken this approach long enough with little in the way of discernible results that would suggest this strategy has had any significant impact on the rates of violence.

If we, as a society, decide that we are serious about reducing violence, then we must take a more holistic approach that draws from many different disciplines. This is precisely why, as mentioned, strong arguments can be made for treating the concept of violence as a public health issue. First, it is a public health issue, and second, a public health approach draws on many disciplines to provide a framework from which to address the issue. As an example, the World Health Organization adopted the following resolution aimed at preventing violence:

A public health approach to violence is interdisciplinary and based on the principles of scientific investigation (Mercy, 1993). Disciplines commonly considered in a public health approach include psychology, sociology, medicine, epidemiology, criminology, and education (Krug et al., 2002).

How, then, is a public health approach to violence operationalized when particular attention is paid to ensuring full compliance with the rigors of science? Theoretically, this is done through the following four postulates:

BOX 1.1 PREVENTING VIOLENCE: A PUBLIC HEALTH PRIORITY (RESOLUTION WHA49.25)

The Forty-ninth World Health Assembly,

Noting with great concern the dramatic worldwide increase in the incidence of intentional injuries affecting people of all ages and both sexes, but especially women and children;

Endorsing the call made in the Declaration of the World Summit for Social Development for the introduction and implementation of specific policies and programmes of public health and social services to prevent violence in society and mitigate its effect;

Endorsing the recommendations made at the International Conference on Population and Development (Cairo, 1994) and the Fourth World Conference on Women (Beijing, 1995) urgently to tackle the problem of violence against women and girls and to understand its health consequences;

Recalling the United Nations Declaration on the elimination of violence against women;

Noting the call made by the scientific community in the Melbourne Declaration adopted at the Third International Conference on Injury Prevention and Control (1996) for increased international cooperation in ensuring the safety of the citizens of the world;

Recognizing the serious immediate and future long-term implications for health and psychological and social development that violence represents for individuals, families, communities and countries;

Recognizing the growing consequences of violence for health care services everywhere and its detrimental effect on scarce health care resources for countries and communities;

Recognizing that health workers are frequently among the first to see victims of violence, having a unique technical capacity and benefiting from a special position in the community to help those at risk;

Recognizing that WHO, the major agency for coordination of international work in public health, has the responsibility to provide leadership and guidance to Member States in developing public health programmes to prevent self-inflicted violence and violence against others;

1. DECLARES that violence is a leading worldwide public health problem;
2. URGES Member States to assess the problem of violence on their own territory and to communicate to WHO their information about this problem and their approach to it;
3. REQUESTS the Director-General, within available resources, to initiate public health activities to address the problem of violence that will:
   (1) characterize different types of violence, define their magnitude and assess the causes and the public health consequences of violence using also a "gender perspective" in the analysis;
   (2) assess the types and effectiveness of measures and programmes to prevent violence and mitigate its effects, with particular attention to community-based initiatives;
   (3) promote activities to tackle this problem at both international and country level including steps to:
      (a) improve the recognition, reporting and management of the consequences of violence;
      (b) promote greater intersectoral involvement in the prevention and management of violence;
      (c) promote research on violence as a priority for public health research;
      (d) prepare and disseminate recommendations for violence prevention programmes in nations, States and communities all over the world;
   (4) ensure the coordinated and active participation of appropriate WHO technical programmes;
   (5) strengthen the Organization's collaboration with governments, local authorities and other organizations of the United Nations system in the planning, implementation and monitoring of programmes of violence prevention and mitigation;
4. FURTHER REQUESTS the Director-General to present a report to the ninety-ninth session of the Executive Board describing the progress made so far and to present a plan of action for progress towards a science-based public health approach to violence prevention.

Source: Adapted from World Health Organization, *Resolution WHA 49.25.* Geneva, Switzerland: World Health Organization, 1996.

1. Uncovering as much basic knowledge as possible about all the aspects of violence through systematically collecting data on the magnitude, scope, characteristics, and consequences of violence at local, national, and international levels
2. Investigating why violence occurs, that is, conducting research to determine
   a. The causes and correlates of violence
   b. The factors that increase or decrease the risk for violence
   c. The factors that might be modifiable through interventions
3. Exploring ways to prevent violence, using the information from the above, by designing, implementing, monitoring, and evaluating interventions
4. Implementing, in a range of settings, interventions that appear promising, widely disseminating information and determining the cost-effectiveness of programmes. (Krug et al., 2002, p. 4)

How have these theoretical postulates been carried out in real-world settings to address problems of violence? One of the best examples is taken from DESEPAZ in Colombia.

Defining Violence

Now that we have a basic framework from which to explore violence, it is necessary to articulate the general parameters that we have chosen to attach to the concept of violence. Admittedly, this was among the most difficult tasks in writing this book. In research, defining a concept is analogous to a police detective creating an affidavit for a search warrant. It must be precise yet general, inclusive but not overly broad, and able to tolerate constant variability among the diverse, culturally relevant perceptions of violence. The basic underpinnings of the definition of violence chosen for this book were again based on the work of the World Health Organization. As noted, although the emphasis of this book is on interpersonal violence, we do retain the concepts of violence against oneself and a group or community largely because it would be difficult to cover the issue of violence without some mention of both. The inclusion of these aspects of violence also becomes more apparent when we discuss the specific theoretical underpinnings of violence. We have added the phrase "and legally proscribed" to the end of our definition to ensure the definition covers not only violence but also violent crime.

> Violence is the intentional use of physical force or power, threatened or actual, against oneself, another person, or against a group or community that either results in or has a high likelihood of resulting in

BOX 1.2 THE PUBLIC HEALTH APPROACH IN ACTION: DESEPAZ IN COLOMBIA

In 1992, the mayor of Cali, Colombia—himself a public health specialist—helped the city set up a comprehensive program aimed at reducing the high levels of crime there. Rates of homicide in Cali, a city of some 2 million inhabitants, had risen from 23 per 100,000 population in 1983 to 85 per 100,000 in 1991. The program that ensued was called DESEPAZ, an acronym for Desarrollo, Seguridad, Paz (development, security, peace).

In the initial stages of the city's program, epidemiological studies were conducted to identify the principal risk factors for violence and shape the priorities for action. Special budgets were approved to strengthen the police, the judicial system, and the local human rights office.

DESEPAZ undertook education on civil rights matters for both the police and the public at large, including television advertising at peak viewing times highlighting the importance of tolerance for others and self-control. A range of cultural and educational projects was organized for schools and families in collaboration with local nongovernmental organizations, to promote discussions on violence and help resolve interpersonal conflicts. There were restrictions on the sale of alcohol, and the carrying of handguns was banned on weekends and special occasions.

In the course of the program, special projects were set up to provide economic opportunities and safe recreational facilities for young people. The mayor and his administrative team discussed their proposals to tackle crime with local people, and the city administration ensured the continuing participation and commitment of the community.

With the program in operation, the homicide rate in Cali declined from an all-time high of 124 per 100,000 to 86 per 100,000 between 1994 and 1997, a reduction of 30 percent. In absolute numbers, there were approximately 600 fewer homicides between 1994 and 1997 compared with the previous three-year period, which allowed the law enforcement authorities to devote scarce resources to combating more organized forms of crime. Furthermore, public opinion in Cali shifted strongly from a passive attitude toward dealing with violence to a vociferous demand for more prevention activities.

Source: Krug, E. G., Dahlberg, L. L., Mercy, J. A., Zwi, A. B., and Lozano, R., eds. *World report on violence and health*. Geneva, Switzerland: World Health Organization, 2002.

injury, death, psychological harm, maldevelopment, or deprivation and is legally proscribed by law.

Most definitions of violence and violent crime found throughout the literature are similar to this definition and vary only to the extent of the specific focus (e.g., see Bartolome-Gutierrez and Rechea-Alberola Young, 2006; Liska and Bellair, 1995; Mersky and Reynolds, 2007; Miller, 1966; Moser, 2004; Police Executive Research Forum, 2006; Rainone, Schmeidler, Frank, and Smith, 2006; Roy, 2000).

Types of Violence

Interpersonal Violence

In addition to defining the concept of violence, it is important to understand the various typologies of violence. This is especially critical when trying to develop and plan intervention. Different types of violence not only are based on different factors but also each of these factors requires specific and strategic methods aimed at reducing their influence and ability to spur violence (Moser, 2004).

The first type of violence, and that with which this book is most concerned, is *interpersonal violence.* Interpersonal violence can be described as "behavior by persons against persons that intentionally threatens, attempts, or actually inflicts physical harm" (Reiss and Roth, 1993, p. 35). An important addendum to this definition, however, would be psychological and emotional harm as opposed to just physical harm. For many people, especially those reared in homes filled with psychological and emotional dysfunction, psychological violence can be extremely debilitating. This type of violence not only occurs in the home but also is common in the workplace. Some of the most damaging psychological and emotional violence occurs as a result of a significant difference in authority and power between two individuals in the workplace (usually involving a supervisor and his or her subordinates), where the person possessing more authority and power places an inappropriate expectation on a subordinate with a direct or indirect demand that it be carried out and backed up with an overt or covert threat. This is considered a form of violence because the damage can be so severe. The subordinate's very survival is at stake (whether this is a real fear or not, it is certainly the perception of most subordinates expected to carry out inappropriate tasks usually designed and meant to forward only the interest of the supervisor.). Within this subtype of interpersonal violence, it is important to highlight the factor of taking some inappropriate action that is ultimately designed to forward someone else's interest or keep them from being exposed as either mediocre or deficient. This is the factor that often makes this type of violence so heinous. Imagine: Your survival within an organization is at stake, you are being asked to do something you should not have to do, and it provides you with absolutely no benefit.

Moser (2004) provided great information pertaining to interpersonal violence and used the term *social violence* to describe the phenomenon. Moser's (2004) focus was primarily in relation to violence in urban settings and covered such concepts as *gender-based violence* and *ethnic violence*. Gender-based violence is primarily concerned with violence in the home, violence pertaining to machismo or masculinity, as well as sexual abuse that takes place in the community. Ethnic violence describes acts that are most associated with street gangs, such as territorial disputes, as well as violence that is related to identity and respect (Anderson, 1993). The World Health Organization (Krug et al., 2002) also recognized these subtypes of interpersonal violence and described them as family and intimate partner violence as well as community violence. The central point is not, however, in the distinction of terms but instead the distinction between violent acts that occur inside the home and within family units and partners and those violent acts that occur outside the home and in the community between people who may or may not know each other.

Weiner et al. (1990) provided some interesting comments regarding interpersonal violence that underpin much of the foundation used in our decision to primarily focus on this type of violence. First, interpersonal violence usually involves smaller groups of people involved in the incident. In addition, the place and time are usually related to the violent incident. For example, consider a brawl that occurs in a parking lot at two o'clock in the morning as a bar is closing. Clearly, the variables are related. This type of interpersonal violence is likely to be brought to the attention of law enforcement, which usually means that there is some information regarding the event that can be later studied and evaluated for possible causes. In essence, as noted by Reiss and Roth (1993), much of the information we have regarding violence is contained within aggregate reports generated by law enforcement officials. Therefore, this is the domain in which much of the existing knowledge originates.

Other Types of Violence

In addition to interpersonal violence, there are other types of violence worthy of mention that are commonly discussed throughout the literature. First, violence aimed at oneself is defined as self-directed violence and generally consists of physical harm to one's body as well as suicide. Self-directed violence is particularly worthy of mention because several of the postulates offered in other chapters meant to explain violence may be just as appropriate for this typology as with interpersonal violence.

Another type of violence common to the literature is collective violence. Collective violence describes a serious phenomenon by which large groups come together to forward a social or political cause and use violence as one of the means to accomplish a task. An example of collective violence related to a criminal justice issue involves the widespread rioting following the beating of Rodney King in Los Angeles, California, March 1991. Collective violence is often difficult to explain due to the enormous number and complexity of interrelated variables that must interact under specific conditions to spur the actual violence. In addition, collective violence is often the result of deep-seated and persistent perceptions of being judged inferior by some other group or subgroup. With these complexities noted, let us explore the collective violence related to the unfortunate incident of Rodney King knowing full well that many variables were at play, all of which possessed complex underpinnings.

First, consider the most important difference between the Rodney King incident and all of those preceding it. The beating endured by Rodney King was captured on video and almost immediately made available for the entire world to see. With the Rodney King incident, the police, the government, and the community were unable to deny the injustice that occurred. People could see it with their own eyes. For years before the event, minorities, especially those in low-income, high-crime areas, were trying to articulate the many cases of abuse that routinely occurred at the hands of the police. In many cases, these reports were eventually ruled unfounded or simply not investigated. Regardless of the findings, what is clear is that many incidents occurred that significantly damaged the trust and relationship between the police department and many of the minority citizens throughout the city. With the infamous video, however, there was an immediate social gathering and uprising based on a central foundation. In essence, the collective group began to say, "You can no longer deny what we have been trying to tell you for years. For years, you have not taken our concerns seriously. With this video we now have proof that allows us to stand up and demand action." And the citizens did stand up. Covertly and now overtly, people felt vindicated. The concept of vindication is often accompanied by the eruption of intense emotion, which before had to be suppressed. In essence, the people were saying that you are going to see us, you are going to hear us, and most important, you are going to respect us. It could be argued that underpinning this particular instance of collective violence was the concept of respect. This is precisely why we have chosen to include the concept of collective violence in this discussion. In other chapters, we present several theories, all of which are related, that posit basic emotion may be at the core of layers that make up the causal factors related to violence.

One final typology of violence is worthy of mention and could be argued to be among the most heinous: economic violence. Economic violence is often described as a subtype of collective violence and generally describes actions meant to interrupt, damage, or even destroy economic systems relating to a society or individual units such as families or persons. The catastrophe surrounding the Enron Corporation provides a good example of economic violence that had a severe impact on the well-being of all those affected. Imagine your entire financial worth and life savings being gone with the click of a mouse; this loss was motivated by individual greed and underpinned by the construct of shame.

Methods of Violence

Generally, there are four methods in which violence can be carried out:

1. Physical
2. Sexual
3. Psychological
4. Deprivation/neglect

Each of these methods of violence can be extremely damaging to a victim, especially under certain circumstances. Interesting questions that often are associated with violent encounters are, Why do they occur? or What characteristics of violence seem to be most heinous and result in the greatest harm to the victim? Of course, a victim's resilience is important, but another factor likely to be strongly related to the degree of damage is the method in which violence was perpetrated and the relationship between the offender and victim. Consider, for example, a crime of rape carried out by the stepfather of a 14-year-old girl and concluding with the threat of physical violence should the young girl decide to tell anyone. In such events, all four methods of violence are actually being carried out. Table 1.1 helps depict the possible interactions between the types of violence and the method used to carry them out. Two primary sources were used to construct the table. First, the World Health Organization (Krug et al., 2002) constructed a useful typology of violence that depicts the fundamental interactions; second, Moser (2004) provided a table that expanded the road map of the various interactions between types and methods of violence.

Violence Prevention Initiative

The Violence Prevention Initiative of the government of Newfoundland and Labrador was designed to address the problem of violence in their communities. The initiative resulted in a six-year, multidepartmental partnership effort to find solutions to the problems of violence against women, children, and other members of the communities (see the Violence Prevention Initiative Web site at http://www.gov.nl.ca/VPI/initiative/index.html).

The researchers concluded that vulnerable populations experience physical, sexual, emotional, psychological, spiritual, and cultural violence as well as verbal and financial abuse and neglect. However, accurate statistics regarding the prevalence of violence are difficult to obtain as approximately only 10 percent of violence or abuse is ever reported.

The following classifications of violence were adapted from the Violence Prevention Initiative report on violence: physical, sexual, psychological, and emotional.

Table 1.1 Interactions between Types of Violence and the Method Used to Carry It Out

Type of Violence	Method of Violence	Example of Behavior
Interpersonal	1. Physical 2. Sexual 3. Psychological 4. Deprivation or neglect	Intimate partner violence; rape; inappropriate sexual touching or fondling, especially that which occurs between stepfathers or other close relatives; excessive physical, psychological, and emotional control or abuse; fistfights, stabbings, and shootings that occur in the home or community
Collective	1. Physical 2. Sexual 3. Psychological 4. Deprivation or neglect	Military conflict; violence on behalf of a state meant to control actions or ideologies of citizens; violence used to protect territory and geographical boundaries as well as economic interests
Self-directed violence	1. Physical 2. Psychological 3. Deprivation or neglect	Suicide; infliction of physical harm on one's body via cutting, burning, exposure to extreme elements; ingestion of harmful substances or chemicals

Physical Violence

Physical violence occurs when an individual uses part of his or her body or an object to control another person's actions. The most common forms of physical violence include

- Murder
- Assault
- Battery
- Stabbing
- Threatening to do bodily injury

- Pushing
- Shoving
- Forcibly holding a person down
- Confinement
- Hair pulling
- Punching
- Slapping
- Arm twisting
- Kicking
- Biting
- Strangling
- Choking
- Burning
- Overmedication

Sexual Violence

Sexual violence occurs when someone forces another person to take part in sexual activity when the other person does not want to do so. The most common forms of sexual violence include

- touching a person in a sexual manner against his or her will (i.e., kissing, grabbing, fondling);
- forcing sexual intercourse;
- forcing a person to perform sexual acts he or she finds degrading or painful;
- using a weapon to make a person comply with a sexual act;
- beating sexual parts of a person's body;
- engaging in exhibitionism (need to expose body parts to others);
- denying of a woman's sexuality;
- humiliating, criticizing, or trying to control a woman's sexuality;
- denying sexual information and education (i.e., birth control);
- withholding sexual affection;
- exposing another to AIDS or other sexually transmitted infections;
- forcing abortion or sterilization;
- forcing prostitution; and
- making unfounded allegations of promiscuity or infidelity.

Psychological Violence

Psychological violence occurs when someone uses threats and causes fear in a person to gain control. Psychological violence includes, but is not limited to, the following:

- threatening to harm you, your children, or your family if you leave;

- threatening to harm themselves;
- threatening violence;
- threatening abandonment;
- destroying your personal property;
- socially isolating you from your family and friends;
- confining you to the home;
- using verbal aggression; and
- engaging in constant humiliation.

Emotional Violence

Emotional violence occurs when someone says or does something to make a person feel stupid or worthless. Emotional violence includes, but is not limited to, the following:

- name calling;
- constant criticism;
- blaming all relationship problems on you;
- humiliating or belittling you in front of others;
- using silent treatment;
- confinement to the home;
- not allowing you to have contact with family and friends;
- destroying possessions;
- threats;
- jealousy;
- intimidation;
- stalking;
- threatening to take the children; and
- threatening to commit suicide.

Cost of Violence

Perhaps the most salient reason for attempting to better understand the phenomenon of violence is due to the fact that it is responsible for an enormous cost to individuals, communities, and society at large. In essence, the consequences of a single incident of violence permeate throughout society and produce a ripple effect that is felt by many far beyond the time and place of the incident. In addition to the physical effects of violence, there will likely be psychological and emotional damage that tends to linger with those victims who do not receive appropriate treatment. And, unfortunately, many victims of violence are not aware of these types of consequences. Sure, they may feel slow, sluggish, and lethargic, but the connection is not made that these symptoms may be a result of the extra energy spent to manage feelings and emotions that can range from fear of a subsequent attack to extreme rage that someone had the audacity and lack of respect to perpetrate the violent encounter. Many people typically assume that once the bruises have healed all is well and forgotten. In many cases, however, there will be serious emotional trauma as well as symptoms of post-traumatic stress disorder (PTSD). Many of our war veterans have returned with PTSD that was never treated or even diagnosed. Even in what may be described as mild violent encounters, the likelihood of one suffering long-term PTSD is great.

Another factor that may aggravate the feelings and emotion associated with violence is if the encounter was random. In other words, if the victim was not in a high-risk environment or engaged in high-risk behaviors, the act of violence can also trigger severe feelings of anxiety. When the violence is random, there is a real perception of loss of control. And, humans do not function well when there is a fear of not being able to control one's environment sufficiently to moderate the likelihood of such violent attacks. "Throughout the literature on the costs of violence, psychological costs greatly outweighed the direct costs of violence" (Waters et al., 2004, p. 13).

Appreciate that in most cases of violence the most severe consequences will be associated with those encounters that are most heinous. For example, victims of stabbings, shootings, and severe beatings will certainly experience significant consequences that will consist of both physical and psychological wounds. With this said, however, it is also critical always to consider a victim's background, culture, and personality. For example, an inner city youth, raised in the street, is likely to interpret and react to being punched in the face much differently from a youth not exposed to the harsh rules of many areas in urban settings. Being punched or even severely beaten may be considered by an inner city youth as normal in some cases or even deserved for breaking the rules of the neighborhood.

An extreme incident of violence was captured on tape and broadcast on the Fox News Network. Several young, black males were involved in a shooting in a local bar. What made this event noteworthy is the manner in which several of the young males portrayed themselves throughout the potentially deadly encounter. In the clip, they appeared calm, collected, and calculating, periodically ducking and looking around the corner of the building to get off a shot. It was as if they were involved in a normal, regular incident that required settling and, if possible, killing their adversaries. The concept that may describe the incident best is that of desensitization. In other words, there was nothing really out of the ordinary. Someone had crossed a line that they should not have, and the response was one of violence. In essence, one can imagine that their response to what had just happened could be, "What else did they expect we would do? They know how things work out here." For a different set of actors, the reactions and consequences may be wholly different. Someone not exposed to the harsh condition of urban settings and suddenly thrust into a life-or-death incident may be permanently affected and in some cases psychologically and emotionally disabled. The person will likely question what he or she did to cause or provoke the incident and in many cases not be able to find the appropriate answer.

Generally, the cost of violence is broken down into two broad categories: direct costs and indirect costs. When attempting to estimate costs resulting from violence, a common error is simply to assume that costs are related solely to those who perpetrate violent encounters and victims who are made to suffer the wrath of the encounter. In reality, however, and as noted, the cost of violence has an impact on the whole of society.

Direct Costs

Direct costs are those described as consisting of actual payments resulting from a specific violent encounter. In the case of physical injury, for example, there will be direct medical costs. Buchart et al. (2008) provided the following examples:

1. Hospital visits and treatment
2. Costs associated with recurring outpatient visits
3. Transport costs, such as for ambulance and life flight services
4. Individual fees directly related to physicians, medication, and laboratory procedures

In addition to the direct costs associated with medical and psychoemotional services, there are direct costs related to the criminal justice system. For every violent encounter reported to the police, especially those encounters that are serious, there will be a significant allocation of resources to investigate the incident. These costs often entail overtime payments to the detectives, transportation costs associated with the investigation, as well as payment for all support services, some of which include crime scene personnel and all attendant costs associated with equipment and laboratory supplies.

In the event a suspect is arrested and charged with a crime, there will be a completely new set of costs related to the judicial system and legal services. The court system is comprised of various professionals, ranging from judges, attorneys, security personnel, court reporters, and administrative staff responsible for managing the docket. In addition, there are often court costs associated with each event that represent a form of direct costs. Even if an offender pleads guilty or accepts a plea bargain, sparing the system from having to conduct a full trial, the costs are substantial.

Finally, if the suspect either pleads guilty or is found guilty through a criminal trial, there are enormous costs for services in association with probation, jail, prison, and parole. Simply stated, correctional costs are staggering. In fact, state corrections departments are often among the largest agencies and are likewise responsible for some of the largest allocations of the overall fiscal budget of a state.

Indirect Costs

Indirect costs are always more difficult to quantify. There is generally not a set of pre-constructed measures that allow one to explain or accurately predict the impact that violence will have on a particular individual. Robust mediators of costs associated with violence include such concepts as resilience and the quality and level of support that is available to someone following a violent encounter. Generally, however, indirect costs are those related to the loss of resources as well as the loss of productivity or output as a result of lost opportunities directly related to a violent encounter.

As noted in Table 1.2, there are a number of variables that represent indirect costs. Most often, they are separated into two groups: tangible and intangible indirect costs. Broadly, tangible indirect costs are mostly associated with one's reduced ability to earn money; intangible indirect costs consist mainly of suffering from a reduced quality of life.

What is critical to understand is that the costs related to violence are broad, general, often overlapping, and anything but a number that can be neatly measured and easily reported in the form of a whole number. Costs related to violence are often hidden. A criminal justice analogy may be helpful. Appreciate that most crime is never reported to the police. Therefore the official statistics that we use to measure and summarize trends and rates of crime are obviously not precise. We know this from the beginning. In essence, we analyze the phenomenon of crime based on the best information we have. The same is true when estimating the cost of violence. Much of the cost is hidden, and much of the cost is never known.

With these limitations in mind, it is still useful to review some of the estimates of costs related to violence. First, understand that when all is considered, direct and indirect, tangible and intangible, the annual estimates reach well into the billions, in fact well over U.S. $100 billion. More recently, the costs associated with violence have been depicted in relation to or as a percentage of the gross domestic product (GDP; Buchart et al., 2008; Krug et al., 2002). The GDP provides a well-understood and widely recognized figure that significantly enhances the meaning of the straight dollar amounts. The real effort is aimed at accurately depicting the cost of violence so that equitable resources are directed toward its prevention. Especially, it has become critical that the phenomenon of violence be shown for its true responsibility and damaging qualities to millions as scarce resources are hotly contested. Consider the amounts provided by Corso, Mercy, Simon, Finkelstein, and Miller (2007), which are delineated next.

Violence-Related Injury in America

- Violence causes approximately 50,000 deaths each year and results in over 2.5 million injuries.
- Homicide and suicide are the second and third leading causes of death, respectively, among Americans aged 15–34.

Table 1.2 Costs of Violence

Interpersonal violence	Direct costs and benefits
• Child abuse and neglect	• Costs of legal services
• Intimate partner violence	• Direct medical costs
• Elder abuse	• Direct perpetrator control costs
• Sexual violence	• Costs of policing
• Workplace violence	• Costs of incarceration
• Youth violence	• Costs of foster care
• Other violent crime	• Private security contracts
	• Economic benefits to perpetrators
	Indirect costs and benefits
	• Lost earnings and lost time
	• Lost investments in human capital
	• Indirect protection costs
	• Life insurance costs
	• Benefits to law enforcement
	• Lost productivity
	• Domestic investment
	• External investment and tourism
	• Psychological costs
	• Other nonmonetary costs

Source: Adapted from Waters, H., Hyder, A., Rajkotia, Y., Basu, S., Rehwinkel, J. A., and Butchart, A. *The economic dimensions of interpersonal violence.* Geneva, Switzerland: Department of Injuries and Violence Prevention, World Health Organization, 2004.

■ Hospital emergency departments treat an average 55 people for injuries every minute.

Costs of Violence-Related Injury in America

■ Americans suffer 16,800 homicides and 2.2 million medically treated injuries due to interpersonal violence annually, at a cost of $37 billion ($33 billion in productivity losses, $4 billion in medical treatment).

■ The cost of self-inflicted injuries (suicide and attempted suicide) is $33 billion annually ($32 billion in productivity losses, $1 billion in medical costs).

■ People aged 15 to 44 years comprise 44 percent of the population but account for nearly 75 percent of injuries and 83 percent of costs due to interpersonal violence.

Result of Violence-Related Injury

■ The average cost per homicide was $1.3 million in lost productivity and $4,906 in medical costs.

■ The average cost per case for a nonfatal assault resulting in hospitalization was $57,209 in lost productivity and $24,353 in medical costs.

■ The average cost per case of suicide was $1 million in lost productivity and $2,596 in medical costs.

■ The average cost for a nonfatal self-inflicted injury was $9,726 in lost productivity and $7,234 in medical costs.

■ Economic costs provide, at best, an incomplete measure of the toll of violence. Victims of violence are more likely to experience a broad range of mental and physical health problems not reflected in these estimates from PTSD to depression, cardiovascular disease, and diabetes.

Conclusion

As a discipline, it is critical that criminal justice make every effort to better understand the concept of violence, especially interpersonal violence among adults. Two central reasons for attempting to better understand violence are the enhancement of our ability, as criminal justice practitioners, to respond to violent encounters appropriately and to identify those areas of violence that require responses from other public service providers better equipped to address the underpinnings of violence. Appreciate that violence is a complex concept that is rooted in a multitude of disciplines, including not only criminology but also psychology, sociology, biology, and other social science disciplines.

Among the most robust reasons for studying violence is the fact that violence is preventable. Within this vein of discussion, the real questions are: What are we as a society willing to sacrifice to reduce or prevent violence? What are we willing to give up? Would we be willing to alter our social and economic system it if were shown that they are causally related to violence? Would we be willing to alter our criminal justice responses to violent encounters if it were shown that jail and prison may not always serve to eliminate future violence? What about our political system—would politicians be bold enough to create and enact policies that are better equipped to respond to violence even though the popular opinion reaches a feverish frenzy at the thought of any response other than longer and harsher prison sentences?

Finally, the impact of violence is profound. Of course, physical wounds are serious, but it has been shown that the psychological and emotional consequences are often more severe and have a significant negative impact on one's future quality of life. Coupled with the personal impact of violence is the impact on society and the enormous financial costs that follow. Billions of dollars are spent each year as a result of direct and indirect costs associated with violence. Imagine if we were able to redirect these funds toward improving the delivery and opportunity for education as well as providing better assistance for those in need, including the sick and elderly.

Ultimately, the question is: What would you be willing to sacrifice to prevent violence?

Review Questions

1. Why is it important to study violence?
2. Discuss the different types of violence. How would you describe the concept of interpersonal violence?
3. Explain the difference between direct and indirect costs. Provide an example of each.
4. Discuss the different methods of violence. Which would you argue is the most severe? Why?
5. Discuss two reasons why it is important to understand the economic cost of violence.

References

Anderson, E. (1999). *Code of the street: Decency, violence, and the moral life of the inner city.* New York: Norton.

Bartolome-Gutierrez, R., and Rechea-Alberola Young, C. (2006). Violent youth groups in Spain. *Nordic Journal of Youth Research,* 14, 323–342.

Brown, R. M. (1969). Historical patterns of American violence. In H. D. Graham and T. R. Gurr (eds.), *The history of violence in America: Historical and comparative perspectives—A report to the National Commission on the Causes and Prevention of Violence* (pp. 45–84). New York: Bantam.

Buchart, A., Brown, D., Khanh-Huynh, A., Corso, P., Florquin, N., and Muggah, R. (2008). *Manual for estimating the economic costs of injuries due to interpersonal and self directed violence.* World Health Organization and Department of Health and Human Services Centers for Disease Control and Prevention.

Buenker, J. (1999). Overview of violence theories: History. In R. Gottesman (ed.), *The encyclopedia of violence in America* (Vol. 3, pp. 314–315). New York: Scribner.

Corso, P. S., Mercy, J. A., Simon, T. R., Finkelstein E. A., and Miller, T. R. (2007). Medical costs and productivity losses due to interpersonal violence and self directed violence. *American Journal of Preventive Medicine,* 32(6), 474–482.

Kalson, S. (2010, January 10). Survey finds gun violence affects youths. *Pittsburg Post-Gazette,* C-1.

Krug, E. G., Dahlberg, L. L., Mercy, J. A., Zwi, A. B., and Lozano, R., eds. (2002). *World report on violence and health.* Geneva, Switzerland: World Health Organization.

Liska, A. E., and Bellair, P. E. (1995). Violent-crime rates and racial composition: Convergence over time. *American Judicature Society,* 101, 578–610.

Mercy, J. A. (1993). Public health policy for preventing violence. *Health Affairs,* 12, 7–29.

Mersky, J. P., and Reynolds, A. J. (2007). Child maltreatment and violent delinquency: Disentangling main effects and subgroup effects. *Child Maltreatment,* 12, 246–258.

Miller, W. B. (1966). Violent crime in city gangs. *The Annals of the American Academy of Political and Social Science,* 364, 96–112.

Moser, C. (2004). Urban violence and insecurity: An introductory roadmap. *Environment and Urbanization,* 16, 3–16.

Police Executive Research Forum. (2006). *A gathering storm: Violent crime in America.* Washington, DC: Police Executive Research Forum.

Rainone, G. A., Schmeidler, J. W., Frank, B., and Smith, R. B. (2006). Violent behavior, substance use, and other delinquent behaviors among middle and high school students. *Youth Violence and Juvenile Justice,* 4, 247–265.

Reiss, A. J., Jr., and Roth, J. A., eds. (1993). *Understanding and preventing violence.* Washington, DC: National Academy Press.

Roy, K. G. (2000). The systemic conditions leading to violent human behavior. *Journal of Applied Behavioral Science,* 36, 389–406.

Waters, H., Hyder, A., Rajkotia, Y., Basu, S., Rehwinkel, J.A., and Butchart, A. (2004). *The economic dimensions of interpersonal violence.* Geneva, Switzerland: Department of Injuries and Violence Prevention, World Health Organization.

Weiner, N. A., Zahn, M. A., and Sagi, R. J., eds. (1990). *Violence: Patterns, causes, public policy.* Washington, DC: Harcourt Brace Jovanovich.

World Health Organization. (1996). *Resolution WHA 49.25.* Geneva, Switzerland: World Health Organization.

Chapter 2

Trends in Violence

Introduction

The purpose of this chapter is to explore trends in violence over the past several centuries and up to the present. This exploration is critical for at least a couple of reasons. First, to make meaningful progress in better understanding the phenomenon of violence, our discussion must be based on fact. We cannot allow popular media outlets to drive our perceptions of violence due to the fact that much of what is broadcast significantly lacks accuracy and rarely is framed in the proper context. Criminality in general, but especially violent crime, is often portrayed with a sense of glamorization, which serves as a very effective tool in the constant struggle of the media for ratings. Of course, we all want to be informed, but when attempting to truly understand the rates and trends of violence, we must look far beyond the media and into the historical data capable of providing a much more accurate depiction of the true parameters of violence.

Second, it is critical to examine trends in violence so that we are able to ask meaningful questions regarding its variance. We must be able to look at specific times in history and identify rates of violence to be better able to associate possible causes for either an increase or a decline in violence. As a society, we are led to believe that current levels of violence are higher and more serious than ever before. Therefore, the main questions regarding violence are centered on factors that are contributing to the increase. And, as an important part of the discussion related to violence, we also must be vigilant in maintaining a broader focus that includes possible factors related to declines in violence.

Fact versus Myth

Before getting into the main content of this chapter, it is necessary to clearly illuminate that which we know to be true about violence and that which has been constructed socially, primarily as a result of what is commonly reported in the media:

1. Is the world more violent today than ever before? No.
2. Is the United States more violent today than ever before? No (Reiss and Roth, 1993). In fact, as discussed in this chapter, there is evidence that suggests trends in violence have been declining since around the year 1200 in Europe and the early 1600s in the United States (Gurr, 1989).
3. Is the United States more violent today than most other countries? Yes, especially in relation to homicide.
4. Who is most likely to perpetrate violence? Young, minority males are most likely to be perpetrators.
5. Who is most likely to be a victim of violence? Young, minority males are most likely to be victims.

Of course, these five points should not be construed as an all-encompassing list of facts related to violence. They are instead a few brief points intended to provide a general foundation from which to frame our discussion. As mentioned above, this necessity is generally related to the vast amount of erroneous information surrounding the concept of violence.

Reliability of the Data

To examine historical and medium- and short-range trends in violence, however, we are quickly confronted with a serious issue that must be presented at the forefront. Much of the data used to construct trends, especially historical trends, is less than reliable and certainly not precise. Instead, much of the data used is best described as general and simply the best we have in an attempt to draw basic conclusions of this phenomenon.

As a result, it quickly becomes difficult to push significantly beyond the five general points and still remain within the domain of fact. To a large extent, it is impossible to guarantee reliability of the data used to construct any trends of violence. Much of what we believe to be true regarding trends in violence has been painstakingly pieced together as a result of scouring through records wherever they could be found. In many cases, there are large gaps of either destroyed or lost records, resulting in periods of time for which we will never know for certain what the actual rates of violence may have been. As noted by Eisner (2003), there are significant periods of missing data for France and Spain, and much more is needed from Italy and the various German-speaking areas of northern and central Europe.

One of the best ways to illuminate the extreme difficulty in gathering reliable data is to consider the United States. In fact, it was not until 1930 that we began systematically collecting crime data. The first attempt, which is still heavily relied on today, consisted of the implementation of the Uniform Crime Report (UCR). The UCR is an annual publication that reports levels of crime throughout the United States for the previous year. The information is gathered locally by participating agencies and then sent to the Federal Bureau of Investigation (FBI), where it is compiled and eventually reported as an aggregate of overall rates and trends. At first blush, this may appear to be a very effective way of gauging the rates of crime and violence, but the truth is that even in the technologically enriched era of today there are still many shortcomings.

The primary shortcoming of the UCR is that it is completely reliant on information that has been reported. This is a significant problem because most of crime and violence is never reported. In an attempt to address this shortfall, another instrument was created, called the National Crime Victimization Survey (NCVS); a sample of households is contacted by phone to ask people if they have been the victim of crime at some point in the past year. The primary goal of the NCVS is to capture what is often called the "dark figure" of crime, or that which is never reported to the police. The NCVS does a pretty good job of enhancing what we know about crime and violence beyond that available through the UCR. In fact, the NCVS typically shows that the number of crimes and incidence of violence are double the figures reported by the UCR.

The NCVS has shortcomings of its own, however. Many victims of crime simply do not trust that the information will be kept confidential. Especially in cases of violence, victims may be so traumatized and fearful of further attack should they tell someone that they simply refuse to provide any information. In addition, the NCVS is completely reliant on the participant's memory. Obvious problems result from this fact. Finally, some participants may simply make up information that contains no factual basis. In essence, we know only what is reported and have no meaningful ways of triangulating or verifying its accuracy.

What does this mean in relation to trends of violence? Ultimately, it means that any information attempting to describe long- or short-term trends should be considered cautiously. There is no way of knowing for sure the exact trends. What we do know is that much more research needs to be directed at more accurately capturing the trends and rates of not only violence but also of crime in general. Think of our economic system as a method for comparison. At any given point, one has myriad measures available to gauge the strength of the economy. Some examples include the NASDAQ, S&P, Dow Jones Industrial Average, wages, gross domestic product (GDP), unemployment numbers, inflation, and so on. The criminal justice system relies largely on two measures, the UCR and the NCVS.

Historical Trends in Europe

Even with these limitations in mind, it is still useful to carefully explore the data we do have regarding trends in violence. Several scholars have produced wonderful work in this area over the past several decades (see, e.g., Cockburn, 1991; Eisner, 2003; Elias, 1976; Given, 1977; Gurr, 1989, 1981). For the purposes of our discussion, the attempt is to summarize some of the major findings and conclusions drawn from the available data. Most of what follows is based on the work of Eisner (2003), Gurr (1989), and Elias (1976). We rely most heavily on their work because it provides the most depth within the area of violent trends and is also the most closely aligned with the general message we are attempting to capture.

For many, the actual trend in violence may be somewhat of a surprise. Based on data provided by both Gurr (1989) and Eisner (2003), there has been a steady decline in the overall rate (number of incidents per 100,000 population) of violence across Europe from about the year 1200 all the way through the late twentieth century. An important note regarding this trend is that it is based only on homicide rates. Therefore, what we do know, based on the available information, is that there has been a steady decline in the number of people killed in homicides. We do not know if other types of violence followed this same trend, but the likely speculation is that they did. There is nothing to suggest any difference in the trends of homicide and other violence-related incidents. According to Gurr (1989), the downward trend can be depicted as an elegant line showing a steady and sustained decrease in violence beginning at an average of 20 homicides a year per 100,000 population in the year 1200 to less than 5 per 100,000 population by the year 2000. According to Eisner (2003), the trend is depicted as a long and sustained decrease in homicides but not until after the 1400s. As the only difference in the findings, Eisner (2003) reported an upswing of violence around the fifteenth century. Afterward, however, the results are consistent with Gurr's (1981) and signal a clear decline in the rate of violence. The safest and most reliable conclusion based on the work of Eisner and Gurr is that beginning in the latter part of the fifteenth century there has been a persistent decline in the rate of violence throughout Europe.

Variation in the Declining Rate of Violence

One of the most interesting aspects of the decline in violence across Europe is also among the most complex. Generally, the overall decline in violence throughout Europe did not take place simultaneously or evenly throughout the past centuries. As noted by Eisner (2003), for example, beginning in the late sixteenth century England and the Netherlands experienced substantial reductions in the rate of interpersonal violence. In Sweden, a similar process occurred, but the rate of decline started later than that of England and the Netherlands, and the decline in Sweden was also reported as sharper. This was not the case in Italy, however, as rates seemed to have moved little from late medieval times, a trend that was even more exacerbated in the southern regions of the country, including the islands.

The question is, Why? Why did the trends differ not only across Europe but also within countries? These same questions are also applied to trends in the United States, where some cities were experiencing declines in violence while others were experiencing a rise. The question becomes, What were the variables associated with the respective increases and decreases that seem to have been occurring simultaneously? Identifying these specific variables is enormously complex largely because we still have much to learn in the area of understanding human behavior. To complicate matters further, we also must consider the interactions of certain variables across space and time, which significantly increases the difficulty in being able to identify causes of noncorrelating trends.

One possible starting point is to approach these questions from the theoretical framework of ecology. Ecology is the study of how people interact with their environment and provides a foundation for better understanding some of the variations. Over the years, a number of authors have engaged in informative research (Chesnais, 1981; Durkheim, 1973; Eisner, 2003; Ferri, 1925; Johnson, 1995) that, when combined, allows us to make a couple of general but important observations. Simply stated, in the mid-to-late nineteenth century and into the twentieth century, rates of violence were lowest in the regions of Europe that were most industrialized and urbanized. Eisner (2003) described this phenomenon with the concept of a "center-periphery dimension" (p. 103). In other words, rates of violence were lowest not only in those regions that were most industrialized and urbanized but in the very center of these regions where literacy and education were highest. "Elevated levels of violence, in turn, were found throughout the peripheral areas with high birth rates, high illiteracy rates, and predominantly rural population" (Eisner, 2003, p. 106).

This is among the most significant of observations because it is contradictory to what we are experiencing today, at least in relation to urbanization in the United States. In modern times, rates of violence are much higher in densely populated inner cities than in the outer regions and suburbs. Today, there are higher birth rates and higher rates of illiteracy within the centers of major cities across the United States.

The question once again is, Why? Pure speculation leads us to ponder whether there is a delicate balance between population and resources and when the population exceeds the available resources rates of violence increase. Could it be that as more and more people migrated toward the centers of education and productivity a threshold was met at which point the physical space in which most violence seems to occur was reversed? It is likely that this is at least part of the foundation from which violence often resonated; however, another important factor that must be considered is culture. For example, many of the Asian countries are much more densely populated, but yet rates of violence are considered lower than many other industrialized countries, especially the United States. Asian culture stresses harmony among groups and possesses subtle methods (one example includes reduced levels of eye contact) for allowing people to maintain a sense of space and independence in spite of their very crowded existence.

Summarizing Historical Trends in Europe

As shown by the discussion, there has been a sustained decrease in the rate of violence throughout Europe over the past several centuries. Of course, this trend fluctuated at various times and in various parts of Europe, but the overall downward trend is clear and significant.

Historical Trends in America

Similar to Europe, there has never been a time in the United States when one could argue that we were free from violence (Courtwright, 1996). In fact, historically America has been among the most violent of nations throughout the world. It is an interesting paradox to ponder when one considers the basic underpinnings of America, which consist of freedom and democracy. One may expect that a country founded on equality and civil rights would be the land of plenty where people could relax and live in peace and harmony. As will be discussed, however, this was not always the case—in fact, not even close.

A few brief examples may help remind us of our violent past. First, recall that the North American continent was inhabited by Native American Indians long before the arrival of English explorers and later settlers. Today, Native American Indians live on and operate reservations that have been provided to them by the U.S. government. How did we go from Native Americans being free to roam and settle the entire continent to life on a handful of small reservations? The answer is through war, bloodshed, and extreme violence. In essence, English settlers systematically pushed the Indians from the east to the west until there was no more land on which to retreat. This entire process was enormously violent as both sides inevitably viewed their position as one of survival.

An interesting final caveat is worthy of mention regarding Native American Indians. For many, gambling is an exciting pastime that produces surges of adrenaline and anticipation. The sheer quantity of people who engage in organized gambling is staggering. For others, gambling becomes an incredibly destructive vice that destroys one's life and relationships. As a result, the history of gambling is fraught with controversy and is rich with moral and ethical ideals that point to its destructive nature. In some parts of the country, gambling is illegal save one exception: the Native American reservation. In essence, "we" do not want this destructive vice on our land, but it is okay if it is on your land and we can use it when we want and when it is convenient.

Unfortunately, the violence contained within the Native American wars was not an isolated event in the United States of America. Other examples of profound violence include the American Revolution, the American Civil War, the two world wars, the Vietnam and Korean wars, and more recently the wars in Iraq and Afghanistan.

Plainly stated, violence is a central part of our very existence. In relation to the American Revolution and Civil War, Brown (1975) made an interesting point: "A salient fact of American violence is that, time and again, it has been the instrument not merely of the criminal and disorderly but of the most upright and honorable." Thus, in our two great national crises—the American Revolution and the Civil War—we called on violence to preserve the nation. And, it appears as though this fact will not soon abate. Currently, the United States is locked in a never-ending struggle with various nations throughout the world who have resorted to terrorism in an attempt to disrupt our democracy and freedom. We are under constant pressure to guard against not only physical attack but also biological, financial, and cyber attacks. The professed reasoning behind the hate leading to the terrorist activities is most often related to religion. In essence, the terrorist ideology is one of saving the world from sinners and infidels. A closer look at this professed ideology, however, begins to paint a different picture. Religion may be a part of the cause and motivation, but it is not able to explain the full picture of modern terrorism and the extreme measures people are willing to take to bring harm and destruction to those who are different. Religion is likely to be a salient driver of action for those willing to carry out the actual events of terrorism. For example, the decision to strap explosive devices on one's body and later detonate these devices in the presence of people to produce as much death and destruction as possible would be hard to justify with any explanation beyond religion. For those leaders, however, responsible for planning and organizing the terrorist acts, the real motivation is likely to extend beyond religion and into the realm of politics, power, and greed. The question is whether the difference is related to religion or really to perceptions of power. In other words, there will always be those groups who will resort to whatever means available in an attempt to balance a real or perceived difference in power, which ultimately equates to access to goods and services.

Before discussing some of the particulars of American violence, however, it is important to note a couple of salient facts that are often overlooked. The quality of any historical analysis is always directly related to the quality of archived data as well as most recent data. Not only do the same problems we discussed regarding data used for European trends apply to trends in America, they are in fact worse. Prior to 1933 and the UCR, there are many gaps in court records, some of which span decades.

In essence, there was no reliable system in place to count on or track the incidents of violence, even those reported to the authorities. And even after 1933, it took many years to appropriately define variables and establish necessary cooperation from agencies throughout the country to submit information on these crimes that had been reported to their jurisdiction. One can almost humorously ponder the look on a police administrator's face in the 1930s when suddenly asked to begin the process of recording all types of criminal activity reported to the organization.

What do we know about violence in America? To begin, it is important to first note the immense diversity within the United States. The "melting pot" is a widely recognized concept that describes the phenomenon of immigrants arriving in the United States from various parts of the world and dispersing throughout the land according to opportunity and in most cases eventually acculturating to the ways and laws of the United States. What makes this point important to this discussion is that this is a somewhat different phenomenon than that experienced in Europe. For example, European trends track rates of violence in aggregate form that are based on different countries throughout the continent. Therefore, the rates consist of what was happening throughout Europe, but they consist of regions or countries made up of people who were mostly alike and shared many of the same cultural values, heritage, and language. This is a very important distinction between Europe and the United States that seems to have had a significant impact on the manner in which trends vary.

In essence, it is likely that differing groups forced to assimilate based on one set of values and cultural expectations experienced an amount of strain that was significantly higher than that experienced by people in other parts of the world. In addition, Europe, especially England, did not (to the extent of America) experience the plight of one particular race, African Americans, who were forced to endure horrendous circumstances of slavery (Gurr, 1989). How does a phenomenon such as slavery have an impact on the rates of violence? In short, the impact is nothing short of profound. Imagine being forced to live in barbaric conditions, treated inhumanely, and violently disrespected all as a result of one characteristic—the color of your skin. The result, as explored in greater detail in another chapter, is anger, resentment, and ultimately shame. These are the factors most robust in producing violent behavior.

In short, violent crime in the United States seems to trend downward historically but at a much higher rate than Europe. Much more important, one could argue that there have been two different rates of violence that need to be illuminated: one for white Americans and one for black Americans, both separately and collectively. In other words, the United States has been and continues to be much more violent than Europe and all other first-world civilizations.

The notion of violence trending downward in the United States is supported by rates of execution beginning in the 13 colonies and then throughout the United States through the year 1980. This information was provided by Gurr (1989), and although certainly not the "smoking gun" resulting in proof positive of a downward trend in violence, an interesting connection can be made. Not only did judicial executions decline, so did the rate of homicides trend downward throughout the same period. Together, there is much more compelling support that in America, just as in Europe, there has been a long-term decline in the most serious of violent offenses: murder.

The highlight of violence rates in the nineteenth century consists of an interesting 20-year span beginning in 1850 and culminating in 1870. First, as noted by Lane (1986) and Hindus (1980), prior to 1850 homicide indictments averaged around 3.3 per 100,000 population in Philadelphia, 2.1 per 100,000 in Boston, which was higher than analogous rates in London but only slightly. What is important to illuminate is that at this point in history rates of violence (especially for murder) were similar in America and Europe (specifically London).

Around 1850, however, things begin to change. Rates of homicide started to increase sharply. The interesting question is why this occurred. Although no definitive answer is discernible, Lane (1986) and Monkkonen (2001) both noted the extremely high rate of representation among Irish immigrants. In fact, Irish immigrants consisted of a large percentage of the offenders appearing in official police records, especially in regard to public disorder.

An additional factor that supports the notion of a greater-than-chance probability that Irish immigrants were responsible or involved in many of the acts of disorder is the fact that Irish immigration peaked around 1840 (Gilse, 1987; Gurr, 1989). In other words, there was a large percentage of Irish immigrants within the population. Monkkonen (2001) noted between 1850 and 1870, 40 percent of the population of New York City consisted of Irish immigrants.

Another interesting circumstance that took place within the 20-year range in question was the American Civil War (1861–1865). Two interesting observations linked to the Civil War appear to be directly related to trends in violence. First, during the war rates of violence (murder) declined. This is not an overly surprising observation as many of the young men (the segment of any population most likely to be engaged in violence) were occupied with fighting.

Also not surprising is the fact that violence began to trend upward immediately following the culmination of the war as the young men returned home. What is interesting, however, is an observation made by Gurr (1989) regarding trends in violence and their correlation with war. Throughout the past 150 years, significant upsurges in violence have been associated with wars, including the two world wars. It will be interesting to look at trends associated with the current state of war and see if the past results apply to modern times. One of the factors posited in regard to elevated rates of violence around years of war is that war serves to legitimize violence. In addition, many of the young soldiers become desensitized to the violence, chaos, and even death. Post-traumatic stress disorder is a common phenomenon among military veteran populations and is responsible for a reduced level of tolerance for commonly considered mundane circumstances and an increased level of agitation. As a result, it is entirely plausible to consider some fluctuation in violence connected to phenomena associated with wartime experience.

Another interesting factor related to violence and war and the influence of desensitization is the connection between violence and abuse, especially physical, sexual, and psychological abuse carried out in the home by primary caregivers. Desensitization is operationalized through the process of one having to mentally and physically disengage from the present. As one disassociates, the abuse is more tolerable. This disassociation is actually a means for survival. Over time and especially with repeated exposure to the negative stimuli, one becomes so removed from the suffering that an emotional numbness begins to set in. As a result of this numbing of emotion and feeling, the perpetration of violence is not experienced as an extreme and toxic event as is usually the case for those who have not had similar experiences. In this framework, violence can be thought of as a dependent variable influenced by external factors that stimulate the concept of desensitization.

Violent Crime in America after 1900

At the turn of the twentieth century, there were a number of factors that contributed to the rate of violence in the United States. One interesting note is that American rates of violence appear to diverge from rates of violence in Europe. Around the turn of the century, European rates, especially in northern Europe, were quite low. In America, however, the homicide rate increased from approximately 5.1 to 10.3 per 100,000 population between 1900 and 1924 (Hoffman, 1925). Some of this increase had to do with the burgeoning auto industry and the massive increase of vehicles on the roadway.

Another factor strongly associated with rates of violence in the early twentieth century was prohibition. The prohibition era consisted of the outlawing of alcohol, which in turn generated a variety of criminal syndicates vying for portions of the lucrative black market trade in alcohol. Similar to the drug trade of today, much violence ensued as competition for territory and market share raged. This was an especially appealing enterprise for those members of society who felt disenfranchised or marginalized based on the changing economic market, which was shifting toward industrialization. Not all members of society were able to adapt to changing times. We are also seeing this phenomenon take place in current times. The current economic market is largely driven by the age of technology and moved in large part beyond the era of industrialism. Every day, more and more factories are becoming automated, and jobs that used to require human input are now handled by the precision of computer-generated applications.

This shift in the capacity in which the economic market is driven is often most felt by immigrant populations not fully versed in the means of production. In the early years of the twentieth century, many of the immigrant population were finding it hard to fit into what was then the new industrial world. During this period, the focus shifted from the Irish immigrants of the 1850s to the Italian immigrants as most likely to be involved with violence, especially murder. As Lane (1986) noted, Italian immigrants in Philadelphia were almost 20 times more likely to be arrested, charged, and imprisoned for murder than any other white group. This is an interesting observation as Italian rates of violence were also among the highest in Europe for several centuries. The question surrounding this phenomenon is what it is about Italian culture that seemed to generate higher-than-normal rates of violence both in the homeland and in the United States of America.

The most perplexing aspect of violence in America, however, and that which supersedes any European group, is the consistently high rate of violence that takes place among African Americans. Lane (1986) noted that in the 1800s the homicide deaths among African Americans was 7.5 per 100,000 population in the city of Philadelphia. This was almost three times higher than the white rate of the same period, which was 2.8 per 100,000 population.

Moving into the twentieth century, the rate of white victimization declined further. As noted by Lane (1986), this was not the case for African Americans because by the 1950s the homicide rate had climbed to an astounding 64.2 per 100,000 population. Relying on the work of Monkkonen, Gurr (1989) provided the rates of murder victimization for the years 1900 to 1930 (Table 2.1). These rates consist of data representing New York. Similar rates were found in data representing homicide arrests in Washington, D.C., for a much longer time frame, 1890–1970 (Table 2.2).

The question concerning this series of rates regards what contributed to the exceptionally high rates of violence among African Americans for sustained periods of time, especially as they compare to the rates of whites. One factor that must be considered is poverty. Throughout the time, African Americans endured much

Table 2.1   Murder Victimization Rates, New York City

	Whites	Blacks
1852–1860	6.5	19.3
1866–1875	5.4	10.7
1881–1890	4.2	10.2
1901–1910	4.2	12.7
1921–1930	4.8	22.2
1931–1940	4.2	31.3
1945–1953	1.9	24.3

Table 2.2   Homicide Arrest Rates, Washington, D.C.

	Whites	Nonwhites
1890–1899	2.9	9.1
1910–1919	5.1	20.0
1930–1939	6.3	36.1
1960–1970	5.0	25.4

higher rates of conditions of poverty than their white counterparts. As Gurr (1989) noted, there is some support for this postulation. An example can be taken from the years surrounding World War II following the Depression. During the Depression, homicide victimization rates among African Americans were extremely high. During World War II, however, the rates subsided. Many African Americans served in the war, but many were also brought into the labor market to support the industries responsible for the creation of equipment used in the war effort. In essence, they were able to work and earn wages. As discussed in more detail in another chapter, poverty breeds shame, which has the ultimate capacity to produce violence.

Other significant events throughout the twentieth century have had an impact on American rates of violence. The civil rights movement of the 1960s spurred rates of violence in different directions. For black Americans, rates of violence declined, while rates of violence among whites increased. This is another interesting observation. Could it be that anger and shame subsided among African Americans as they began to make inroads into the mainstream of American society? Could it be that as African Americans became more recognized as counterparts or equals to whites some of the anger was replaced with security in relation to economic conditions and opportunity? Was the increase in rates of violence among whites due to insecurity as power and control were shifting to a more equal status?

The late 1970s to 1980 was also a period of change as rates of violence increased sharply. In 1985, another upsurge in violence has been documented throughout several regions of the country with the onslaught of crack cocaine, a very potent and cheap form of cocaine hydrochloride, that swept through country. During the 1990s and into the early years of the twenty-first century, overall rates of violence subsided. Some have attributed this decline to better economic conditions. Table 2.3 provides a good depiction of actual rates of violence and murder from 1960 to 2008.

Theoretical Postulations Concerning Changing Rates of Violence

First, it is important to reiterate that generally there has been a long-term decline in rates of violence in Europe, and it appears as though this trend loosely applies to the United States of America. In America, however, the factors are much more complex, especially in regard to different cultural groups. As noted by Gurr (1989), the real questions consist of which factors are associated with declines in violence and which factors are associated with increases in rates of violence.

In Europe, there is little question that the rates of violence have trended downward for centuries. In America, this same trend can be argued; however, clarification is needed. In essence, America consists of two different trends: one for white Americans and one for minorities, especially African Americans. The trend for

Table 2.3   U.S. Crime Index Rates Per 100,000 Inhabitants

Year	Population	Violent	Murder
1960	179,323,175	160.9	5.1
1961	182,992,000	158.1	4.8
1962	185,771,000	162.3	4.6
1963	188,483,000	168.2	4.6
1964	191,141,000	190.6	4.9
1965	193,526,000	200.2	5.1
1966	195,576,000	220.0	5.6
1967	197,457,000	253.2	6.2
1968	199,399,000	298.4	6.9
1969	201,385,000	328.7	7.3
1970	203,235,298	363.5	7.9
1971	206,212,000	396.0	8.6
1972	208,230,000	401.0	9.0
1973	209,851,000	417.4	9.4
1974	211,392,000	461.1	9.8
1975	213,124,000	487.8	9.6
1976	214,659,000	467.8	8.7
1977	216,332,000	475.9	8.8
1978	218,059,000	497.8	9.0
1979	220,099,000	548.9	9.8
1980	225,349,264	596.6	10.2
1981	229,146,000	594.3	9.8
1982	231,534,000	571.1	9.1
1983	233,981,000	537.7	8.3
1984	236,158,000	539.2	7.9

—continued

Table 2.3 (Continued) U.S. Crime Index Rates Per 100,000 Inhabitants

Year	Population	Violent	Murder
1985	238,740,000	556.6	8.0
1986	240,132,887	620.1	8.6
1987	243,400,000	609.7	8.3
1988	245,807,000	637.2	8.4
1989	248,239,000	663.1	8.7
1990	248,709,873	731.8	9.4
1991	252,177,000	758.1	9.8
1992	255,082,000	757.5	9.3
1993	257,908,000	746.8	9.5
1994	260,341,000	713.6	9.0
1995	262,755,000	684.5	8.2
1996	265,284,000	636.6	7.4
1997	267,637,000	611.0	6.8
1998	270,296,000	566.4	6.3
1999	272,690,813	523.0	5.7
2000	281,421,906	506.5	5.5
2001	285,317,559	504.5	5.6
2002	287,973,924	494.4	5.6
2003	290,690,788	475.8	5.7
2004	293,656,842	463.2	5.5
2005	296,507,061	469.0	5.6
2006	299,398,484	473.6	5.7
2007	301,621,157	466.9	5.6
2008	304,059,724	454.5	5.4

Source: The information was provided by the Uniform Crime Report compiled and produced by the Federal Bureau of Investigation.

white Americans has been much more stable and much lower throughout the late 1800s through the twenty-first century. For African Americans, the trend has been much less stable and much higher. Within the African American population, there have been much sharper increases in violence, and the increases have been sustained for longer periods of time.

In regard to the long-term decline, Elias (1976) proposed the concept of a civilizing process. In essence, he argued that throughout time human beings have continuously evolved mentally, physically, and emotionally to a state in which more often people are able to respond to aversive stimuli without resorting to violence. A central component in Elias's theory of civilization is self-control. He believed that much of the past violence has been reduced as a result of more refined and humane methods of dealing with conflict.

Elias's (1976) theory has been largely supported (Spierenburg, 1996), but it is not accepted unanimously. Schuster (2000), for example, found the theory completely void of any real or meaningful explanation. For Europe, the civilizing theory appears to have strong merit. The downward trend in European violence is now supported by robust, ample research, and certainly one could argue that over time standards of decency have evolved. Elias (1976) went to great lengths to describe macroprocesses that demand transformation of individual behavior from gunfights and knife fights to settle minor disputes to a more humane response of either voicing one's displeasure or simply avoiding the altercation altogether. The macroprocesses that have aided or spurred this civilizing process are in large part related to the production of goods and the growth of industry. As the economy has developed in ways that demand interaction and cooperation among participants, less violence has resulted. People have had to employ greater levels of self-control or be forced out of the economic market. Consider, for example, two traders on the floor of the European Stock Exchange. One bumps the other, words are exchanged, and the decision is made to each walk 10 paces, turn, and fire a weapon. The slower of the two is now dead. Centuries past, this was a common and acceptable practice to resolve disputes. Today, it is not.

In America, the civilizing process is probably a part of the violence picture, but it is not as significant as in Europe. America is still such a young country that there are many other factors associated with rates of violence. In addition, as noted, the rates of violence in America do not trend in the same fashion as Europe. As noted by Gurr (1989), European rates of violence can be described as a reversing U-shape, while the rate of violence in America is mostly stable with three pronounced explosions of violence. Monkkonen (1999), for example, studied rates in New York between 1830 and 1990 and discovered the first pronounced increase in 1860, the second in the 1930s, and the most significant explosion between 1970 and 1990.

Because of the enormous complexity surrounding human behavior, it is impossible at this point to definitively point to one, two, or even three factors that may be associated with these pronounced upswings in violence and describe them as causal and capable of eliminating rival variables. Honestly, we just do not know for certain.

With this said, are there any postulates that can be provided regarding the rate of violence in America? Thome (2001), for example, focused on modernization and described it as a series of conflicts. On the one hand, there is anomic contribution to violence and on the other civilizing forces. The thesis is that during times of rising rates of violence, especially those noted (1860, 1930, 1970–1990), it could be that anomic contributions were more dominant. As people tired of the violence, the civilizing process gained back some ground.

Another interesting factor highlighted by Gurr (1989) is the connection between waves of violent crime and times of war. Gurr (1989) even went as far as to say, "In fact, war is the single most obvious correlate of the great historical waves of violent crime in England and the United States"(p. 132). Of course, there are other factors, but the main upswings in violence throughout the United States have been associated with times of war:

1860s–1870s: Civil War
1930s: decade after World War I
1960s–1990s: Vietnam War and the baby boom (population increase associated with World War II)

A final note, again provided by Gurr (1989), captures the essence of what may be occurring in times of war and how it relates to the civilizing process. "If the civilizing process has been accompanied by sensitization to violence, then war, including internal war, temporarily desensitizes people to violence" (p. 48).

Predicting Violence

Can We Predict Which Individuals Will Be Involved in Violent Behavior?

According to Tikkanen (2009), many negative effects of violence could be alleviated by improving the accuracy of predicting violent behavior. Tikkanen noted that the lack of knowledge about the root causes of violence is an impediment for such predictions. Tikkanen, in his doctoral dissertation on the subject, analyzed the risk factors of violent reconvictions and mortality, using research data that was previously collated by Professor Matti Virkkunen and based on court-ordered mental status examinations carried out in Finland during 1990–1998.

The data indicated that the majority of the 242 men participating in the study suffered from alcoholism and severe personality disorders. The control group comprised 1,210 Finnish males matched by sex, age, and place of birth. Following a nine-year follow-up period, the risk analyses were conducted based on criminal register and mortality data.

Risk variables used in the study were antisocial personality disorder (ASPD), borderline personality disorder (BPD), the comorbidity of ASPD and BPD, childhood adversities, alcohol consumption, age, and the monoamine oxidase A (MAOA) genotype. In addition to these factors, the temperament dimensions were assessed using the Tridimensional Personality Questionnaire (TPQ).

The prevalence of recidivistic acts of violence (32%) and mortality (16%) was high among the offenders. Severe personality disorders and childhood adversities increased the risk of recidivism and mortality both among offenders and in comparison to the controls. Offenders with BPD and a history of childhood maltreatment stood out as having a particularly poor prognosis.

The MAOA genotype was associated with the effects of alcohol consumption and aging on recidivism. With high-activity MAOA (MAOA-H) offenders, alcohol consumption and age affected the risk of violent reconvictions—alcohol increasing it and aging decreasing it—while with low-activity MAOA (MAOA-L) offenders no such link existed.

How Should We Use Predictions of Future Violence?

Based on the study (Tikkanen, 2009) and similar ones, does this mean that if there is a possibility that a person will commit a violent act in the future, the individual should be locked up and not released in society?

In *Murr v. Marshall*, a California appellate court stated:

> The paramount consideration for both the Board of Prison Hearings and the Governor of California under the governing statutes is whether the inmate currently poses a threat to public safety and thus may not be released on parole.

Excerpts from the U.S. Supreme Court Case O'Connor v. Donaldson

> A former patient of a state mental hospital, who throughout his nearly 15 years of confinement in the hospital had repeatedly demanded his release, claiming that he was dangerous to no one, that he was not mentally ill, and that the hospital was not providing treatment for his supposed illness, brought an action under 42 USCS 1983, in the United States District Court for the Northern District of Florida, alleging that the hospital superintendent and other members of the hospital staff had intentionally and maliciously deprived him of his constitutional right to liberty. The testimony at trial demonstrated that the former

patient posed no danger to others or to himself during the time he had been confined, and also showed that his requests for release had been supported by responsible persons willing to provide any care he might need on release. The superintendent's principal defense was that he had acted in good faith and was therefore immune from any liability for monetary damages. Although rejecting a proposed instruction reflecting the superintendent's contention, the District Court did instruct the jury that monetary damages could not be assessed against the superintendent if he had believed reasonably and in good faith that the patient's continued confinement was proper, and that punitive damages could be awarded only if the superintendent had acted maliciously or wantonly or oppressively. The jury returned a verdict assessing both compensatory and punitive damages against the superintendent and a codefendant, and the Court of Appeals for the Fifth Circuit affirmed (493 F2d 507).

[Facts as recited in the Court's opinion] The respondent, Kenneth Donaldson, was civilly committed to confinement as a mental patient in the Florida State Hospital at Chattahoochee in January 1957. He was kept in custody there against his will for nearly 15 years. The petitioner, Dr. J. B. O'Connor, was the hospital's superintendent during most of this period. Throughout his confinement Donaldson repeatedly, but unsuccessfully, demanded his release, claiming that he was dangerous to no one, that he was not mentally ill, and that, at any rate, the hospital was not providing treatment for his supposed illness. Finally, in February 1971, Donaldson brought this lawsuit under 42 U.S.C. § 1983, in the United States District Court for the Northern District of Florida, alleging that O'Connor, and other members of the hospital staff named as defendants, had intentionally and maliciously deprived him of his constitutional right to liberty. After a four-day trial, the jury returned a verdict assessing both compensatory and punitive damages against O'Connor and a codefendant.

A finding of "mental illness" alone cannot justify a State's locking a person up against his will and keeping him indefinitely in simple custodial confinement. Assuming that that term can be given a reasonably precise content and that the "mentally ill" can be identified with reasonable accuracy, there is still no constitutional basis for confining such persons involuntarily if they are dangerous to no one and can live safely in freedom.

Jackson v. Indiana

Theon Jackson was a mentally defective deaf mute with a mental level of a preschool child. He could not read, write, or otherwise communicate except through limited sign language. In May 1968, at age 27, he was charged in the Criminal Court of Marion County, Indiana, with separate robberies of two women. The offenses were alleged to have occurred the preceding July. The first involved property (a purse and its contents) with a value of $4. The second concerned $5 in money. The trial court determined that Jackson was not mentally competent to stand trial. Could he just be locked up without being convicted because he may be a danger to society?

In *Jackson v. Indiana*, the U.S. Supreme Court held that a person charged by a state with a criminal offense who is committed solely on account of his incapacity to proceed to trial cannot be held more than the reasonable period of time necessary to determine whether there is a substantial probability that the individual will attain that capacity in the foreseeable future. If it is determined that this is not the case, then the state must either institute the customary civil commitment proceeding that would be required to commit indefinitely any other citizen or release the defendant. Furthermore, even if it is determined that the defendant probably soon will be able to stand trial, the defendant's continued commitment must be justified by progress toward that goal.

Conclusion

Across Europe, rates of violence have trended downward for several centuries. Within this downward trend, however, there have been periods of increased violence embedded within the long-term historical decline. Therefore, the study of violence really consists of questions aimed at two different phenomena: factors associated with the decline and factors associated with the increases.

In the United States, the historical rate of violence is much more complex. Part of this rate complexity lies in the fact that two different rates have coexisted—one rate for whites and a separate one for minorities, especially black Americans. The rate of violence for nonwhites has been much higher and much more prone to rapid and very sharp increases in violence. As we progress throughout this book, the goal is somehow to understand better the variables associated with violence.

Review Questions

1. Discuss the general trend of violence throughout Europe over the past several centuries.
2. Throughout premodern Europe, where were the rates of violence higher, in rural or urban areas? Is this still the area in which most violence takes place today?
3. Discuss what we know about violence in America. How has the American trend of violence differed from that of European trends?

4. What is the most significant factor influencing rates of violence in America that was not experienced to the same degree in Europe?
5. Discuss the three major upswings in violence that have taken place in America. During which years did they occur, and what are the variables common to each?

References

Brown, R.M. (1975). *Strain of violence: Historical studies of American violence and vigilantism.* New York: Oxford University Press.

Chesnais, J. C. (1981). *Histoire de la violence en occident de 1800 a nos jours.* Paris: Laffont.

Cockburn, J. S. (1977). The nature and incidence of crime in England, 1559–1625: A preliminary survey. London: Methuen.

Courtwright, D.I. (1996). *Violent land: Single men and social disorder from the frontier to the inner city.* Cambridge, MA: Harvard University Press

Durkheim, E. (1973). *Le suicide: Etude de sociologie.* Paris: Presses University de France.

Eisner, M. (2003). *Long term historical trends in violent crime.* Chicago: University of Chicago Press.

Elias, N. (1976). *Uber den Prozess der Zivilisation: Soziogenctishe und psychogenetische Untersuchungen.* Frankfurt, Germany: Suhrkamp.

Ferri, E. (1925). *L'omicida nella psicologia e nella psicopatologia criminale.* Turin, Italy: Unione tipografico-editrice torinese.

Given, J. B. (1977). *Society and homicide in thirteenth-century England.* Stanford, CA: Stanford University Press.

Gurr, T. R. (1981). Historical trends in violent crime: A critical review of the evidence. In M. Tonry and N. Morris (eds.), *Crime and justice: An annual review of research* (Vol. 3). Chicago: University of Chicago Press.

Gurr, T. R., ed. (1989). *Violence in America.* Newbury Park, CA: Sage.

Hindus, M. S. (1980). *Prison and plantation: Crime, justice and authority in Massachusetts and South Carolina.* Chapel Hill, NC: University of North Carolina Press.

Hoffman, F. (1925). *The homicide problem.* San Francisco: Prudential Press

Jackson v. Indiana, 406 U.S. 715, 720 (U.S. 1972).

Johnson, E. (1995). *Urbanization and crime: Germany, 1871–1914.* Cambridge, UK: Cambridge University Press.

Lane, R. (1986). *The roots of violence in black Philadelphia.* Cambridge, MA: Harvard University Press.

Monkkonen, E. H. (1989). Diverging homicide rates: England and the United States, 1850–1875. In T. R. Gurr (ed.), *Violence in America.* Newbury Park, CA: Sage, 121–142.

Monkkonen, E. H. (2001). New standards for historical homicide research. *Crime, histoire et Societe* [crime, history and society], 5(2), 7–26.

Murr v. Marshall, 673 F. Supp. 2d 1028 (C.D. Cal. 2009).

O'Connor v. Donaldson, 422 U.S. 563 (U.S. 1975).

Reiss, A. J. and Roth, J. (1993). *Understanding and preventing violence,* Washington, DC: National Academy Press.

Schuster, P. (2000). *Eine stadt vor Gericht: Recht und Alltag im spatmittelalterlichen kon Stanz.* Paderbor, Germany: Schoning.

Spierenburg, P. (1996). Long-term trends in homicide: Theoretical reflections and Dutch evidence fifteenth to twentieth centuries. In E. A. Johnson and E. Monkkonen (eds.), *The civilization of crime: Violence in town and country since the Middle Ages* (pp. 63–108). Urbana, IL: University of Illinois Press.

Thome, H. (1995). Modernization and crime: What is the explanation? *IAHCCJ Bulletin,* 20, 31–47.

Thome, H. (2001) Explaining long term trends in violent crime. *Crime, History, and Society Journal* vol. 5, no. 2, pp. 69-82.

Tikkanen, R. (2009, September 27). New ways to predict violent behavior? *Science Daily.* Retrieved April 30, 2010, from http://www.sciencedaily.com/releases/2009/09/090925092646.htm.

Chapter 3

Correlates of Violence

Introduction

Identifying correlates of violence is among the most important task of any work attempting to better understand the phenomenon. The reason the correlates are so important is that it is through the correlates that we are able to approach the concept of violence from a macro level. In this chapter, five correlates are identified as closely related to violence. Of course, this is not an exhaustive list. The fact is that human behavior is so complex and multifaceted it is nearly impossible to construct an exhaustive list of correlates without confounding the relationships to the point of uselessness.

As a result, we have selected five correlates that appear to be robust in contributing to the likelihood of someone engaging in violence. The ultimate attempt is to demonstrate a pattern among these correlates by which one leads to another and ultimately produces a state of being in which violence becomes an almost predictable response. In Figure 3.1, the depiction shows how each correlate can be related to violence individually. The depiction in Figure 3.2 shows the relationship between violence and the correlates in a circular manner. It is when each of the correlates is present and contributing to the next that violence becomes so likely and often so damaging.

Values and Violence

Values, in this context, are meant to describe the relative worth or importance assigned to some possession or state of being. A person's values therefore provide a part of the

45

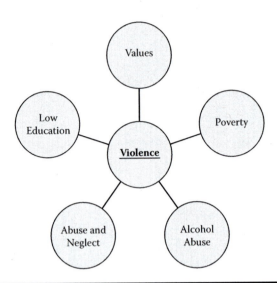

Figure 3.1   Relation of each correlate individually.

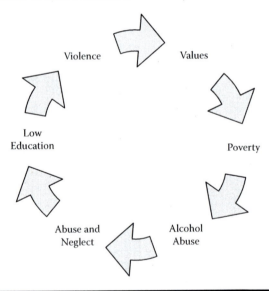

Figure 3.2   Relationship between violence and the correlates circularly.

most basic foundation from which feeling and assessments of worth resonate. In essence, if one is able to obtain possessions deemed valuable, then one's global assessment of self is positive. If not, one's global assessment is negative, which often leads to anger, resentment, and shame, all of which contribute to potential violence.

What are some of the dominant features of the current system of values in the United States and many other parts of the world? Unfortunately, the most dominant value held is the extreme significance placed on material possessions—inanimate objects that possess no ability to provide meaningful feeling. Especially in the United States, people are inundated on a daily basis with powerful messages consisting of what it means to be successful. For example, we are told that to be successful one must live in a certain neighborhood, possess a certain type or style of vehicle, own certain types of clothing, and even achieve a certain physical stature that is considered attractive.

In essence, the emphasis of current values is squarely rooted within the domain of materialism or "fine things." The ultimate problem with this psychological framework is that true happiness is unable to be securely achieved. Even when a person is able to obtain certain material possessions, the satisfaction is often brief and quickly dissipates. The possession is likely to serve as a short-term buffer to one's ego but is quickly deflated as one identifies "something else" that is bigger, better, faster, and shinier than the current possession. One concept widely discussed in sociological literature that is closely related to this phenomenon is relative deprivation. Relative deprivation, according to Messner and Rosenfeld (1994), describes the economic and social gap between the rich and the poor, especially those who live in close proximity to one another. In essence, one is constantly evaluating his or her place in the social and economic structure according to the possessions of others. This is a dangerous phenomenon mostly because there is no end point. A person firmly in the grasp of evaluating personal worth according to the material possessions he or she is able to acquire will eventually find the process exhausting because there will always be "something else" "out there" more valuable.

An important point regarding relative deprivation is that it does not have to be reserved for describing the relationship between only the rich and the poor. The concepts of "rich" and "poor" are elusive and within this context do not properly capture the true phenomenon under scrutiny. This is because relative deprivation can be experienced by those who would be described as "well off." For example, someone may live in a nice neighborhood, drive a nice vehicle, and own fashionable clothes. To others, they may be considered and looked on as the epitome of success. To the individual, however, their possessions may be perceived as wholly inadequate in comparison to their neighbor's slightly bigger home, nicer car, and more extravagant possessions.

Goldberg (2006) wrote an interesting article in the *New York Times,* "Materialism Is Bad for You, Studies Say." A particularly interesting point is that people enveloped in the quest for material goods, beyond those needed to meet basic needs, lose the ability to engage in meaningful human connection. According to Goldberg (2006, p. 12), "They are so exhausted from the pursuit of nice things—a big house, private school for the kids, fancy cars—that they are time starved and depleted. Life is luxurious but unsatisfying and simply no fun." Goldberg (2006) noted that there are more serious consequences beyond having no fun for those engaged in the perpetual quest for material possessions. "In recent years researchers have reported an ever growing downside to getting and spending—damage to relationships and self esteem, a heightened risk of depression and anxiety, less time for what the research indicates truly makes people happy, like family, friendships, and engaging work."

How do materialistic values contribute to the phenomenon of violence? First, it must be noted that the relationship between material values and eventual violence is complex. There are many mediating variables that can influence the cognitions and actions that propel one toward or away from violent responses. The basic postulate, however, is that societies largely governed by material possession will experience a long-term erosion of the basic foundation from which happiness is attainable. This postulate is also complex; however, evidence does support a relationship. Our most basic attempt is to position the concept of valuing material possessions as a means of achieving happiness and worth as a contributing factor in the processes that may lead to violence. Of course, this postulate assumes an inverse relationship between the variables happiness and violence. Future studies would be well served in further exploring this relationship. Intuitively, it makes sense that a person who purports to be genuinely happy and content would be less inclined to engage in violence and more inclined to seek out alternative responses to various stimuli.

Poverty and Violence

Closely related to the idea of valuing material possessions as a means of achieving happiness and success is the long-held discussion of the relationship between poverty and violence. Again, according to Goldberg (2006) there are some studies that showed that poor people who place a high value on materialistic goods are especially prone to experience high degrees of unhappiness. Similar to the relationship between material values and violence, however, the relationship between poverty and violence is complex.

To begin, we must establish a working definition of poverty. Generally, poverty is a state or condition of having little or no money, goods, or means of support. Poverty is also analogous to a condition of being poor or, in the case of relative poverty, a perception of insufficient desirable possessions. According to Crutchfield and Wadsworth (2003), poverty is widely believed to cause violence. The use of the word *cause* is a powerful implication because it suggests that for there to be violence there must also be poverty. Of course, this contention is hotly debated because there are certainly some people who live in conditions of poverty who do not engage in violence.

Another well-established line of thought proposes the opposite relationship in some circumstances. Staley (1992), for example, made the claim that violence can cause poverty. The basis for this postulation is that areas inundated with violence serve to destabilize the environment to the degree that business ventures or attempts at economic development seek alternative locations.

An additional area of debate concerning the relationship between poverty and violence is the precise method with which to measure poverty. The debate here is generally in relation to whether it is poverty or income inequality that is most responsible for violence. For income inequality, one may not be in the defined category of poverty but may experience or perceive an unequal distribution of wealth in relation to society at large as well as both inter- and intraracial inequality. As a result, violence may be a response to inequality and not necessarily poverty.

In this context, the general concept of relative deprivation is again applicable. Even though a person is not considered to be living in poverty, the person may still experience strain and dissatisfaction due to their real or perceived unequal status with those seen on television and in media outlets.

Irrespective of this debate, however, there is agreement among scholars that an important relationship exists between those considered extremely disadvantaged within society and the amount of violence that takes place within the areas in which they reside (Crutchfield and Wadsworth, 2003). The focus on the connection between violence and the extremely disadvantaged is likely to be most measurable for a couple of reasons. First, those considered to be extremely disadvantaged are also the most likely to have limited emotional and psychological resources to deal with stressors, whereas those not classified as extremely disadvantaged may possess sufficient, albeit limited, resources to moderate certain stressors without having to resort to violence.

Overall, much of the literature points to a fairly stable connection between higher levels of violence and the poor, especially among the poorest of the poor (Crutchfield and Wadsworth, 2003). In addition, there is support for a relationship between violence and place. The poor engage in more violence, but they also live in more violent locations. As a result, violence and place serve as factors that appear to be related to other variables that also contribute to continued violence. An example may help to illuminate this point. A violent act in a neighborhood not normally associated with violence is likely to be addressed quickly and directly by both law enforcement and the citizens who reside there. On the other hand, a violent act perpetrated in a poorer area where violence is more common is likely to receive different or reduced attention simply because it is not out of the ordinary and much more expected. In essence, many of the social controls, both formal and informal, that are normally employed to keep the peace are deteriorated (Crutchfield and Wadsworth, 2003; Sampson and Groves, 1989; Stark, 1987). Staley (1992) provided a good synthesis of this area of the literature using the concept of a multidirectional relationship. Poverty breeds illegal markets, which often lead to violence, and culminates in community and neighborhood instability. Once the community is destabilized, the process becomes circular via the discouragement of economic development. In the end, poverty and violence continue.

Alcohol Abuse and Violence

Closely associated with the variables discussed thus far—values (material possessions) and poverty—is the concept of alcohol abuse. We focus specifically on alcohol in this discussion because it is the one drug that is most closely connected to violence (and the one that is legal to possess and consume). Of course, violence is carried out while under the influence of other drugs but not at the same rate as alcohol.

What is the logic behind the connection of alcohol abuse with values and poverty? First, the abuse of any drug, including alcohol, is a direct result of an attempt to alter mood. In essence, the current state of being is one that is consumed with emotional and psychological discomfort. The degree of discomfort, or more precisely the degree of emotional and psychological pain, is an important consideration and is likely to distinguish between those who abuse alcohol and those who use alcohol. Many individuals consume alcohol on a daily basis yet are never involved in any criminal or violent incidents. Our mention of alcohol abuse as a correlate of violence is reserved for those users and abusers of alcohol who are much more likely to engage in violence while under its influence. Ultimately, offenders most likely to engage in violence are those most strained emotionally and psychologically. The consumption of alcohol represses cognitive mechanisms used to keep violent reactions in check. Once these mechanisms are numbed through a sufficient rate of consumption of alcohol, the negative and painful emotion is free to radiate largely unchecked. Violence, within this framework, can be experienced as catharsis as negative emotion is released from the body. This is a dangerous phenomenon as those who experience relief or pleasure as a result of some action are much more likely to repeat the action, in this case violence.

Greenfield (1998) provided the following statistical information regarding the influence of alcohol in a multitude of violent encounters:

1. About 3 million violent crimes occur each year in which victims perceive the offender to have been drinking at the time of the offense. Among those victims who provided information about the offender's use of alcohol, about 35 percent of the victimizations involved an offender who had been drinking. About two-thirds of the alcohol-involved crimes were characterized as simple assaults.
2. Two-thirds of victims who suffered violence by an intimate (a current or former spouse, boyfriend, or girlfriend) reported that alcohol had been a factor. Among spouse victims, three of four incidents were reported to have involved an offender who had been drinking. By contrast, an estimated 31 percent of stranger victimizations, in which the victim could determine the absence or presence of alcohol, were perceived to be alcohol related.
3. For about one in five violent victimizations involving perceived alcohol use by the offender, victims also reported that they believed the offender was using other drugs as well.

4. Data for 1995 from the National Incident-Based Reporting System (NIBRS) of the FBI indicated that about half of the incidents described by the investigating officer as alcohol related were between offenders and victims who were intimates.
5. NIBRS data showed that 7 of 10 alcohol-involved incidents of violence occurred in a residence; the hour beginning at 11 p.m. was the most frequent time of occurrence; and about 2 in 10 incidents involved the use of a weapon other than hands, fists, or feet.

Alcohol therefore can be described as a cathartic substance that significantly contributes to violent responses to aversive stimuli. Especially, when used to mask or numb the negative feeling associated with the need to achieve material possessions and the strain of poverty, alcohol becomes a powerful variable strongly associated with violent eruptions.

Abuse and Neglect Effect on Violence

Thus far, the correlates of violence we have presented have been mainly aimed at adults. The attempt has been to provide a connection between adults who are struggling to achieve material values deemed important by society yet simultaneously reduced to conditions of poverty. The strain of this phenomenon or circumstance will lead many to engage in a variety of abusive behaviors, all meant to alleviate the powerful pangs of negative emotion. As shown, those who engage in alcohol abuse are especially susceptible to engaging in violence as an adaptive response.

In this section, our focus shifts toward the children of those adults who engage in violence and general dysfunction as a result of their experiences. Adults who are experiencing significant psychological and emotional pain, regardless of whether this pain is a result of the emphasis placed on material values, poverty, or alcohol abuse, are more likely to raise children in circumstances described as neglectful and abusive.

Children reared in neglect and abuse-ridden environments are much more likely to experience significant trauma that has a negative impact on their development. Children who are not able to develop in loving and caring environments will be especially prone to emotional and behavioral problems that make it difficult to conform to accepted societal views and values. As a result, these children represent the next iteration of the perpetual cycle of those human beings especially vulnerable to engaging in violence in an attempt to reduce negative emotion.

Neglect and abuse, especially that which is persistent and prolonged, will often lead to psychological trauma. Van der Kolk and Streeck-Fischer (2003) described a *psychological trauma* as "an event that both overwhelms a person's psychological and biological coping mechanisms and that is not responded to by outside help to compensate for the inability of the organism itself to cope" (p. 218). What makes trauma so central to this discussion is that there is strong evidence demonstrating a significant connection of abuse and neglect with subsequent violence (Lewis, 1992; Lewis, Lovely, Yeager, and Femina, 1989).

According to van der Kolk et al. (1996) as well as Putnam (1997), those who have experienced trauma are prone to experience a numbing of emotion. In relation to violence, this is especially problematic as empathy, understanding, flexibility, and tolerance are all necessary to moderate one's actions and serve to direct one to alternative courses of action instead of violence. People who have experienced significant trauma are also vulnerable to hyperarousal or states of hypersensitivity to certain conditions. A child who has been abused or controlled through certain mechanisms, especially physical abuse, may respond harshly or even savagely to stimuli that are similar to their past experiences even when the perception of the intent of the stimuli is completely misguided.

The defense mechanisms within those people who experienced abuse, neglect, and trauma are often so developed and held in a constant state of readiness that, from an emotional standpoint, every ounce of their being is poised to protect them from further trauma. The attempt to articulate to one in this state that they are overreacting is often futile. To them, the essence of their very survival is at stake.

The employment of defense mechanisms is a reaction to a physiological state that results from the presentation of an environmental stimulus. When these physiological reactions are extreme, the result may be engagement in violence. The most salient point thus far is that in many circumstances in which children are raised in abusive and neglectful conditions they will experience trauma that leads to a great expenditure of energy aimed at avoiding the return of a traumatic experience. Energy toward this quest is energy that cannot be used in other areas of development, such as secure attachment, leisure activities, games, learning, and fun.

A traumatized child is one who is forced to grow up quickly, well beyond his or her time. Again, a traumatized child's main concern is survival, survival of the self, and certainly not a neighborhood game of tag. And, as is the case with any organism whose major expenditure of energy is aimed at survival, these children will be prone to overreact to any circumstance that is even slightly ambiguous. Because traumatized children rarely trust others, a little ambiguity could be more than sufficient to spur a violent outburst.

As children grow older, their exposure to violence becomes especially problematic. Boys who have experienced abuse and neglect in the form of violence in the home are most likely to mimic this violence in the form of a response to neighborhood or community stimuli (Selner-O'Hagan et al., 1998). Kalmuss (1984) provided powerful support for this postulation. He reported that boys who witnessed their fathers engage in violence were 1,000 times more likely to later abuse their own partners than boys not exposed to the same violence.

Education and Violence

The final correlate, low levels of education, is largely related to experiences of abuse, neglect, and trauma. Especially when the trauma is a result of violence, children spend a great deal of time trying to cognitively manage their situation in an attempt to alleviate heightened states of physiology and emotion. Really, they are trying to manage anxiety associated with the insecurity and destabilizing effect of a violent surrounding. The point, as mentioned, is that much of their vital energy is spent trying to figure out how to reduce the chances of reexperiencing the trauma and violence.

One of the profound consequences of a child's energy being spent on minimizing future episodes of violence and conflict is that little remains available to be directed toward a meaningful education. As noted by Bion (1962), it is only when children feel secure that they are able to engage in the concept of curiosity, which is a significant prerequisite for learning.

Making matters worse is the fact that children who have experienced trauma and violence are also much more likely to engage in violence in a school setting. In a sense, traumatized children have a difficult time delineating between information that is relevant and that which is irrelevant (McFarlane, Weber, and Clark, 1993).

Van der Kolk and Ducey (1989) as well as Bower and Sivers (1998) made an interesting connection. Traumatized children often misinterpret stimuli. In some cases, they erroneously interpret nonthreatening stimuli as traumatic, to which they will respond. In other cases, when the stimuli are not interpreted as traumatic, they ignore them. This is profound insofar as it illuminates a cycle in which traumatized children have little chance at success.

The thesis to this line of reasoning is that children who have experienced significant trauma are only able to be stimulated if presented with stimuli they perceive as traumatic. Anything less than traumatic is disregarded as unimportant and ignored. The question then is how it is possible to educate a traumatized child whose physiological system has become so desensitized to any presentation of stimuli that is not perceived as threatening or capable of producing further trauma. The result is that traumatized children within an educational setting miss out on critical skills needed to be successful. Because the bulk of their energy is spent on managing the effects of trauma, abused children have a limited capacity to engage in complex tasks, including the ability to read and write.

Ultimately, it is difficult to properly educate a child who has experienced prolonged abuse and neglect. A vicious and deteriorating cycle often ensues. As the child grows older, the problems become more complex as the basic skills needed to learn were never appropriately set in place.

Consider the example of a fifth grader living in a foster home. The boy had been severely abused by his parents, who were poor, alcoholics, and unable to gain meaningful employment as a result of not finishing high school. Every time the boy was called on to read, he became disruptive and sometimes violent.

After extensive intervention on behalf of school counselors, it was finally learned that the boy could not properly read at a fifth-grade level. The boy was already two years behind his age group and still could not read at the appropriate level. Once it became known that he could not read, he was further stigmatized by his peers, resulting in more violence. The boy was eventually expelled as the school could no longer deal with his violent outbursts, some of which resulted in severe injury to other children. What ultimately happened to this boy is unknown. At last contact, he had been sent to a maximum security juvenile detention facility after being adjudicated for a violent crime in which he struck a neighborhood kid with a metal pipe.

Some statistics may help to further illuminate the connection between not only violence but also criminality in general and education:

- The United States spends an average of $9,644 a year to educate a student (National Center for Education Statistics, 2006).
- The average annual cost per inmate is $22,600 (Stephen, 2004).
- The United States spent almost $50 billion in incarceration costs in 2004 (Bureau of Justice Statistics, 2005; Stephen, 2004).
- A 10 percent increase in the male graduation rate would reduce murder and assault arrest rates by about 20 percent, motor vehicle theft by 13 percent, and arson by 8 percent (Moretti, 2005).
- Of black males who graduated from high school and went on to attend some college, only 1 percent were incarcerated in 2000 (Raphael, 2004).
- State prison inmates without a high school diploma and those with a GED (general equivalency diploma) were more likely to be repeat offenders than those with a diploma (Harlow, 2003).
- Over a third of jail inmates said the main reason they quit school was because of academic problems, behavior problems, or lost interest (Harlow, 2003). This point is especially important as each of these variables is likely a direct result of trauma, abuse, and a neglectful upbringing.

Conclusion

The task of identifying variables associated with violence is daunting. The problem is that the number of variables that could be considered and could be related to violence is legion. The variables presented in this discussion, however, appear in much of the literature, and strong associations have been made. The one variable that has been added is the concept of values. The intent behind the addition of this variable is to provide a foundation on which the other variables interact. A value system rooted in the possession of material goods is one that serves to accentuate the relationship among poverty, alcohol abuse, neglect, and abuse and low levels of education. A different value system stressing healthy interaction and acceptance of others would possibly serve to mitigate the relationship between violence and the remaining variables to the extent that each could be more sufficiently addressed. To not address the concept of values is like releasing an inmate incarcerated for the last 20 years and sending him back to the environment from which he came with no additional skill sets.

In addition, the effort has been to present these variables in a manner in which they create a circular pattern by which each leads to the next and is a result of the previous. We fully understand, however, that the order in which we have presented the variables may not be agreed on by all. In fact, we welcome this exploration as several different orders may be appropriate, and many more variables may be applicable, depending on the individual. For example, with some people who engage in violence, the presence of alcohol may not appear until after the incident has been perpetrated. For others, violence may be a response not as a result of abuse in the conventional sense but as a result of neglect because caregivers were not being present and available, leaving them to roam freely with no supervision.

Review Questions

1. Discuss the concept of values. How do values contribute to violence?
2. Analyze the concept of poverty and its relation to violence.
3. What is the relationship between poverty and alcohol abuse? How does this relationship contribute to violence?
4. Discuss the consequences of neglect and abuse. How do these relate to violence?
5. Analyze the relationship between low education and violence.
6. Analyze and discuss the interrelatedness of each of the variables discussed in this chapter. Which do you think is capable of explaining the most variance in violence?

References

Bion, W. R. (1962). *Learning from experience.* London: Heinemann.

Bower, G. H., and Sivers, H. (1998). The cognitive impact of traumatic events. *Development and Psychopathology,* 10, 625–653.

Bureau of Justice Statistics. (2005). *Prison statistics.* Washington, DC: U.S. Department of Justice, Bureau of Justice Statistics.

Crutchfield, R. D., and Wadsworth, T. (2003). Poverty and violence. In W. Heitmeyer and J. Hagan (eds.), *International handbook of violence research* (pp. 67–82). Dordrecht, the Netherlands: Kluwer Academic.

Goldberg, C. (2006, February 8). Materialism is bad for you, studies say. *The New York Times,* A-18.

Greenfield, L. A. (1998). *Alcohol and crime: An analysis of national data on the prevalence of alcohol involvement in crime.* Washington, DC: U.S. Department of Justice.

Harlow, C. (2003). *Education and correctional populations.* Bureau of Justice Statistics Special Report. Washington, DC: U.S. Department of Justice.

Kalmuss, D. (1984). The intergeneration transmission of marital aggression. *Journal of Marriage and the Family,* 46(1), 11–19.

Lewis, D. O., Lovely, R., Yeager, C., and Femina, D. D. (1989). Toward a theory of the theory of violence: A follow up study of delinquents. *Journal of American Academy of Child Adolescent Psychiatry,* 28(3), 431–436.

Lewis, M. (1992) *Shame: The exposed self.* New York: Free Press.

McFarlane, A. C., Weber, D. L., and Clark, R. (1993). Abnormal stimulus processing in posttraumatic stress disorder. *Biological Psychiatry,* 34(5), 311–320.

Messner, S. F., and Rosenfeld, R. (1994). *Crime and the American dream.* Belmont, CA: Wadsworth.

Moretti, E. (2005, October). Does education reduce participation in criminal activities? Research presented at the 2005 symposium on the Social Costs of Inadequate Education. New York: Teachers College, Columbia University.

National Center for Education Statistics. (2006). *The condition of education 2006.* Washington, DC: U.S. Department of Education.

Putnam, F. W. (1997). *Dissociation in child and adolescents.* New York: Guilford Press.

Raphael, S. (2004). *The socioeconomic status of black males: The increasing importance of incarceration.* Berkeley, CA: Goldman School of Public Policy, University of California, Berkeley.

Sampson, R. J., and Groves, B. W. (1989). Community structure and crime: Testing social disorganization theory. *American Journal of Sociology,* 94(4), 774–802.

Selner-O'Hagan, M. B., Kindlon, D. J., Buka, S. L., Raudenbush, W., and Earls, F. (1998). Assessing exposure to violence in urban youth. *Journal of Child Psychology and Psychiatry and Allied Disciplines,* 39(2), 215–224.

Staley, S. (1992). *Drug policies and the decline of American cities.* New Brunswick, NJ: Transaction.

Stark, R. (1987). Deviant places: A theory of the ecology of crime. *Criminology,* 25(4), 893–909.

Stephen, J. (2004). *State prison expenditures, 2001.* Bureau of Justice Statistics Special Report. Washington, DC: U. S. Department of Justice.

Van der Kolk, B. A., and Ducey, C. P. (1989). The psychological processing of traumatic experience: Research patterns in PTSD. *Journal of Traumatic Stress,* 2(3), 259–274.

Van der Kolk, B. A., Pelcovitz, D., Roth, S., Mandel, F., McFarlane, A. C., and Herman, J. L. (1996). Dissociation, somatization, and affect dysregulation: The complexity of adaptation to trauma. *American Journal of Psychiatry,* 153, 83–93.

Van der Kolk, B. A., and Streeck-Fischer, A. (2003). Trauma and violence in children and adolescents: A developmental perspective. In W. Heitmeyer and J. Hagan (eds.), *International handbook of violence research* (pp. 817–832). Dordrecht, the Netherlands: Kluwer Academic.

Chapter 4

Sociological Aspects of Violence

Introduction

> In cities, suburban areas, and even small towns, Americans are fearful and concerned that violence has permeated the fabric and degraded the quality of their lives. The diminished quality of life ranges from an inability to sit on the front porch in neighborhoods where gang warfare has made gunfire a common event to the installation of elaborate security systems in suburban homes where back doors once were left open.

> **Reiss and Roth, 1993, p. 1**

In this chapter, violent crime causation is examined using the sociological themes. First, informal social controls are discussed. The conflict and strain theory of crime causation is explored, followed by a discussion of the relationship between economy and trends of violence. Next, periods of war and their relationship to violence are examined, and then the effects of poverty as a factor in violent crime causation are explored.

In the United States, the causes of violent crime are often explained by the use of sociological theories. August Comte is credited with founding the discipline of sociology in the early 1800s (Vold and Bernard, 1986). Comte studied the turmoil caused by the French Revolution of 1789 and the rapid industrialization of the French society along with the decline of the traditional French society. Later in the

1800s, Emile Durkheim became the clear leader in the development of sociological causes of violent crime.

Life Inside a War Zone

In one South Memphis neighborhood, a violent crime was reported nearly every other day for almost a decade, says the *Memphis Commercial Appeal*. Across the city, more than 30,000 residents in roughly 40 neighborhoods live with the constant threat of violence, said examination of a decade of police records by the newspaper. These are neighborhoods where a violent crime occurs one to three times every 10 days; where there are more than three violent incidents per every five residents. (Goetz, 2009 A-1)

Social Controls

Sociologists contend that our behavior within our society is controlled by formal and informal social controls. Formal social controls are statutes, laws, and the like that are formally enacted to control conduct. For example, a homicide statute prohibiting the unlawful killing of a human being is a formal social control. Thus, California Penal Code, Section 187, which provides that murder is the unlawful killing of a human being or a fetus with malice aforethought, is a formal social control.

Sociologists contend that most of our behavior in society is controlled by informal social controls or norms of conduct. William Summer (1906), in his classic text *Folkways*, divided informal social controls into three types of norms: mores, customs, and folkways. Summer defined *norms* as rules that govern our behavior in a given situation.

Summer (1906) noted that mores are the strongest form of social control and the norms that give society its moral standards of behavior. Many mores are also written into formal social controls. Most violent behavior against another human being would be considered as a violation of a more. According to Summer, violation of a more causes intense feelings and extreme consequences. Killing or sexual assault would be the violation of a basic more in our society.

Summer (1906) classified customs as the second-strongest form of informal social control. He saw that the violation of a custom was not as serious as the violation of a more, but it still caused disgust and shock to those witnessing such an act. An example of a custom violation would be watching someone spit out half-eaten food on the floor during dinner.

The least serious of the norms are folkways. *Folkways* are defined as the traditional methods of doing things because they are accepted behavior. When someone violates a folkway, he or she may be subject to criticism or ridicule. There are times when the violation of a folkway causes another to react in a violent manner. For example, cutting in line at a music concert is a violation of a folkway. There are reports that such behavior has triggered riots and brutal confrontations.

Emile Durkheim

Emile Durkheim (1858–1917) has been called "one of the best known and one of the least understood major social thinkers" (Roberson and Wallace, 1998, p. 94). Durkheim rejected the concept that prevailed in Europe in the late 1800s that human beings were free and rational in society. His theories on the cause of violent behavior are complex, overlapping with different approaches to the causes of violent behavior.

Durkheim was born of Jewish parents in a small French town near the German border. He went to school in Paris and taught philosophy in various secondary schools in France. After spending a year studying under the famous German psychologist Wilhelm Wundt, he was appointed to a professorship at the University of Bordeaux. At the university, he taught the first course on sociology in a French university. Later, he received the first doctoral degree in sociology awarded by the University of Paris. He accepted an appointment to the faculty at the University of Paris and taught there until his death in 1917. Durkheim's first major publication, which was based on his doctoral dissertation, was published in 1893 and titled *De la Division du Travail Social* (The Division of Labor in Society) (Roberson and Wallace, 1998).

Division of Labor in Society

In Durkheim's first major publication (*De la Division du Travail Social*; Roberson and Wallace, 1998), he described the processes of social change involved in the industrialization of societies. The processes were part of the development of societies from primitive societies that he labeled as "mechanical" to the more advanced societies that he labeled as "organic." Durkheim saw the mechanical society as one in which each social group is relatively isolated from all other social groups. Each group in a mechanical society is basically self-sufficient and works largely under identical circumstances. They also do identical work and have relatively identical values. Since there is little division of labor, there is social solidarity among the members of the clan. In the mechanical society, the social controls of the group have far stronger influence on the members of the group; therefore, there is more pressure on the members to conform to certain behaviors.

As societies developed, they moved from mechanical societies to organic ones. In the organic societies, different segments of the society depend on each other in a highly organized division of labor. For example, a family, rather than growing grain to make bread as they would in a mechanical society, now buys the bread from a bakery. Individuals no longer have similar jobs and duties, and there is less social solidarity. Durkheim (Roberson and Wallace, 1998) noted that, as societies became more organic, the society as a whole had less influence on the behavior of individual members. In the mechanical society, Durkheim stated that law functions to enforce uniformity of the members of the group and is oriented toward repressing deviations from the norms. In an organic society, the law functions to regulate the interaction of the various groups within the society and provide restitution when there are transgressions. There are more deviations among societal members in an organic society. Durkheim indicated that all societies are in some stage between the mechanical and the organic structures, with no society totally organic or mechanical (Roberson and Wallace, 1998). In Durkheim's later works, including *The Rules of Sociological Method* (1982) and his most famous work, *Suicide*, he developed the concept that crime is normal in both mechanical and organic societies. He also developed the concept of anomie.

Anomie

Anomie is a Greek term that may loosely be defined as "lawlessness." According to Durkheim (1982), anomie is a state or condition that exists within people when a society evolves from a mechanical to an organic entity. Anomie results because of wide-sweeping scientific, technological, and social change. Anomie may be described as a condition of normlessness rather than a lack of norms. Under the condition of normlessness, norms have lost their meaning and have become inoperative for large segments of the society. According to Durkheim, anomie may also be described as the fragmentation or disassociation of one's center; the feeling of being a number, not a person; social isolation; or social loneliness. A modern-day example of anomie would be an individual who grows up in a small town. As the individual is growing up, if he or she commits a violation of a norm, a neighbor would inform his or her parents. The individual, aware that his or her misconduct would be brought to the attention of his or her parents, was less likely to engage in the misconduct. But, if the individual moves to New York City and gets drunk and disorderly, there is little chance that any of the individual's family back in the small town would be aware of his or her conduct. Thus, the informal social controls have less influence on the individual's behavior.

Durkheim opined that anomie was a product of societal transition. Accordingly, when society is in transition and anomie is high, institutions and laws become less effective in controlling behavior, and violence results. Durkheim used his concept of anomie to explain the phenomenon of suicide and also violent crime. According to him, all the uniformity that exists in a society is the "totally of social likenesses" or the "collective conscience." He contended that pressure is exerted in varying degrees for uniformity within the society. The pressures result in certain conduct being designated as criminal behaviors and as morally reprehensible. The rules of social conduct are constructed in a manner that certain individuals cannot fulfill them. The number who cannot fulfill the demands must be large enough to constitute an identifiable group but not so large that they include a substantial portion of the society. Accordingly, those in society who fulfill the demands of the collective conscience feel a sense of moral superiority by identifying themselves as good and righteous and those who fail as criminals. The criminals play an important role in the maintenance of the social solidarity because they are identified as inferior and allow the rest of society to feel superior (Roberson and Wallace, 1998).

Durkheim stated that even punishment plays a role in the maintenance of social solidarity. When the rules of the collective conscience are violated, society tends to respond with repressive sanctions, not for retribution or deterrence, but because those of us who conform will be demoralized if the sanctions are not imposed. He contended that when a criminal is punished, those of us who are not punished receive the award of "not being punished" because of our "good behavior." In a crimeless state, society would punish any deviation from the social norm; therefore, social progress would be impossible. In addition, according to Durkheim, the elimination of misbehavior would also eliminate the possibility of independent growth (Vold and Bernard, 1986).

If there were no violent crime, would we be bored to death? If so, then does violent crime have a function in society? Durkheim discussed these questions. He contended that it would be a pathological state of society if there were no crimes. He also contended that if the most violent crime, murder, was eliminated, then society would impose the most severe punishments on the next most violent crime. Under Durkheim's logic, as we eliminate the most serious crime, the next most serious would then receive the harshest punishment. This would continue, and finally society would punish jaywalking with the harshest punishment (Williams and McShane, 2004).

Using Durkheim's logic in today's world, note that the leading television shows and most of the current movies shown in the theaters are based on or include violence. A common complaint about television and movies is their violence. Even the most popular sport in America, football, is a violent sport. And the new sport involving a combination of boxing and wrestling, ultimate fighting, is one of the fastest-growing spectator sports in America. Accordingly, violence is a major part of present-day entertainment.

Strain Theory and Violence

Strain theorists contend that individuals commit violent acts because of the pressures placed on them by society. According to them, if an individual fails to conform to social norms and laws, it is because there is excessive pressure or strain that causes the individual to commit criminal behavior. And, lawbreaking and deviance are not normal, but the misconduct is caused by immense pressures on the individual. The strain theorists see people as basically moral and innately desirous of conforming to the norms of society. Those theorists contend that we should attempt to discover the nature of the strains or pressures that cause individuals to stray from their law-abiding behavior and commit violent crime (Roberson and Wallace, 1998).

Robert Merton

American sociologist Robert Merton (1910–2003) revised Durkheim's concept of anomie and applied it to American society. Merton was born to working-class Jewish eastern European immigrants in Philadelphia. He never discussed why he changed his name from Schkolnik to Merton. He was educated at South Philadelphia High School; during his high school time, he was a frequent visitor to the nearby Andrew Carnegie Library and other cultural and educational centers. He studied sociology at Temple University in Philadelphia and later at Harvard University. He taught at Harvard, Tulane, and Columbia (Sztompka, 2003).

Merton's (1938) article "Social Structure and Anomie" is probably the most frequently quoted article in modern sociology and criminology. In the article, he examined the question of how malintegration in society is related to deviance. Merton defined anomie as a discontinuity between cultural goals and the legitimate means available for reaching them. When applied to the United States, Merton contended that the American dream emphasizes the goal of monetary success but without a corresponding emphasis on the legitimate avenues to meet this goal. He saw this discontinuity as leading to deviant behavior.

Merton (1938) contended that the American culture is based on egalitarian ideology, in which it is maintained that all people have an equal chance to achieve wealth. However, only the most talented and the most hard-working individuals in the lower socioeconomic class have a chance to obtain the goal of achieving wealth in the accepted method (lawful method). The others must use illegal means to obtain wealth. Accordingly, the high level of crime and violence in American society is caused by a cultural imbalance—imbalance between the cultural forces that drive the individual toward criminal behavior and the cultural forces restraining the individual from criminal behavior. He believed that the distribution of criminal behavior is inversely related to the distribution of legitimate opportunities.

Middle-Class Measuring Rod

Using an approach similar to Merton, Albert Cohen (1960) concluded that American society primarily consisted of middle and working classes, and this places a high premium on ambition, getting ahead, and achievement. Cohen contended that both the middle and working classes tend to teach certain values to their children and that both classes believe in ambition, getting ahead, and achievement. The lower-class boys are measured or evaluated by the standards and aspirations of the middle class, but for this they are not properly trained and lack the resources to fulfill this expectation. He referred to this process as the "middle-class measuring rod." By that, he was referring to the fact that success is measured using the middle-class goals for which the lower-class boys are not trained and lack resources to achieve. As the results of the failure to achieve, the lower-class boys often turn to violence and crime in an attempt to reach the goals.

Table 4.1 Cohen's Values

Middle-Class Values	*Lower-Class Values*
Self-control	Toughness
Postponement of immediate gratification in favor of long-term goals	Instant gratification
Planning for the future	Lack of order
Individual responsibility	Lack of punctuality
Ambition	Ethic of reciprocity
Control of aggression and anger	Retaliation

While Cohen contended that both classes believe in ambition, getting ahead, and achievement as goals, the two classes have different value systems. His value comparisons between the two classes are listed in Table 4.1.

Opportunity Structure

Two other strain theorists, Richard Cloward and Lloyd Ohlin, attempted to explain violent crime by young males and subcultural delinquency using an "opportunity theory" concept. The researchers explored the linkage between the socially structured patterns of youth opportunity in the communities and the dominant patterns of subcultural formulation among youth that would occur in response to that system. Cloward and Ohlin opined that lower-class boys share the American dream for success, and that to them success can be measured in material gains. But, the lower-class boys do not have access to the legitimate means to attain the success goals, and they perceive that their chances of reaching the goals by legitimate means are slim. This creates strain or pressures on the youths, and they turn to illegitimate means, including violent crime, to achieve their goals. Cloward and Ohlin divided lower-class boys into three basic types of subculture (Roberson and Wallace, 1998):

- **Criminal subculture.** To achieve success, this subculture primarily conducts illegal activities, such as drug sales, robberies, and carjacking.
- **Conflict subculture.** This subculture is characterized by forming violent and aggressive gangs in unstable transient neighborhoods. According to the researchers, these subcultures are under great pressure and perceive that legitimate opportunities to obtain wealth are blocked for them.
- **Retreatism subculture.** This subculture is made up of individuals who, having failed to find a place for themselves in either the criminal or the conflict subcultures, have withdrawn from society. The drug addict would fit within this subculture.

Control Theories and Violence

As noted in this chapter, strain theorists believe that human beings are basically moral and deviate because of societal pressures or strain placed on them. Control theorists take the opposite approach. They contend that human beings are basically animals and commit selfish and violent acts when societal controls are relaxed or broken. According to the control theorists, if the socialization process is effective, our societal bonds will prevent us from committing violent acts. However, when our socialization process is ineffective or our social bonds are weak, we will not be restrained from committing violent acts. Under this concept, most people conform to social norms because they are restrained by their relationship to conventional institutions and individuals such as families, school, friends, and peer groups. A strain theorist asks why individuals commit violent acts, whereas the control theorist asks why anyone conforms to social norms, that is, why we all do not commit violent acts.

Both the strain and the control theories are not really theories in the sense of rigorous scientific procedures that provide for developing and testing hypotheses. These theories are only approaches in a search for explanations regarding why people commit violent crime. Control theories may be broadly classified into three types: containment, social control, and social learning theories. The social learning theories are also considered as a psychological approach, as discussed in the next chapter. All three types have the following common assumptions:

- Humans require nurturing.
- Differences in nurturing account for the variations in bonds to others and commitment to the accepted way of living.
- Bonds and commitment are internal controls commonly called "conscience" and recognized in "guilt."
- External controls are usually tested by the presence or absence of "shame."

Albert Reiss

In some 200 years of national sovereignty, Americans have been preoccupied repeatedly with trying to understand and control one form of violence or another.

Albert Reiss, 1993

Albert Reiss (1951) conducted a study of Chicago working-class boys between the ages of 11 and 17 who were involved in the juvenile justice system and who were on probation. He concluded that the boys with weak egos and superego concepts were more likely to engage in violent criminal behavior than those with strong ego and superego concepts. (Note that he borrowed the ego and superego concepts from psychiatry, which is discussed in the next chapter.) Reiss stated that the primary control mechanism was their attachment to others, and if those others were law abiding, then the youths were more likely to conform to the norms of society. According to him, violent delinquent acts and delinquency were caused by the failure of personal and social controls that produce conformity with the norms of the social system.

Collective Violence in America

In the 1960s, Albert Reiss used the assassination of President John F. Kennedy to raise the question of why Americans so often resort to violent means. Reiss concluded that much collective violence in America is systematically organized. He noted that organized crime, especially resulting from conflicts over the control of illegal territorial markets, is a continuing preoccupation of national, state, and local governments. Reiss pointed out that the National Commission on Law Observance and Enforcement (known as the Wickersham Commission after its chair) was established in 1929 by then President Herbert Hoover to inquire into the lawlessness and violent and organized criminal activity associated with prohibition. Reiss noted that because of the repeal of prohibition in the 1930s, most of the recommendations of the commission to reduce violent crime went unheeded. He also noted that in the 1950s and 1960s, violent criminal activity was linked to labor racketeering and to the control of illegal trafficking in drugs (Reiss and Roth, 1993).

According to Reiss and Roth (1993, p. 5), while a few individuals commit violent crimes frequently, these offenders account for only a small share of total violence in the United States. They noted that "serial murderers" are responsible for only about 1 or 2 percent of homicides in any given year. The researchers noted that most recorded violent crimes occur in the course of long, active criminal careers dominated by property offenses, so that arrests for violent crimes accounted for no more than one in eight of all arrests in European and American cohorts whose records they analyzed. They concluded that the general pattern is that while few offenders begin their criminal careers with a violent crime, most long arrest records include at least one, but that it was inaccurate to portray this as an "escalation" from property to violent crimes. They also concluded that predictions of future violent behavior from past arrests are generally highly inaccurate.

Reiss and Roth (1993) concluded that aggressive childhood behaviors correlate with elevated potentials for adult violent behavior. However, the researchers noted that while many young children display aggressive behavior patterns, only a few become violent adults, and most do not. Reiss and Roth concluded that why the few became violent adults was unknown. They concluded that the distinguishing factors may be related to socioeconomic status because adult violent behavior is so much more concentrated than aggressive childhood behavior in lower-income neighborhoods. They opined that identifying the relevant characteristics of communities, families, and persons should be of highest priority in future research.

Reiss and Roth (1993) noted that blacks are more likely to be homicide victims than whites and looked at what social factors accounted for the variation. They noted that, for at least 50 years, sociologists have pointed to three structural factors: low economic status, ethnic heterogeneity, and residential mobility. Reiss and Roth concluded that research has supported these findings and refined them. They concluded that the major points were as follows:

- Concentrations of poor families in geographic areas and greater income differences between poor and nonpoor (income inequality)
- Measures associated with differential social organization, such as population turnover, community transition, family disruption, and housing/population density—all of which affect the capacity of a community to supervise young males
- Indicators of opportunities associated with violence (e.g., illegal markets in drugs and firearms)

In addition to these factors, Reiss and Roth (1993) concluded that some individual-level risk factors for violent crimes point to possible community-level causes. The community-level causes include ineffective parenting, drug use, school failure, and a poor employment history. They concluded that it was more likely that these causes would occur in communities in which illegal markets are nearer at hand than are prenatal and pediatric care, good schools protected from violence, and legitimate employment opportunities.

Containment

To the containment theorists, we live in a society that provides us with a variety of opportunities for conformity or nonconformity. They contend that both illegal and legal opportunities are available, and not everyone will choose to commit criminal behavior. They also examine the question of why two boys growing up on the same street under similar circumstances will choose different patterns of life, with one becoming the mayor of Chicago and the other spending life in prison for a violent crime.

Walter Reckless (1970) attempted to answer this question using his containment theory. His theory is based on the assumption that there is a containing external social structure that holds individuals in line, and that there is also an internal buffer that influences individuals from committing violent conduct. The external social structure and the internal buffer act as a defense mechanism against deviations from social norms. If there are causes that lead to violence and the two mechanisms are strong and healthy, they motivate the individual not to violate social norms. If the mechanisms are negated, neutralized, or rendered impotent, the individual may be prone to commit violent behavior.

Reckless (1970) stated that there were two types of containment: outer (external social structure) and inner (internal buffer). The outer containment represents the structural buffer in a person's intermediate social world and includes such items as a consistent moral front to the person and institutional reinforcement of his or her norms, goals, and expectations. The inner containment consists of self components, such as self-control, good self-concept, ego strength, well-developed superego, high tolerance for frustration, high sense of responsibility, and strong goal orientation. Reckless stated that the inner containments provided the most effective controls on a person's behavior.

Reckless (1970) stated that while the inner and outer containments work to prevent a person from committing violent criminal acts, there are many social pressures that pull and push a person toward criminal behavior and interact with their containments. The pulls toward violence include such factors as poverty, poor family life, and deprived education. The pushes include hostility, personality, and aggressiveness.

Social Control

Travis Hirschi (1969) stated in his book *Causes of Delinquency* that the real question was why with so many opportunities and pressures to commit crime and other violent acts the vast majority of citizens conform to social norms. He concluded that the strength of our social bonds to society is what determines whether we commit violent behavior. To him, there were four components of the social bonds: attachment, commitment, involvement, and belief. According to him, we are more likely to commit violent acts if our social bonds are weak or ineffective.

Hirschi's (1969) four components are as follows:

- **Attachment:** Attachment refers to the affective ties that a person has to people who are important to him or her and to his or her sensitivity to their options.
- **Commitment:** Commitment was considered by Hirschi as the rational component of the bond. It refers to the time and energy that a person invests in the way of living of the community. Individuals who are not committed are more likely to commit acts of violence.
- **Involvement:** The more a person is involved in conventional things and events, the less motive the person has to commit violent behavior.
- **Belief:** If a person's belief in the values that are held by the society or group is weakened, criminal behavior is more likely to happen.

Social control theorists do not consider humans as basically evil, a blank state, or inherently good. To them, the human spirit is a "free spirit"—free to be good or bad depending on what is more convenient and advantageous for him or her. According to these theorists, we all have nonconformist impulses and would all deviate if given the opportunity. If the person's socialization is effective, the individual will have a strong social bond that gives the person a stake in conformity and prevents the individual from being aggressive and violent (Roberson and Wallace, 1998).

Delinquency and Drift

Gresham Sykes and David Matza (1957) concluded that individuals who commit violent behavior have no commitment to either societal norms or criminal norms. They concluded that those individuals are "normless." The two researchers concluded that individuals who committed violent behavior drift in and out of delinquent behavior. The researchers pointed out that the majority of delinquents spend most of their time in law-abiding behaviors and tend to drift in and out of violent crimes. They noted that the delinquents are flexible in their commitment to societal values.

Sykes and Matza (1957) contended that people need to neutralize their morals before violating conduct in which they believe. To explain this concept, they formulated "techniques of neutralization." These techniques act to lessen the effects of social control. The techniques as formulated by Sykes and Matza are as follows:

- **Denial of responsibility:** The offender defines him- or herself as lacking responsibility for the behavior in question. The offender feels that he or she is being pulled or pushed into situations beyond his or her control. A typical response is "I didn't mean to do it, but … ."
- **Denial of injury**: There is no harm to the victim; for example, fights between gangs are only private quarrels and nobody else's business.
- **Denial of the victim**: The victim deserves the injury, or the victim had it coming to him or her.
- **Condemnation of the condemners:** The persons complaining are hypocrites. The police are corrupt, stupid, and brutal.
- **Appeal to a higher loyalty:** The rules of the gang are more important than those of society. The group is justified in bombing an abortion clinic in the name of God.

Cliff Roberson, one of the authors of this text, once taught a course in criminology to prisoners in federal prison. Often during the discussions on the causes of crime, he would ask the prisoners if they agreed with a certain theory on crime and how that theory related to any crimes that they were convicted of having committed. The usual answer was that they agreed with certain theories, but these theories did not apply in their case "because … ." They would then attempt to rationalize their conduct and to neutralize it.

Cultural Conflict

Most cultural conflict theories can be traced to the "Chicago school." Thorsten Sellin (1938) was one of the first to discuss the relationship between culture and

crime or violent behavior. Sellin noted that different cultures have different conduct norms. To him, conduct norms are the rules that reflect the attitude of a
group about the manner in which a person should act in a given situation. Sellin
noted that the dominant class in a society decides what the conduct norms should
be and which conduct is criminal and which is not. He concluded that there were
two types of cultural conflict: primary and secondary. A primary conflict occurs
when one's native culture conduct norms conflict with those of the new culture. A
secondary culture conflict occurs in complex societies with a variety of subcultures
when behavior required by the conduct norms of one group violates the conduct
norms of another group.

Subculture of Violence

Subculture theories are based on the concept that there are subcultures with different value systems from the conventional value systems in a society. The subcultures differ from the larger culture because they have similarities such as ethnic
background, age, and so on. Marvin Wolfgang and Franco Ferracuti (1978) contended that there is a "subculture of violence." Their theory may be summarized
as follows:

- Members of the subculture hold values different from those of the dominant
  parent culture.
- Those who belong to the subculture of violence have values that are not, however, totally different from those of the dominant culture.
- Individuals who belong to the subculture of violence have a favorable attitude
  toward the use of violence and learn a willingness to resort to violence to
  solve conflicts.
- Members of the subculture have different psychological traits from those who
  are not members of the subculture.
- Persons who commit violent acts are distinctly more pathological and display
  more guilt and anxiety than those persons who do not commit violent acts.

Differential Association

Edwin Sutherland (1934) contended that all behavior is learned, and that we
learn criminal behavior the same way that we learn noncriminal behavior. For
example, the young male learns to be violent the same way that he may also learn
to play baseball. He contended that a person can be trained to adopt and follow
any pattern of behavior that he or she is able to execute. Sutherland stated that a
person's failure to follow a prescribed pattern of behavior is due to the inconsis-
tencies and lack of harmony in the influences that direct the individual. By the

term *differential association*, Sutherland meant that the content of the patterns presented in association would differ from individual to individual. He did not mean that mere association with criminals would cause one to commit criminal behavior. Instead, he meant that the content of the communications from others were given different degrees of significance depending on the relationship with the person making the verbal or nonverbal communication. For example, a communication from a buddy would have more significance in affecting a young male's behavior than communication from a stranger. His theory may be summarized as follows:

- Criminal behavior is learned.
- It is learned in interaction with other persons in a process of communications.
- The principal part of the learning of criminal behavior occurs within intimate personal groups.
- When criminal behavior is learned, the learning includes the techniques of committing crime and the specific direction of motives, rationalizations, and attitudes.
- A person becomes a criminal because of an excess of definitions favorable to the violation of the law over definitions unfavorable to violation of the law.
- Differential associations may vary in frequency, duration, priority, and intensity.
- The process of learning criminal behavior by association with criminal and noncriminal patterns involves all of the mechanisms that are involved in any other learning.
- While criminal behavior is an expression of general needs and values, it is not explained by those general needs and values since noncriminal behavior is an expression of the same needs and values.

Review Questions

1. Explain the differences between formal and informal social controls.
2. What role did Durkheim play in establishing the discipline of sociology?
3. Explain Durkheim's concept of anomie.
4. How did Merton redefine anomie?
5. Explain Cohen's middle-class measuring rod.
6. What are the informal social norms?
7. What is meant by the phrase *social bonding*?
8. Which of the social theories discussed in this chapter do you believe better explains violence and criminal misconduct?
9. Explain Reiss's explanation of the causes of collective violence.
10. How did Reckless explain violent behavior?

References

Cohen, A. (1960). *Delinquent boys: The culture of the gang*. New York: Free Press.

Durkheim, E. 1982. *Durkheim: The rules of sociological method and selected texts on sociology and its method*. edited and introduction by Steven Lukes, select translations by W. D. Hallis. New York, NY: The Free Press.

Goetz, K. (2009, October 18). Living with crime: Life inside a war zone. *Memphis Commercial Appeal*, A-1.

Hirschi, T. (1969). *Causes of delinquency*. Berkeley, CA: University of California Press.

Merton, R. K. (1938, October). Social structure and anomie. *American Sociological Review*, 3(5), 894–904.

Reckless, W. (1970). Containment theory. In M. Wolfgang, L. Savitz, and N. Johnson (eds.), *The sociology of crime and delinquency* (2nd ed., pp. 402–409). New York: Wiley.

Reiss, A. J., Jr. (1951). Delinquency and the failure of personal and social controls. *American Sociology of Crime and Delinquency*, 16, 196–207.

Reiss, A. J., Jr., and Roth, J. A. (1993). *Understanding and preventing violence*. Washington, DC: National Academy Press, 13.

Roberson, C., and Wallace, H. (1998). *Criminology*. Incline Village, NV: Copperhouse.

Sellin, T. (1938). *Culture conflict and crime*. New York: Social Science Research Council.

Summer, W. G. (1906). *Folkways*. New York: Dover.

Sutherland, E. (1934). *Principles of criminology*. Philadelphia: Lippincott.

Sykes, G. M., and Matza, D. (1957). Techniques of neutralization: A theory of delinquency. *American Sociological Review*, 22, 664–670.

Sztompka, P. (2003). R. K. Merton. In G. Ritzer (ed.), *Blackwell companion to major contemporary social theorists*. Malden, MA: Blackwell, 821–851.

Vold, G., and Bernard, T. J. (1986). *Theoretical criminology* (3rd ed.). New York: Oxford University Press.

Williams, F. P., and McShane, M. D. (2004). *Criminological theory* (4th ed.). Upper Saddle River, NJ: Pearson.

Wolfgang, M. E., and Ferracuti, F. (1978). The subculture of violence. In L. D. Savitz and N. Johnson (eds.), *Crime in society*. New York: Wiley, 545–561.

Chapter 5

Psychological/Psychiatric Approaches to Understanding Violence

Introduction

In Chapter 4, the sociological approaches to understanding violence were discussed. In this chapter, the psychological approaches are examined. The key difference between the two approaches is that the sociological approach looks at groups of people, whereas the psychological approach focuses on causes within the individual. Included within the microlevel approaches are those causes based on the biological makeup or nature of the individual; the biological aspects are examined in Chapter 6.

Most of the approaches discussed in this chapter argue that violent criminal behavior originates primarily in the personalities of the offender rather than from the environmental situations they encounter. In addition, some of the approaches argue that violence is the result of normal learning patterns.

Nature of Violent Behavior

The ancient Hebrews considered laws as expressions of God's commands. Accordingly, any violation was a transgression against God. Deviant behavior, if left unchecked, would destroy the bonds of society. Under this concept, any violent crime on any member of God's chosen people could incur God's wrath on everyone (Schafer, 1969).

Early Greek philosophers considered violent criminal behavior as an offense against the society or the state. Persons who committed crimes were infected with corruption and evil. Plato (428–348 BC) explained violent behavior by the fact that humans have a dual character. The individual is rational and seeks perfection but is limited by his or her own weaknesses and imperfections. He concluded that violent behavior was present because of the greedy nature of humans. Plato advocated that punishment was a human's right to cleanse him- or herself of evil. Aristotle (384–322 BC) contended that our ability to reason separates us from animals, and that crime is caused by our irrational acts. However, he was not clear on what causes the irrational acts of violent behavior (Schafer, 1969).

The early European churches saw the violent criminal as a person who was possessed by the devil. St. Augustine (AD 354–430) contended that crime and violent behavior resulted from influences of the devil. If the devil was driven out, then people would no longer be bad. St. Thomas Aquinas (1225–1274) contended that the "soul," which is implanted in the unborn child by God, is the source of our reasoning power. Aquinas explained that the conscience part of the soul drives us toward rational and just behavior. When our human appetites are influenced by the devil, then our appetites overrule our conscience, and evil occurs (Vold and Bernard, 1986).

During the fifteenth and sixteenth centuries, the concept that astral influences (moon and stars) caused an individual to commit violent behavior was popular. Hohenheim (1493–1541), a Swiss physician, was a leading proponent of the concept that violent behavior was caused by influences of the stars and moon. Hohenheim argued that people acted strangely and irrational because of astral influences. Consider that the word *lunatic* comes from the Latin word *luna*, meaning moon. Even today, it is a common saying that there must be a "full moon" because a lot of crazy things are happening (Schafer, 1969).

Cesare Beccaria

In the eighteenth century, Cesare Beccaria, in writing on the concept of the contractual society and the need for punishment, stated that laws are the conditions under which independent and isolated people unite to form a society. People, weary of living in a continual state of war and enjoying a liberty rendered useless by the uncertainty of preserving it, sacrificed some of their liberty so that they might enjoy the rest of it in peace and safety. Tangible motives in the form of punishments are needed to protect society and to prevent it from plunging into its original chaos. According to Beccaria, individuals committed violent crime because they felt that they had more to gain by committing the crime than they would lose because of the reaction of society against the violent behavior. Accordingly, he stressed that violators of the law (individuals who commit violent crime) must be punished to protect society (Monachesi, 1973).

To Beccaria, the true measure of violent crimes was the harm that they do to society. It is erroneous to believe that the true measure of crimes is to be found in the intention of the person who commits them. Sometimes, people with the best intentions do the greatest injury to society, and at other times, with the worst intentions, they do the greatest good. To determine the severity of the criminal conduct, especially when it involves violent behavior, we should consider the extent of the harm that is done to society. Since it is common interest that violent crimes not be committed and that they be less frequent, there must be a proper proportion between crimes and punishments. Obstacles that deter people from committing crimes should be stronger in proportion as the crimes are contrary to the public good. Thus, the greater the harm to society, the harsher the punishment should be for that conduct. If punishments are too severe, however, people will be driven to commit additional violent behavior, such as killing witnesses to avoid punishment for a single crime. For punishment to attain its goal, the evil that it inflicts has only to exceed the advantage derived from the crime (Monachesi, 1973).

Beccaria contended that one of the greatest curbs on crime is not the cruelty of the punishments, but their certainty. Do you want to prevent crime? To prevent crime, the laws should be clear and simple, with the entire force of the nation united in their defense. The laws should favor not the classes of people but people themselves. People should fear the laws and fear nothing else. Fear of the law is salutary, but one's fear for another human is fertile for crime. He stated that it is better to prevent crime than to punish individuals for them, and that the ultimate goal of all good legislation should have that as its ultimate end. Laws should be published so that the public may know what they are and support their intent and purpose. Torture and secret accusations should be abolished. Capital punishment should be abolished. Jails should be made more humane institutions. The law should not distinguish between wealthy and poor or between nobles and commoners. A person should be tried by a jury of his or her peers; when there is a class difference between the offender and the victim, one-half of the jury should be from the class of the offender and the other half from the class of the victim. Beccaria concluded that for punishment not to be an act of violence of one or many against a citizen, it must be public, prompt, necessary, the least possible under the circumstances, proportionate to the crimes, and dictated by the laws (Beccaria as translated by Paolucci, 1963).

Capital Punishment

An area of debate today is the effect of capital punishment on reducing violent behavior. There is no easy answer to this issue. From a psychological point of view, Cesare Beccaria (as translated by Paolucci, 1963) claimed that capital punishment actually increases violent crime in a society. He stated:

> Was there ever a man who could have wished to leave to others the choice of killing him? It is conceivable that the least sacrifice of each person's liberty should include sacrifice of the greatest of all goods, life? ... The punishment of death, therefore, is not a right, for I have demonstrated that it cannot be such; but it is the war of a nation against a citizen whose destruction it judges to be necessary or useful. If, then, I can show that death is neither useful nor necessary I shall have gained the cause of humanity.
>
> There are only two possible motives for believing that the death of a citizen is necessary. The first: when it is evident that even if deprived of liberty he still has connections and power such as to endanger the security of the nation—when, that is, his existence can produce a dangerous revolution in the established form of government. ... I see no necessity for destroying a citizen, except if his death were the only real way of restraining others from committing crimes; this is the second motive for believing that the death penalty may be just and necessary laws. (pp. 43–45)

Becarria's ideas were quite radical for his time. In 1766, the book was condemned by the Catholic Church. The essay was, however, extremely well received. It was first translated into French in 1766 and into English in 1767 (Monachesi, 1973).

Utilitarianism

Jeremy Bentham (1748–1832) put great emphasis on the practical problem of eliminating or at least decreasing violent crime (Atkinson, 1905). This principle of utilitarianism is that an act is not to be judged by an irrational system of absolutes but by a supposedly verifiable principle of the greatest happiness for the greatest number. Bentham said that an act possesses "utility" if it tends to produce benefit, advantage, pleasure, good, or happiness or prevents pain, evil, or unhappiness. According to him, the "goodness" or "badness" of an act should be judged by its utility. To Bentham, all human action is reducible to one simple formula of motivation: the pursuit of pleasure and the avoidance of pain. He contended that motive necessarily refers to action. Pleasure, pain, or another event prompts the action. There is no such thing as any sort of motive that is bad. It is only the consequence of the motive that can be bad because of its effect on others, because of its ultimate influence (Geis, 1973).

Bentham contended that it was obvious that all persons might derive considerable pleasure from uncontrolled orgies of criminal behavior if there were no pains attached to this criminal behavior. Bentham recognized that any legal sanction must be acceptable to the majority of people before it would be effective. He advocated social engineering to establish effective punishments for criminal behavior. He dismissed any recourse to natural law. He caustically labeled "natural law" as "nonsense on stilts" (Geis, 1973).

Bentham saw punishment as an evil, but a necessary evil to prevent greater evils from being inflicted on society and thus diminishing happiness. Punishment should not be an act of anger, resentment, or vengeance according to him. Punishments should not produce any more pain than necessary to accomplish their purpose. He advocated two principles regarding punishment: the general concept that the less certain the punishment, the more severe that it must be to have any possibility of deterrence and that overtly equivalent punishments are not really equivalent because of the variations among the offenders. Regarding the second principle, a fine to a rich man is a mild punishment compared to a similar fine against a poor man (Geis, 1973).

Psychiatric Explanations of Violence

Psychiatry grew out of the experiences of medical doctors in dealing with basic problems of mental disease. *Psychiatry* may be defined as a field of medicine that specializes in the understanding, diagnosis, treatment, and prevention of mental problems. Psychiatry has divided the mental disorders into organic disorders and functional disorders. Organic disorders are those disorders that can be traced to a physical problem (e.g., head injuries, distorted vision, or problems due to disease or degeneration). Functional disorders are those disorders for which there is strange behavior but no known organic problems. An example of a functional disorder would be a person with no apparent brain pathology who hears voices or who sees things that others do not see.

Psychoanalysis is a branch of psychiatry that is based on the theories of Freud and a particular method of treatment involving individual case study. While psychiatry is as old as medicine, psychoanalysis is a relatively recent development with the work of Sigmund Freud (1856–1939), Alfred Adler (1870–1937), and Carl Jung (1875–1961). The psychological approaches tend to focus not only on the mental but also on the behavioral characteristics of a person. Despite the differences in the approaches studied in this chapter, the basic connecting theme is the concept that the person is a unique personality, and that the only way that a person can be understood is through a thorough case study.

Before the development of the scientific theories of violent criminal behavior involving mental illness, demonology was used to explain criminal behavior. Individuals were thought to be "possessed" by evil spirits, and their behavior could not be changed until the evil spirits were exorcized. Methods of exorcism included the drinking of horrible concoctions, praying, and making strange noises to scare away the evil. Many considered that the only way to drive out the evil spirits was to insult them or to make the body an unpleasant place to inhabit. Flogging and other types of corporal punishment were also used in an attempt to drive out the evil spirits. By the eighteenth century, the discovery of an organic basis for many physical illnesses led to the discovery of an organic basis for some mental illnesses as well. As the organic view replaced the demonological theory of crime causation, the concept that psychological problems could also cause mental illness became popular.

William Healy is credited with taking the positivists' emphasis on studying anatomical characteristics and shifting it to the psychological and social elements. He believed that the only way to find the causes of violence was to deeply study the individual's background, including emotional development. He measured personality disorders and environmental pathologies with the thesis that criminal behavior was purposive behavior resulting when individuals were frustrated in their attempts to fulfill their basic needs. Healy also noted that delinquents had a higher frequency of personality defects and disorders than nondelinquents (Reid, 1991).

The psychological/psychiatric theories of crime causation include emotional problem theories, mental disorder theories, sociopathic personality theories, and thinking pattern theories.

Psychoanalytic Approaches

Sigmund Freud

Sigmund Freud was born in Freiberg, Moravia, in 1856 of Jewish parents, and he died in 1939. He was a distinguished student at the University of Vienna, where he graduated in 1881 with a medical degree. From 1881 to 1885, he did research in physiology while on the staff of the Vienna General Hospital. He then was in private practice until 1902, when he was appointed professor of neuropathology at the University of Vienna School of Medicine. Freud remained there until 1923, when he was forced to retire because of cancer in his jaw. Freud was one of the most controversial and influential persons of the twentieth century.

While Freud did not discuss criminal behavior to any great extent, he did suggest that the criminal wants to be caught and punished for his or her guilt. According to him, criminals are their own worst punishers. Freud focused on the pathological, not the healthy, part of human beings. He was concerned with the unconscious mental life of the individual.

Freud believed that aggression and violence have their roots in instinct. According to him, violence is a response to thwarting the pleasure principle. He developed the idea that each of us has a "death wish." This death wish is a constant source of aggressive impulses and tries to reduce the organism to an inanimate state. Freud contended that this death wish may be expressed directly, manifested indirectly as in hunting, or sublimated into sadomasochism.

Freud contended that behavior based on "guilt" arising from the Oedipus conflict was the basis of criminal activity. The conflict was named for a character in Greek mythology who killed his father and married his mother. Freud contended that we have a hidden desire to act out similar behavior. The equivalent complex for girls is known as the Electra complex and is taken from a classic tragedy in Greek mythology. Both the Oedipus and Electra complexes are based on the Freudian premise that incest is a basic human desire.

Freud's concepts of the id, ego, and superego are well known. According to him, these form the basis of personality. The id is the primary, rash, impulsive part of the personality. It is governed by the pleasure principle. The id is hedonistic and has no regard for responsibility and sensible things. The ego is considered the sensible and responsible part of the personality. It is governed by the reality principle. The ego appraises the external situation and then enables the person to make rational decisions. The ego should repress unacceptable social impulses or drives into the unconscious. The superego is the "conscience." It is unconscious. This part of the personality allows a person to feel pride, shame, or guilt. It is the person's moral faculty and sets moral and ethical standards.

Freud's contribution of the concept of human developmental phases are also important. According to him, there are certain developmental stages that humans go through: oral, phallic, latency, and neophallic or genital stages. The oral stage is the first stage and occurs during infancy and the first year of life. During this stage, the child is totally antisocial and laden with primitive urges. The infant is beset by a variety of oral urges. The urges can be sadistic, cannibalistic, and antisocial.

The second stage is the anal stage, which lasts until the child is about three years old. During this stage, the child is stubborn, spiteful, and cruel. The phallic stage is next, and during this stage, the genitals are a major focus. This stage lasts until approximately the age of six. During the latency period, which lasts from age six to puberty (approximately twelve years of age), it appears that no urges are present. The last stage is the genital or neophallic stage, in which the preteenager is again obsessed with his or her genitals, sex, oral urges, and anal urges.

Freud invented the technique of psychoanalysis to treat problems caused by traumatic experiences in early childhood of which the individual was not consciously aware. He used the concept of free association, by which the patient relaxed completely and talked about whatever came to mind. By exploring these associations, the individual was able to reconstruct earlier events and bring them to consciousness.

Juvenile Delinquency

According to Schoenfeld (1975), the adolescent who is likely to commit delinquent or criminal behavior is a person whose superego has criminal tendencies and does not oppose the antisocial instincts of early childhood. Delinquent behavior may also occur in a youngster whose superego is rigid, prim, and proper. This child's superego is so offended by the reactivated urges that his or her superego becomes guilty. To deal with the overwhelming guilt, the youth commits crimes with the unconscious aim of being caught and punished.

Most psychoanalytic theories take the position that criminality and delinquency are caused by insecurity, inadequacy, inferiority, unconscious motivation, and conflict within the person.

Violent Crime Causation

The psychoanalytic theories of violence were summarized by Yablonsky and Haskell (1988, pp. 355–357) as follows:

■ An inability to control violent drives (id) because of a deficiency in ego or superego development. Because of the faulty development, the criminal is believed to possess little capacity for repressing instinctual (criminal) impulses. The individual who is dominated by the id is consequently criminal.
■ Antisocial character formation resulting from a disturbed ego development. This occurs during the first three years of life.
■ An overdeveloped superego, which makes no provision for the satisfaction of the demands of the id. Offenders of this type are considered neurotic.
■ An inability to control criminal drives (id) because of a deficiency in ego or superego development. Because of the faulty development, the criminal is believed to possess little capacity for repressing instinctual (criminal) impulses. The individual who is dominated by the id is consequently criminal.
■ Antisocial character formation resulting from disturbed ego development. This occurs during the first three years of life.
■ An overdeveloped superego, which makes no provision for the satisfaction of the demands of the id. Offenders of this type are considered neurotic.

The psychoanalytic theorists assume that violence is a part of human nature. Most assume that the difference between a violent person and a nonviolent one is that the nonviolent person can control his or her criminal drives and find other socially acceptable outlets for them, whereas the violent criminal cannot.

Emotional Problem Theories

The emotional problem theories assume that the violent criminal commits crimes because of the inability to cope with everyday emotional problems. Instead of possessing gross pathological problems, the criminal is responding to subtle psychological factors that prevent him or her from functioning normally. Generally, these theorists assume that the criminal is normal in psychological makeup, and that he or she is not psychotic, neurotic, or sociopathic. The deterioration of coping skills caused by emotional problems is the root of the criminal behavior. The emotional problems could spring from any number of events, such as problem relationships, crises, finances, employment, sickness, lack of adequate self-concept, and so on. Once the criminal's coping ability is restored, it is unlikely that he or she will commit additional crimes.

There is considerable overlap between the emotional problem theories and the mental disorder theories discussed in the next section. Both groups contend that there is something mentally wrong with the criminal (i.e., the criminal is not a normal person).

Mental Disorders

Mental disorders have been studied for years, but there is still much disagreement regarding the definitions, classifications, causes, and methods of identification, diagnoses, and treatment. There is also difficulty in determining the extent of any disorders diagnosed. Accordingly, any conclusions should be viewed with caution.

The mental disorder theories attempt to classify criminal behavior by the use of certain mental disorders, such as psychosis, neurosis, and impulse disorders. Psychosis is a common category of mental disorder used to explain criminal behavior. Psychoses can be functional or organic. Psychotic people lose contact with reality and have difficulty distinguishing reality from fantasy. Neurosis is a common type of mental disorder that was first used to cover a class of diseases that referred to "affections of the nervous system."

Neuroses have no demonstrable organic cause, and neurotic behaviors are behaviors that do not grossly violate social norms or represent severely disordered personalities. Impulse disorders are sudden, explosive, and driven to action. A person with an impulse disorder does not necessarily lose touch with reality or lose communication. Impulse disorders include kleptomania (compulsive thievery), pyromania (an irresistible impulse to burn), and explosive disorder (sudden assaultive or other destructive behavior that occurs in a person who otherwise demonstrates good control).

As noted, there are two general types of mental disorders: organic disorders, which have an identifiable physiological cause, and functional disorders, which are characterized by no apparent brain pathology that can be identified by existing techniques.

There is a popular tendency to view deviant irrational behavior as psychologically abnormal behavior. Often, the public confuses socially unacceptable behavior with "mental illness"; therefore, the psychotics and schizophrenics are guilty by association. As noted by Bartol (1980), unpredictable, irrational, bizarre, disoriented people are frightening and thus dangerous. It is important to note, however, that murderers and violent offenders, although socially deviant, are not necessarily psychotic or crazy. In fact, the research literature, according to Bartol, is highly consistent in pointing out that psychotic or severely disturbed individuals are no more likely to commit serious crimes against others than the general population.

Sociopathic Personality Theories

Psychiatrists use the term *psychopath* to describe an individual who exhibits a certain group of behaviors and attitudes. The term *psychopath* is also considered synonymous with the more modern terms of sociopath and antisocial personality. The three terms are often used interchangeably. Working definitions of them are provided next.

The term *psychopath* is reserved for individuals who are basically unsocialized and whose behavior patterns bring them repeatedly into conflicts with society. They are incapable of significant loyalty to individuals, groups, or social values. They are grossly selfish, callous, irresponsible, impulsive, and unable to feel guilt or to learn from experience and punishment. Frustration tolerance is low. They tend to blame others or offer plausible rationalization for their behavior.

The preceding definition implies that the behaviors originate in the personality of the individual. Others contend, however, that it is possible that the behaviors may be explained by factors other than personality. Yablonsky and Haskell (1988) contended that core members of violent gangs tended to be sociopaths and lead their gangs in mob-like violence while acting out their own hostility and aggression. Samuel Guze (1992) argued that sociopathy, alcoholism, and drug addiction are the only psychiatric conditions consistently associated with criminal behavior. He also contended that psychiatry has no consistently effective methods of treating individuals who are sociopaths and recommended that they be confined until they reach middle age.

The *Diagnostic and Statistical Manual of Mental Disorders* (*DSM*) refers to a sociopathic disorder. The third edition (*DSM-III*; American Psychiatric Association, 1980) replaced the terms *psychopath* and *sociopath* with the term *antisocial personality disorder*. The fourth and revised edition of the DSM, commonly referred to as DSM-IV-TR, again referred to such behavior as antisocial personality disorder.

Hervey Cleckley (1976) pointed out that the terms *psychopath* or *antisocial personality* are so broad that they might be applied to almost any criminal. He contended that psychopathy is distinctly different from criminality, that the majority of psychopaths are not criminals, and that the majority of violent criminals are not psychopaths.

He also stated (Cleckley, 1976) that psychopaths may be found in any profession, including business, science, and medicine. He believed that the typical psychopath differs from the typical criminal in that his or her actions are less purposeful and his or her goals more incomprehensible; while the psychopath causes him- or herself needless sorrow and shame, he or she usually does not commit criminal behavior. Vold and Bernard (1986) stated that the terms *psychopath, sociopath,* and *antisocial personality* may have some use for psychiatrists who want a shorthand way to describe a certain type of person with whom they come in contact in the practice of their profession, that the terms seem to be simply labels that psychiatrists attach to more serious offenders, and the terms do not seem to add anything to our ability to identify these offenders in the first place or to understand why they behave this way.

Future Dangerousness

Should we, as recommended by Guze (1992), lock up sociopaths until they reach middle age? Many states have enacted "violent sexual predator" laws that allow for the confinement of individuals based on the concept of future dangerousness. In general, these laws rely on a psychiatric evaluation of the individual and a prediction of the future dangerousness of that individual.

Baxstrom v. Herold

In *Baxstrom v. Herold* (1966), the U.S. Supreme Court considered the validity of the statutory procedure under which a prisoner was committed to a state hospital at the expiration of his criminal sentence in a state prison. While serving his prison term, the prisoner was transferred to a state hospital that was used to confine and care for male prisoners who were declared mentally ill while serving a criminal sentence. The state hospital director filed a petition in which he stated that the prisoner's prison term would soon end and requested that the petitioner be civilly committed pursuant to N.Y. Correctional Law § 384. The court held that the prisoner was denied equal protection of the laws by the statutory procedure under which a person could be civilly committed at the expiration of his penal sentence without the jury review that was available to all other persons who were civilly committed in the state and by his civil commitment to the institution beyond the expiration of his prison term without a judicial determination that he was dangerously mentally ill under N.Y. Mental Hygiene Law § 74.

As a result of the decision, the state of New York was required to transfer to a regular mental hospital 967 patients held in a New York State hospital for the criminally insane because they were "dangerous." During the next five years, only 26 of them were returned to hospitals for the criminally insane. One-half of the original group were later discharged from the hospital. Of those discharged, only 17 percent had any additional arrests. Accordingly, the prediction of dangerousness was incorrect for 83 percent of those released. Prior to release, they had been held an average of 13 years.

Charles Whitman, the University of Texas tower killer, while on active duty with the U.S. Marines, was tried by a special court-martial several years before his killings in Austin. He was charged with assault and battery. A psychologist testified on Whitman's behalf that he was a nondangerous person and not the type of person who would commit assault and battery. He was nevertheless convicted. On August 1, 1966, Charles Whitman, shooting from a tower located on the University of

Texas campus in Austin, Texas, killed 14 individuals and wounded 32 others before he was killed.

Post-Traumatic Stress Disorder

Post-traumatic stress disorder (PTSD) was first recognized in the 1980s. It is considered a brain dysfunction. The PTSD defense has been raised by war veterans, who contend that they suffer nightmares, flashbacks, depression, and survivor guilt. They contend that they lose their orientation and believe that they are back in the war, and that their actions are taken to protect their buddies by shooting, attacking, or maiming the people around them. Their attorneys argue that the flashbacks appear so real to the veterans that they have destroyed their ability to distinguish right from wrong. The defense has been used in murder cases, cases involving battered women, and in cases involving armed robbery and drug law violations.

Behavior and Social Learning Theories

The social learning theory was developed by Albert Bandura (1973). Using the works of B. F. Skinner and Skinner's operant learning theory, Bandura focused on violent and aggressive behavior. He asserted not only that learning is reinforced through actual rewards and punishments but also that we learn by watching others receive rewards and punishments for certain forms of behavior. We then imitate or model those behaviors that are rewarded.

Earlier learning theories saw violent criminal behavior as normal learned behavior and were focused on how learning takes place. The later versions of the learning theories also considered the social environment. *Learning* refers to habits and knowledge that develop as the result of the experiences of the individual in entering and adjusting to the environment. Learning is distinguished from unlearned or instinctive behavior, which seems to be present in the individual at birth and determined by biology. Bandura (1973) recognized that all persons have self-regulatory mechanisms and thus can reward and punish themselves according to internal standards for judging their own behavior. Aggression may be inhibited in some people (e.g., high moral standards, religious beliefs, etc.); however, these people may still engage themselves in aggressive behavior through the process of disengagement.

Disengagement may result from

1. "Attributing blame to one's victims" (p. 181)
2. "Dehumanization through bureaucratization, automation, urbanization, and high social mobility" (p. 181)
3. "Vindication of aggressive practices by legitimate authorities" (p. 183)
4. "Desensitization resulting from repeated exposure to aggression in any of a variety of forms" (p. 182)

Social learning theory considers the concept of imitation or modeling central to the learning process. Accordingly, as per the learning theorists, we learn criminal behavior by observing the behavior of others in the context of the social environment.

The learning theories rely on behavioral psychology and are based on Skinner's operant learning theory (Skinner and Fream, 1997). Operant learning theory is concerned with the effect that an individual's behavior has on the environment and the consequences of that effect on the individual. Behavior therefore is shaped and maintained by its consequences. An individual is the product of present and past events in his or her life. The determination regarding whether the frequency of any particular behavior is increased or diminished is based on the contingencies of reinforcement and punishment (aversive stimuli). There are six basic principles: positive reinforcement, negative reinforcement, positive punishment, negative punishment, discriminative stimuli, and schedules. *Reinforcement* is any event that follows the occurrence of behavior and that alters and increases the frequency of the behavior. Those that directly increase the behavior are positive reinforcers, and those that remove something undesirable are negative reinforcers. Punishment is the opposite of reinforcement. Discriminate stimuli do not occur after the behavior but are present either before or as the behavior occurs. The schedules refer to the frequency with which, and the probability that, a particular consequence will occur. Learning takes place because of the consequences associated with behavior.

Burgess and Akers's (1966) differential reinforcement theory accepted the six basic principles and adds satiation and deprivation to them. They contended that a stimulus will be more or less reinforcing depending on the individual's current situation. For example, a person who already has money (satiated) will be less reinforced by robbing someone than a person who is impoverished (deprived). Since individuals do not have the same past experiences, their conditioning histories are different. Accordingly, some stimuli that people experience daily will produce different responses in different individuals.

Thinking Pattern Theories

The thinking pattern theories are psychological theories that are focused on the offender's cognitive processes. For the most part, the theories focus on the criminal's intellect, logic, mental processes, rationality, and language usage. They explore the concept that a link between crime and intelligence exists. It has been argued many times that low intelligence causes crime. Research in this area has not demonstrated that low intelligence causes crime, only that low intelligence and crime often appear together in the same groups.

Cognitive Development Theories

The cognitive development theorists contend that the way in which people organize their thoughts about rules and laws results in either criminal or noncriminal behavior. This organization of thoughts is referred to as *moral reasoning* by psychologists. When that reasoning is applied to law issues, it is termed *legal reasoning*, although this term has a different meaning to lawyers.

Some cognitive development theorists developed the thesis that both criminal and noncriminal behaviors are related to cognitive development, and that people choose the behaviors in which they wish to engage, just as the classical theorists did several centuries posited earlier. They argued that criminal behavior exists because of the way people think, and either the criminal must be confined forever or the criminal must be taught how to change his or her ways of thinking. According to these theorists, the root causes of violence and crime are thought and choice (Walters and White, 1989).

The cognitive development theories are based on the early works of Jean Piaget, who believed that there are two stages in moral reasoning. The first is the belief that rules are sacred and immutable. The second is the belief that rules are the products of humans. Piaget contended that we leave the first stage at about the age of 13. The second stage leads to behavior that is more moral than the first.

Lawrence Kohlberg (1958) called the first stage "preconventional" and the second "conventional." He also added a third and higher stage called "postconventional reasoning." According to him, those who do not make this transition from preconventional to conventional may be considered arrested in their development of moral reasoning, and they may become delinquents. He noted that the progression to higher stages should preclude criminal behavior, and that most criminals do not progress beyond the preconventional stage.

The Criminal Personality

The most detailed study on the way that offenders think and the mind of the criminal was conducted by Samuel Yochelson and Stanton Samenow (1976) and was discussed in their book, *The Criminal Personality*. They conducted their study over a 15-year period, and it involved intensive interviews, therapy, and follow-up studies of 255 male patients committed to the Saint Elizabeth's Hospital in Washington, D.C. The researchers concluded that traditional psychiatric ideas and treatment modes did not work with criminals. They concluded that criminals use language differently from noncriminals, and that the criminal has a different frame of reference when compared to the noncriminal. They concluded that to change the criminal, we need to change the criminal's way of thinking. They identified 52 criminal thinking errors. They also concluded that the criminals told self-serving stories and tended to tell what they thought the authorities wanted to hear. Yochelson and Samenow recognized that most offenders are aware of the ways of thinking in society, but many used the adversities of life to justify their behavior.

Some of the common thinking errors listed by Yochelson and Samenow are as follows:

1. The criminal's mental life includes fantasies of triumph, power, and control over others.
2. The criminal has a different concept of normal energy. If the criminal's energy level is not full of vitality and energy, he or she thinks something is wrong with him or her.
3. Criminals are preoccupied with and fear death.
4. The criminal is fearful of being put down or being a "zero." The criminal believes that everyone can see how worthless he or she is.
5. Criminals have an unyielding criminal pride and think that they are better than and above others.
6. Criminals are concrete thinkers. They tend to think in terms of isolated events. In addition, their thinking is fragmented.
7. Criminals view themselves as one of a kind and as unique.

Yochelson and Samenow (1976) have been criticized since they do not answer the question of why criminals think in certain ways and others do not and what causes criminal thinking patterns. They appear to be more concerned with a description of criminal thinking. In addition, they researched only criminals confined to institutions and never looked at criminals who were never confined.

Substance Abuse as a Cause of Violence

According to the National Youth Violence Prevention Resource Center, while violence and substance use are both part of a lifestyle that involves antisocial and delinquent behavior, in many cases the violent behavior actually comes before the substance use. The drug use is just one aspect of a risky and dangerous lifestyle. While the use of drugs does not generally cause teens to become involved in violence, those violent teens who do use illegal drugs tend to engage in violent behavior more frequently and to continue to engage in violence much longer than those violent youth who do not use drugs. The center did note that some teens may become violent under the influence of drugs. It is also likely that some teens engage in violence to get money to buy drugs. In most cases, however, it appears that the use of drugs does not cause violent behavior (Elliot, Huizinga, Menard, 1989).

Teens who use alcohol or other drugs are much more likely to attempt and to die by suicide. According to one study, drug and alcohol abuse was the most common characteristic of those who attempted suicide: Seventy percent of the youth who died by suicide frequently used alcohol or other drugs. The researcher noted that research has not proven that drug and alcohol use actually causes suicidal behavior, only that the two behaviors are associated. It may be that teens that have emotional problems are more likely to use drugs and to contemplate suicide or that the use of drugs aggravates preexisting depression or other emotional problems.

Drugs and alcohol may also impair the judgment of teens considering suicide, making suicide attempts more likely (Shaffer et al., 1996).

Intergenerational Transmission of Violence

Wallace and Roberson (2010) noted that many scholars contend that the most effective method of stopping child abuse is to break the intergenerational cycle of violence. They were looking at the cycle in their chapter on child abuse. They noted that the cycle fails to provide a definitive answer to why people commit violent acts, but that it is singled out for examination because professionals and laypersons constantly refer to it as a scientifically accepted fact. According to them, there is no way to prove or disprove the theory of the intergenerational cycle of violence.

The intergenerational cycle of violence concept has generated controversy among researchers for several decades. Wallace and Roberson (2010) noted that scholars have attempted to determine whether violent tendencies can be inherited from the family of origin as a result of observing it or being a victim. Other scholars have attempted to explain criminal behavior by reference to this cycle.

Previously, the most common term used to describe the process involved in this concept was cycle of violence; however, the theory is now known as the *intergenerational transmission of violence theory*. The intergenerational cycle of violence theory is based on the concept that violent behavior is learned within the family and bequeathed from one generation to the next, and children who are victims of child abuse or who witness violent aggression by one spouse against the other will more likely grow up and react to their children or spouses in the same manner. According to this theory, a child who survives growing up in a violent family develops a predisposition toward violence in his or her own family. Thus, so this theory holds, we have a never-ending chain of violence that is passed from one generation to the next.

The sources for most studies of the intergenerational cycle of violence theory are case studies, clinical interviews, self-reports, and agency records. Joseph Carroll (1980) studied 96 violent patients at a community guidance center in an attempt to determine the effects of intergenerational transmission of violence. He concluded that 37 percent of respondents who had experienced a high degree of punishment as children were involved with the use of physical violence within their own families, whereas only 15 percent of those who had not been subject to severe punishment as a child reported that violence was a problem for their families. He concluded that there was a strong association between first-generation physical punishment and second-generation violence. Individuals from families characterized by low warmth and high parental punishment were found to have the highest frequency of family violence, with a significant main effect of family warmth. Individuals from high-stress and high-punishment families also had a high frequency of family violence. Carroll concluded from these analyses that the absence of family warmth and the presence of highly stressful family relationships contributed to the intergenerational transmission of violence, but that the lack of warmth seemed to play a greater role in this cycle than did stressful family ties.

A group of researchers from the Department of Psychiatry at the Columbia University College of Physicians and Surgeons and the New York State Psychiatric Institute conducted a 20-year study of the effects of domestic violence on the children in the household (Ehrensaft et al., 2003). They used a sample of 543 children to test the independent effects of parenting, exposure to domestic violence between parents, maltreatment, adolescent disruptive behavior disorders, and emerging adult substance abuse disorders on the risk of violence to and from an adult partner. The researchers concluded that conduct disorder presented the strongest risk for perpetrating partner violence for both sexes, followed by exposure to domestic violence between parents and power assertive punishment. Exposure to domestic violence between parents conferred the greatest risk of receiving partner violence; conduct disorder increased the odds of receiving partner violence but did not mediate this effect. Child physical abuse and conduct disorder in adolescence were strong independent risks for injury to a partner (Ehrensaft et al., 2003).

Review Questions

1. What are the basic concepts of the psychological theories of violent crime causation?
2. How did Freud explain violent behavior?
3. How do mental disorder theorists explain violent crime causation?
4. How does intergenerational transmission of violence explain violent behavior?
5. Explain the difference between the social learning theories and the emotional problem theories.

References

American Psychiatric Association. (1980). *Diagnostic and statistical manual of mental disorders* (3rd ed.). Washington, DC: American Psychiatric Association.

Atkinson, C. M. (1905). *Jeremy Bentham: His life and work*. London: Oxford University Press.

Bandura, A. (1973). *Aggression: A social learning approach*. Englewood Cliffs, NJ: Prentice Hall.

Bartol, C. R, (1980). *Criminal behavior: A psychosocial approach*. Englewood Cliffs, NJ: Prentice Hall.

Baxstrom v. Herold, 383 U.S. 107 (U.S. 1966).

Beccaria, C. (1963). *On crimes and punishment*, H. Paolucci, trans. New York: Bobbs-Merrill.

Burgess, R., and Akers, R. L. (1966). A differential association-reinforcement theory of criminal behavior. *Social Problems, 14*, 363–383.

Carroll, J. C. (1980). The intergenerational transmission of family violence: The long-term effects of aggressive behavior. *Advances in Family Psychiatry*, 2, 171–181.

Cleckley, H. (1976). *The mask of insanity.* St. Louis, MO: Mosby.

Ehrensaft, M. K., Cohen, P. J., Brown, J., Smailes, E., Chen, H., and Johnson, J. G. (2003, August). Intergenerational transmission of partner violence: A 20-year prospective study. *Journal of Consulting and Clinical Psychology*, 71(4), 741–753.

Elliot, D. S., Huizinga, D., and Menard, S. (1989). *Multiple problem youth: Delinquency, substance use, and mental health problems.* New York: Springer-Verlag. As cited in U.S. Department of Health and Human Services. (2001). *Youth violence: A report of the surgeon general*, Washington, DC: U.S. Department of Health and Human Services, 49.

Geis, G. (1973). Jeremy Bentham. In H. Mannheim (ed.), *Pioneers in criminology*. Montclair, NJ: Patterson Smith, 249–267.

Guze, S. B. (1992). *Why psychiatry is a branch of medicine.* New York: Oxford University Press.

Kohlberg, L. (1958). *The development of modes of moral thinking and choice in years 10 to 16.* Cambridge, MA: Harvard University Press.

Monachesi, E. (1973). Cesare Beccaria. In H. Mannheim (ed.), *Pioneers in criminology*. Monclair, NJ: Patterson Smith, 192–203.

Reid, S. T. (1991). *Crime and criminology.* Fort Worth, TX: Harcourt Brace Jovanovich.

Schafer, S. (1969). *Theories in criminology.* New York: Random House.

Schoenfeld, C. G. (1975). A psychoanalytic theory of juvenile justice. In E. Peoples (ed.), *Correctional casework and counseling.* Pacific Palisades, CA: Goodyear, 141–157.

Shaffer, D., Gould, M. S., Fisher, P., Trautment, P., Moreau, D., Kleinman, M., and Flory, M. (1996). Psychiatric diagnosis in child and adolescent suicide. *Archives of General Psychiatry*, 53, 339–348.

Skinner, W. F., and Fream, A. M. (1997). A social learning theory analysis of computer crime among college students. *Journal of Research in Crime and Delinquency*, 34(4), 341–359.

Vold, G. B., and Bernard, T. J. (1986). *Theoretical criminology* (3rd ed.). New York: Oxford University Press.

Wallace, H., and Roberson, C. (2010). *Victimology* (3rd ed.). Columbus, OH: Pearson.

Walters, G. D., and White, T. W. (1989). *The thinking criminal: A cognitive model of lifestyle criminality.* Criminal Justice Research Bulletin No. 4. Washington, DC: U.S. Department of Justice.

Yablonsky, L., and Haskell, M. R. (1988). *Juvenile delinquency.* New York: Harper and Row.

Yochelson, S., and Samenow, S. (1976). *The criminal personality, Vol. 1. A profile for change.* Northvale, NJ: Aronson.

Chapter 6

Biological Factors and Violence

Introduction

The evidence is very firm that there is a genetic factor involved in crime.

Sarnoff A. Mednick (as quoted by Winkler, 1986)

Today positive school criminology dominates academic studies of crime and criminology. ... Despite the resurgence of classical criminology with its current "get tough on crime" emphasis, positive school ideals continue to be practiced in both adult and juvenile corrections in the United States.

Ronald Hunter and Mark L. Dantzker (2002)

Biological factors refer to a wide array of neurological, physiological, or chemical influences on aggression and violence. As Bartol and Bartol (2007) noted, recent advances in the neurosciences have revealed that biological factors, interacting with the social environment, may have some significant influences on child development. The exact nature of these influences remains largely unknown.

Currently, biological explanations of violence are in vogue. Part of the reason for this surge in popularity is that scientists studying the brain and its genetic underpinnings have learned a lot in recent years. Many researchers believe that a person's tendencies toward violence may reside in his or her genes or be hardwired into his or her brain. Some neuroscientists have mapped brain abnormalities in laboratory animals and human murderers that seem to correlate with aggressive behavior. Other neuroscientists have teased out apparent connections between violent behavior and brain chemistry. Charles Darwin's work on animal evolution was a major impetus to the rise of positivism. Many of the individuals during that period were strongly influenced by his theory of evolution (Bartol and Bartol, 2007).

Modern biological theories of violence are far more sophisticated than those that preceded them. Unlike the early biological theories, modern theories are concerned with behavior in individuals rather than groups and tend to allow for environmental factors. These studies are discussed in this chapter after an examination of the traditional biological theories of violent causation.

Charles Darwin's book *On the Origin of Species*, written in 1859, was considered by most researchers as the final break with the Age of Enlightenment (Vold and Bernard, 1986). In his famous book, Darwin presented evidence in an attempt to prove that humans were the same general kind of creatures as other animals but were more highly evolved or developed; humans were merely one type of creature with no divinity links. According to his view, our ancestors were less highly evolved and were part of a continuous chain linking humans to the earliest and simplest forms of animal life. As creatures, they could be understood by biological and cultural antecedents rather than as individuals with "free will." Accordingly, free will was replaced by the concept of determinism. Determinism was based on the notion that behavior is governed by physical, mental, environmental, and social factors beyond the control of the offender.

Table 6.1 provides an overview of the various biological schools of thought on violence causation.

Positivist Approach to Violence

Auguste Comte

Auguste Comte was born in January 1798 in southern France near the city of Montpellier. His father was a devout Catholic and a low-level government employee. His father despised the French Revolution and its attack on the Catholic Church.

Comte was frail and in poor heath as a young boy. He was, however, a good student. Early, he became disillusioned with his father's attacks on the evils of a republican form of government and the supremacy of the church. After developing a strong belief in the republican form of government, he advocated a return to those principles. He spent two years at the prestigious Ecole Polytechnique University in Paris. He left after being upset with the handling of six students who objected to the antiquated methods of administrating examinations (Coser, 1971).

Table 6.1   Schools of Thought on Causes of Violence Associated with Biological Reasons

School	*Early Positivism*	*Body Chemistry Theories*	*Constitutional Theories*	*Sociobiology*
Time frame	1880s–1930	1940s to present	1930s–1940s and 1960s to present	1975 to present
Overview	The early biological approaches were built on the evolutionary principles of Darwin and were the first to apply scientific techniques to the study of crime and criminals. They saw the criminals as throwbacks to the earlier evolutionary periods.	Use chemical influences, including hormones, food additives, allergies, vitamins, and other chemical substances, to explain human behavior. Some included the impact of weather.	Criminal conduct was explained by reference to the offenders' body types, inheritances, genetics, and external observable physical characteristics.	By studying the biological basis of all social behavior, we can determine why individuals commit criminal acts.
Leaders	Franz Joseph Gall, Cesare Lombroso, Charles Goring, and Earnest Hooton	Ellen Cohn and James Rotten	Ernst Kretschmer, William H. Sheldon, Richard Dugdale, and Henry Goddard	Edward O. Wilson

In 1827, while presenting a series of lectures on his philosophy, Comte had a mental collapse. During that time, he tried to commit suicide. During this period, his marriage also ended. He later blamed his problems on his preoccupation with the elaboration of his positivist philosophy. He resumed lecturing in 1829 and died in 1857.

Comte originally labeled his methods of research "social physics." He quickly abandoned this term when the Belgian social statistician Adolphe Quetelet also referred to his work as "social physics" (Coser, 1971). Comte contended that there were three stages in the evolution of human thinking:

- **Theological stage**—characterized by mythological thinking
- **Metaphysical or abstract stage**—characterized by classical thinking
- **Scientific or positive stage**—which he considered as the highest stage in human thinking

Comte repudiated the metaphysical and speculative concepts. He envisioned a society in which all social problems are solved by scientific methods and research. He contended that by studying large groups of people, we could learn the specific laws that govern human behavior. This concept became known as *empiricism*. Under empiricism, it was thought that all social sciences could be dealt with by empirical research and scientific methods, not by the abstract intuitive philosophy that was relied on by the classical thinkers (Gould, 1969).

Cesare Lombroso

More has been written by and about Cesare Lombroso (1835–1909) than any other criminologist. Lombroso is generally referred to as "the father of modern criminology." His influence is still alive in European contemporary research. In America, he is often used as a straw man for an attack on biological analyses of crime causation.

Lombroso was born in Venice of a Jewish family. He was educated in medicine and became a specialist in psychiatry. At the age of 15, he had two noteworthy historical papers published. At the age of 16, he published a review of Paolo Marzolo's *Introduction to Historical Monuments* (Vold and Bernard, 1986). Marzolo, a leading philosopher and physician, was impressed by the review and requested an interview with Lombroso. Marzolo was shocked to learn that a 16-year-old schoolboy had written a comprehensive review of his works.

After graduating from medical school in 1859, Lombroso volunteered for medical service in the army. While serving in the army, he began systematic measurement and observation of over 3,000 Italian soldiers. His purpose was to ascertain and analyze the physical differences that he had noted among Italian soldiers from various regions of Italy. During this time, he concluded that the practice of tattooing was a characteristic of criminals.

His personal life was rather typical. At the age of 34, he married a young Jewish girl. They had two daughters. Both daughters married professional men who were involved in Lombroso's work. With his daughter Gina's husband, G. Ferrero, he spent many hours examining human skulls. Together, Ferrero and Lombroso published *The Female Offender* (Vold and Bernard, 1986).

While a professor of legal medicine at the University of Turin, Lombroso's name became prominent with the publication of his book *L'uomo Delinquente* (The Criminal Man) in 1876 (Vold and Bernard, 1986). In the book, Lombroso proposed that criminals were biological throwbacks to an earlier evolutionary stage when people were more primitive and less highly evolved than their noncriminal counterparts. He described those people as "atavistic." The word is apparently taken from the Latin word *atavus*, which means ancestor. Darwin had previously written that "with mankind some of the worst dispositions which occasionally and without any assignable cause make their appearance in families, may perhaps be reversions to a savage state, from which we are not removed by many generations" (Darwin, 1871, p. 137).

As noted, Lombroso is given credit for founding the positivist school of criminology. Some researchers (e.g., Vold and Bernard, 1986) contended that it is something of an anomaly that it was Lombroso's fate to be known principally for the earliest formulation of his theory of criminality of the atavistic criminal because the real basis for the positivist school is the search for the causes of criminal behavior. The search is based on the multiple-factor causation approach, and some of the factors may be biological, others psychological, and still others social. Lombroso's thinking changed over the years, and in later years, he looked more and more to environmental rather than biological factors (Vold and Bernard, 1986).

Lombroso was the first clinical criminologist who "got his hands dirty" by spending numerous hours measuring criminally insane persons and epileptics' skulls. He was referred to as a "scientific Columbus." He attempted to categorize and classify types of offenders. Although his system of classification is considered crude by today's standards, he developed the first criminal topology. His general theory suggests that criminals are different from noncriminals because of the manifestation of multiple physical anomalies that are of atavistic or degenerative origin. Lombroso classified criminals as follows:

- Epileptic criminal
- Insane criminal
- Born criminal
- Occasional criminal

Lombroso designated the epileptic criminal, the insane criminal, and the born criminal as separate types, all stemming from an epileptoid base. Lombroso believed that the moral imbecile and the criminal were fundamentally alike in physical constitution and mental characteristics. In addition to the physical stigmata, Lombroso also noted that the born criminal had sensory and functional peculiarities, including greater insensitivity to pain and touch, more acute sight, and less-than-average acuteness of hearing, smell, and taste. The born criminal also had a lack of moral sense, including an absence of repentance and remorse. The occasional criminal, which he added later, referred to a large number of individuals who do not seek the occasion for the crime but who are almost drawn into it or fall into the meshes of the criminal codes for very insignificant reasons. He subdivided the occasional criminal types into categories: pseudocriminals, criminaloids, habitual criminals, passionate criminals, and political criminals.

Lombroso, like Beccaria, advocated that the first objective of punishment should be the protection of society. The second objective should be toward the improvement of the criminal. He maintained, however, that we should not treat crime in the abstract, and that we should make the punishment fit the offender. Like a physician applying remedies according to the illness, we should adapt the punishments to each individual. We must, according to him, make a difference according to whether we have under our eyes a born criminal, an occasional criminal, or a criminal by passion. He recommended the concept of indeterminate sentencing and restraining the criminal until he or she has been corrected.

Gabriel Tarde

While Lombroso concentrated on the biological and physical causes of criminal behavior, Gabriel Tarde (1843–1904) examined the sociopsychological factors. Even though he was not a positivist advocate, a discussion of Tarde is included in this section. He did advocate the scientific investigation of crime causation and many of the other attributes of the positivist school of thinking. He attempted to arrive at a happy marriage between psychology and sociology. Tarde did not lead the usual scholar's life. For 15 years, he was a provincial magistrate in the small village of Sarlat, his birthplace and home. Later, he directed the Bureau of Statistics in the Department of Justice in France. Unlike Lombroso, Tarde indicated that individual choice played a limited role in the crime causation process. Tarde's major contribution was his concept of the criminal as a professional type. He was of the opinion that most criminals went through an apprenticeship before becoming a criminal, and it was an accident of birth or chance that put them in an atmosphere of crime. He also attempted to classify criminals and was critical of Lombroso's classifications.

Raffaele Garofalo

Raffaele Garofalo (1852–1934) was one of the three leading exponents of the positivist school of criminology. Often referred to as one of the "unholy three of criminology" because of his Darwinistic beliefs (the other two were Lombroso and Ferri). He was born a member of Italian nobility in Naples. He worked as a lawyer, prosecutor, and magistrate. Later in life, he was a professor of criminal law and procedure. Garofalo also enjoyed a long and productive scholarly career. He is known principally for his major work, *Criminology*, first published in 1885 (Hoffer, 1978).

Criminology contained the influence of social Darwinism and the speculations of Herbert Spencer. Garofalo rejected the definition of crime as conduct for which the law has provided penalties and denominated as criminal. His concept of "natural crime" was substituted for the general definition of crime. To him, *natural* was defined as that which was not conventional that existed in human society independently of the circumstances and exigencies of a lawmaker's concepts of crime. Natural crime thus consisted of conduct that offends the basic moral sentiments of pity and probity. *Pity*, in this case, refers to a revulsion against the voluntary infliction of suffering on others. *Probity* is the respect for property rights of others. To be a criminal act, he stated that the act must be harmful to society. The concept of natural crime, however, does not consist of a catalogue of acts that are universally conceived to be criminal. True crime is conduct that, on evaluation by the average person's moral sense, is deemed offensive to society.

According to Garofalo, the criminal has a "moral" deficiency that is of an "organic" basis and transmissible by heredity. He believed in the biological transmission of criminality but not necessarily in the physical manifestation of criminality, as did Lombroso. Garofalo classified criminals as murderers, violent criminals, thieves, and lascivious criminals. He accepted Darwin's theory of survival of the fittest, and if the criminal did not adapt or conform to society, the criminal should be eliminated. He supported capital punishment for those who would not adapt. Garofalo viewed criminality as something organic and innate.

Enrico Ferri

Enrico Ferri (1856–1929) was one of the most colorful and influential figures in the history of criminology. He was born in the province of Mantua, Italy, and his active life spanned more than 50 years. During a substantial portion of that time, he was the acknowledged leader of the positivist school of criminology. He was also a highly successful trial lawyer and a member of Parliament. He was even the editor of the socialist newspaper Avnati. His book, *Principles of Criminal Law*, which was published in 1928, was his most important contribution to the legal principles of the positivist school (Sellin, 1972). According to him, the concept of free will had no place in criminal law, the social defense was the prime purpose of criminal justice, criminals should be classified into five categories, and penal substitutes should be used as a means of indirect social defense. He also saw three principal types of factors in crime causation. He is actually credited with coining the term *born criminal*, which Lombroso used in his theory (Sellin, 1972).

Ferri's three principal types of crime causation factors are anthropological, physical, and social. Anthropological factors are the offender's age, sex, civil status, occupation, residence, social class, degree of training, and education. The physical factors include race, climate, fertility and the distribution of soil, the daily cycle, the seasons, the meteorological factors, and annual temperature. The social factors include an increase or decrease in population, customs and religion, the nature of the family, and political, financial, and commercial life.

Ferri's five types of criminals are as follows:

1. The born or instinctive criminal, who carries from birth an evident and precocious propensity to crime
2. The insane criminal, who is affected by a mental disease
3. The passional criminal, who commits the crime through a prolonged and chronic mental state of passion or emotion (explosive and unexpected mental state)
4. The occasional criminal, who constitutes the majority of lawbreakers and is the product of family and social conditions and therefore has less-deviating psychological traits from those of the social class to which he or she belongs
5. The habitual criminal, who is a criminal by habit and is mostly a product of the social environment in which he belongs

Ferri clearly recognized that not every criminal fits neatly into his classification system.

Later, Ferri added a sixth type of criminal, the involuntary pseudocriminal, who causes damage by his or her lack of foresight, imprudence, negligence, or disobedience of regulations rather than through malice.

In support of the positivist school, Ferri contended that the principal reason for the rise of a positivistic view of criminal justice was the necessity to put a stop to the exaggerated individualism in favor of the criminal to obtain a greater respect for the rights of honest people who constitute the greatest majority. The positivist school first studies the natural origin of crime and then its social and legal consequences to provide, by social and legal means, the various remedies that will have the greatest effect on the various causes of crime (Sellin, 1972).

Determinism

As noted, the classical school emphasized the concept of free will and the position that punishment should be based on the crime that was committed. The positivists rejected the free will concept and substituted the doctrine of determinism and the position that punishment be tailored to fit the needs of the criminal. Determinism is based on the concept that the individual has no choice in his or her behavior, and because of biological or other factors, the concept of choice has been removed. The criminal is propelled by social, biological, emotional, or spiritual forces beyond his or her control. Accordingly, the criminal did not voluntarily commit the crime. *Hard determinism* is based on the concept that the individual has no freedom of choice. *Soft determinism* is based on the concept that the individual has limited choice in the matter.

Importance of Positivism

The positivist approach was a reaction to the inflexible and harshness of the classical school. The positivists emphasized not the crime as had the classical thinkers, but the criminal as an individual and the concept that the punishment should be tailored to fit the criminal. They contended that the criminal had no choice in the crime because of determinism. Only by treating the criminal, not punishing the criminal, could crime be eliminated. The positivists advocated scientific methodologies for studying the cause of crime. Accordingly, by careful study and scientific observation, the causes of crime could be determined and thus eliminated. One of their important contributions is evidenced by the juvenile justice system, in which treatment and punishment are directed toward what is best for the juvenile.

Biological Approaches to Violence Causation

Until recently, the biological theories enjoyed more popularity in Europe than in the United States. The common assumption of the biological theories is that crime is caused by a biological process. The process could be the product of our genetic makeup or the things we eat. The biological approaches to crime causation that are discussed in this section include heredity and crime, inferiority and body-type theories, difference and defectiveness theories, and nutrition.

Heredity and Violence

Do criminals inherit bad genes that cause their violent or antisocial behavior? The concept of the "bad seed" was popularized by *The Bad Seed*, a 1950s play and later movie about a prepubescent pigtailed blond girl who was a multiple murderer. According to the tale, she appeared to be an angelic girl whose parents were homicidal, antisocial people. She was raised by a foster family and had no contact with her biological parents. While she appeared to have model behavior, her bad seed or aberrant gene eventually took control, and she committed deceptive, shocking, atrocious criminal acts. The public tended to forget that the tale was fictional.

Two studies of bad seeds were compiled in the early part of the twentieth century. One was about the famous Juke family, and the other involved the Kallikak family. Henry Goddard, a leading U.S. advocate on heredity and crime, conducted the research on the Kallikak family. Researchers concluded in both studies that there was evidence of hereditary transmission of criminology. Today, most researchers who have reviewed the two studies concluded that there is little evidence to support the findings of hereditary transmission of criminology. Henry Goddard also taught that the feebleminded were a form of undeveloped humanity, "a vigorous animal organism of low intelligence, but strong physique" (as quoted by Winkler, 1986, p. 9).

A 1992 publication by the National Research Council discussed the findings of a team of Dutch and American scientists who had discovered a Dutch family in which, for the past five generations, the men had been unusually prone to aggressive outbursts, rape, and arson. According to the report, the men in that family had a genetic defect that made them deficient in an enzyme that regulates levels of the neurotransmitter serotonin. The report, however, cautioned that the results concerned only one family and should not be generalized to the population at large.

Edward O. Wilson's book, *Sociobiology: The New Synthesis,* received a great deal of attention when it was published in 1975. Sociobiology is the study of genetic explanations for such behaviors as altruism, homosexuality, male dominance, and conformity. Wilson's book examined crime causation based on sociobiology concepts. As the result of his book, the subdivision of criminology known as "biosocial criminology" developed (Marsh and Katz, 1985). Biosocial criminology deals with the study of crime from a biological perspective. Biosocial theories assume that criminal behaviors cannot be understood unless the interaction between the offender's biology and his or her environment is understood.

Biological explanations of crime causation are based on the assumption that structure determines behavior. People behave differently because their body structures are different. The structural differences may be the result of chromosomes, genes, chemistry, hormones, or even body type. The biological theories assume that the causes of criminal misconduct are often beyond his or her control because the person is "different."

According to many researchers, brain scans seem to give a dramatic view into the biological dynamics of violence. In the 1980s, brain scan studies indicated that the brains of many convicted criminals had areas of inactivity relative to the brain scans of control subjects. In 1997, one psychologist at the University of Texas, Medical Branch, conjured up red-and-blue reconstructions of the brains of violent offenders and used them to support his thesis that hair-trigger tempers are the result of an impairment of the frontal and parietal lobes of brains. Neuroscientists are attempting to isolate and study the roles of several neurotransmitters in suicidal patients, depressives, and people prone to impulsive violence (Kevles and Kevles, 1997, pp. 58–64).

Inferiority Theories

According to the inferiority theories, the criminal is different from the noncriminal. The criminal is inferior because of constitutional, intellectual, or mental reasons. The first inferiority theories focused on the criminal's physical characteristics (constitutional). At the time that the inferiority theories developed (sixteenth century), unusual physical characteristics were considered inherently evil. J. Baptiste della Porte (1535–1615) is considered one of the first researchers to study the relationship between a person's physical characteristics and crime causation. He concluded that thieves had small ears, small noses, slender fingers, and bushy eyebrows.

Physiognomy became popular in the latter part of the eighteenth century. Physiognomy is the study of judging a person's character by studying facial features. According to the thoughts of that day, a person's facial features were related to his or her conduct. Later, physiognomy gave way to phrenology. As noted, phrenology is the study of bumps on the skull.

Franz Joseph Gall (1758–1828) investigated the bumps and other irregularities of the skulls of criminals in the late 1700s. It was then that phrenology emerged as a discipline. Phrenology is based on the concept that the exterior of the skull corresponds to the interior and the conformation of the brain, that the brain can be divided into functions and those functions are related to the shape of the skull. By examining the shape of a person's skull, one can measure behavior. While these concepts developed about 70 years before the contributions of Lombroso, most look to Lombroso as beginning the positivist school of criminology. The positivist or positive school was probably founded by Auguste Comte (1798–1857), but Lombroso made it popular.

Cesare Lombroso examined and measured many Italian prisoners' craniums before and after their deaths to determine character traits and development. He concluded that criminals were physically inferior to noncriminals, and that criminals possessed certain physical stigmata that distinguished them from noncriminals. He also concluded that many criminals were born inferior, and for the most part, they were helpless to do anything about their differences. According to Lombroso, criminals have excessive dimensions of the jaw and cheek bones, eye defects, ears of unusual size, asymmetry of the face, and fleshy lips.

Phrenology was short-lived as a science. It disappeared as a scientific discipline because no one was able to substantiate its conceptions of physiological organs of the mind and their relationship to human conduct.

Charles Goring (1870–1919), based on a study of 3,000 convicts, refuted Lombroso's concept of criminal atavism but never rejected the idea that serious criminality was the result of a constitutional, physical, mental, or moral proclivity. He believed that this proclivity was biological and inherited. He concluded that criminals were physically smaller in stature and weight than the general population. Goring, in his study, attempted to control for some environmental influences but ignored others. His work is only considered as evidence of an association between crime and heredity.

Many of the later inferiority theories assumed that the criminal is inferior to the noncriminal in intelligence. There is some evidence that intelligence is inherited, and there appear to be a number of studies that found "a clear and consistent link" between criminal behavior and low intelligence. One of the problems in this area is that of measuring intelligence. There are numerous studies that attacked the credibility of the most frequently used IQ measurement instrument (Benet and Simon test). In addition, it appears that IQ scores are affected by socioeconomic and cultural factors.

Some of the arguments that are used to reject the link between criminal behavior and low intelligence include the following:

- Low mentality is not a significant cause of criminal behavior because there are smart criminals and dumb criminals.
- Intelligence appears to be more of a factor in the type of crime the individual will commit rather than whether he or she will become a criminal.

Body-Type Theories

The body-type theories have been popular with the general public. We seem to believe that fat people are always jolly, and redheads are hot tempered. The criminal, therefore, should be hard in appearance with a malformation in general facial structure or have a scar. Who were the criminals in the Dick Tracy comic strips? They were all deformed.

Ernst Kretschmer (1888–1964) studied the relationship between physique and mental illness. After researching 4,417 cases, he concluded that bodies could be divided into three distinct body types:

1. **Asthenic type**: The asthenic person has a thin and narrow build, with long arms and delicate bone structure and appearance. He concluded that this type of person tended to be idealistic, introverted, and withdrawn. This body type he also associated with schizophrenia. He concluded that this type of person is generally associated with violent crimes.
2. **Pyknic type**: The pyknic-type person has a round body and is fat and fleshy. This body type is associated with manic depressiveness. He concluded that the pyknic-type person tended to exhibit moodiness, extroversion, joviality, and realism. He concluded that pyknic types are generally associated with the crimes of larceny and fraud.
3. **Dyplastic type**: The dyplastic-type person has a body type that is part pyknic and part asthenic. He did not indicate an identifiable mental illness for this type of person (Kretschmer, 1925).

Earnest A. Hooton, a Harvard physical anthropologist, studied 17,000 people, including 13,873 prisoners. He was attempting to corroborate Lombroso's biological theories. Hooton concluded that there were differences between criminals and noncriminals. Criminals were more likely to have long, thin necks; thinner beards and body hair; more red-brown hair; and thinner lips than noncriminals. Criminals also had low foreheads, compressed faces, and narrow jaws. Criminals were physically inferior to noncriminals, and differences were due to hereditary factors. His theories were often criticized because his famous book was published in 1939 and supported the Nazi belief of a "superior race" (Hooten, 1939).

In 1949, William H. Sheldon studied delinquent male youth between the ages of 15 and 21. He concluded that delinquents had greater mesomorphy (tendency to be big boned and muscular) than did nondelinquents. He developed his own method of body typing. He attempted to isolate three poles of physique, which he called somatotypes, and devised three classes of them:

1. **Endomorph**: a person who is fat, round, and fleshy with short tapering limbs and small bones
2. **Ectomorph**: a person who is thin, small, and bony with a small face, sharp nose, fine hair, and relatively little body mass and relatively great surface area
3. **Mesomorph**: a person who is big boned and muscular and tends to have a large trunk, heavy chest and large wrists and hands (Sheldon, 1949).

Later, William Sheldon, in his text on delinquent youth, listed both physique and temperament types. He then concluded that each person possesses the characteristics of the three types of physique and temperament. Sheldon used three numbers, each between one and seven, to indicate the extent to which the characteristics of the various types were present in a given individual. He also concluded that most delinquent youth were significantly more mesomorphic than those least involved in delinquent behavior.

Sheldon and Eleanor Gluecks, a husband-and-wife research team, studied the association between physical body types and delinquency. They concluded that strength, physical ability, and activity level of mesomorphy can, under certain circumstances, be a factor in whether a juvenile becomes antisocial and criminal (Glueck and Glueck, 1950).

The body-type theories have been criticized for the following reasons:

■ The theories have not actually demonstrated the relationship between physique and behavior.
■ In most studies of body types, cultural factors were not considered.
■ Most body-type tests were conducted exclusively on males.
■ Most body-type theories were conducted on confined individuals and probably do not represent a normal sample.

The test may really indicate which body types are more likely to be detected when involved in criminal behavior.

Difference and Defectiveness Theories

The difference and defectiveness theories are based on the concept that criminals are biochemically different from noncriminals. Linus Pauling, who twice won the Nobel Prize in chemistry, suggested that behavior disorders are mostly caused by "abnormal reaction rates" in the body that result from constitutional defects, faulty diets, and abnormal concentrations of essential body elements (Hoffer, 1978). The concept of biochemical imbalances may be traced to Fredrick Wohler, a German chemist. In 1828, Wohler demonstrated that the organic compound "urea" could be synthesized. This led to the concept that people were chemical beings. Earlier, researchers had been able to identify some physiological and psychosocial effects caused by secretions of the endocrine glands (hormones). Max Schlapp and Edward Smith, in 1928, presented the theory that crime was the result of emotional disturbances caused by biochemical imbalances. The imbalances were in the secretions of endocrine glands. According to them, if the secretions were the product of chemical imbalances, the physiological and psychosocial effects of these secretions on individuals could cause irrational behaviors. They also contended that over 30 percent of all prison inmates suffered from irregular glandular functioning (Schlapp and Smith, 1928).

Research has also been conducted on the relationship between high levels of testosterone and criminal conduct. Since females tend not to be as aggressive as males, maybe males with high levels of testosterone, a hormone secreted by the testes that simulates the development of masculine characteristics, would be more aggressive than males with low levels.

Premenstrual Syndrome/Premenstrual Tension

Premenstrual syndrome (PMS) and premenstrual tension (PMT) have been considered as factors in violent personal crime by women. However, the rate of violent personal crime by women is much lower than the rate of males. Researchers estimated that approximately 40 percent of woman between the ages of 20 and 40 years are affected by PMS/PMT. Generally, the symptoms begin 10 to 14 days prior to the onset of the menstrual period. In some cases, it continues until the onset of menstruation. Some researchers contend that severely afflicted women are most vulnerable to extreme behavior during this period. One study of 249 female prison inmates indicated that 62 percent of the violent crimes committed by the females were during the PMT period, and only 2 percent were committed in the postmenstrual week.

The popularity of the PMS theory exceeds the empirical evidence supporting the theory. The PMS/PMT defense has been successful in reducing murder to manslaughter in several English cases. One famous case involving this defense was that of Sandie Smith, an English barmaid. She had previously been convicted of carrying a knife and threatening a police officer. She was also on probation for having stabbed another barmaid to death. Her background included nearly 30 convictions for assault and battery and 18 attempted suicides. Her attorney was successful in getting the British court to accept PMT as a mitigating factor (Masters and Roberson, 1990, pp. 251–253).

Chromosomal Abnormality

In a normal person, there are 23 pairs of chromosomes in each cell, including a pair of sex chromosomes, X and Y for men and XX for women. A relatively small number of males have the extra Y chromosome (XYY individuals). Over 200 research studies have failed to support the thesis that the XYY men are more aggressive and violent than XY men. In addition, the XYY condition is so rare in the population that it cannot be a major factor in criminality.

In the 1960s, a team of British researchers reported that a disproportionate number of male inmates in a Scottish hospital for the criminally insane had an extra Y chromosome accompanying the normal male complement of one X and one Y chromosome. Next, attorneys for Richard Speck, the notorious Chicago multiple murderer, announced that they planned to appeal his case based on the fact that he was XYY and therefore not responsible for his actions. It was later determined that Speck was not an XYY individual. Several popular novels, including *The XYY Man* (1965) and *The Mosley Receipt* (1968), came out in the late 1960s and featured XYY characters who struggled against their compulsion for violence.

Central Nervous System

The central nervous system (CNS), which includes the brain and the spinal column, is involved in conscious thought and voluntary motor activities. Some researchers have concluded that criminals have an excessive amount of slow brain-wave activity when compared to noncriminals. Accordingly, criminal behavior in some cases is the result of brain damage. As with many other theories, there is a definite lack of clear evidence that criminal behavior is the direct result of brain damage.

Nutrition and Criminal Behavior

Nutrition as a causative factor in criminal behavior is generally traced to biochemical imbalance, with the imbalance being caused by nutrition. Generally, nutrition is considered the primary cause of an individual's chemical imbalance. A number of studies have maintained that delinquents and criminals suffer from vitamin deficiencies, cerebral allergies, and low blood sugar. Like the studies of hormone imbalances, much of this research was based on case histories, with reports of spectacular changes in behavior attributed to changes in a person's diet (Vold and Bernard, 1986).

Problems with Biological Explanations

The use of biological factors to predict an individual's tendency to commit violent crimes causes difficult problems for our society. Suppose it was determined that males with certain biological factors were twice as likely to commit a violent crime as males without this factor. Would this give us the right to take precautionary measures against someone discovered with this factor? Should this fact be made public and violate the individual's right of privacy? What about the concept of "self-fulfilling prophecy"? Telling individuals, especially children, that they are prone to violence might just encourage them to commit violence.

Summary

Biological explanations of violence are popular today because of recent discoveries regarding the brain and its genetic underpinnings. The positivist school of criminology grew out of the Age of Realism and Darwinism. The concept of free will was replaced by the concept of determinism. Determinism was based on the notion that behavior is governed by physical, mental, environmental, and social factors beyond the control of the individual. Cesare Lombroso is referred to by many as the father of modern criminology. He is credited with the founding of the positivist school of criminology. He was also the first criminologist who got his hands dirty by spending many hours in labs studying criminals' bodies. He concluded that criminals are biologically different from noncriminals. Positivism was a reaction to the inflexibility and harshness of the classical school. The school is based on the scientific study of the causes of crime.

Biological approaches to criminal behavior were more popular in Europe than in the United States. The biological approaches to crime causation include heredity, inferiority, body-type, difference and defectiveness, and nutrition theories. The positivist's approach is based on the concepts of determinism, indeterminate sentences, punishment designed to fit the criminal, rejection of the legal definitions of crime, and inductive reasoning with empirical research. According to the inferiority theories, the criminal is biologically inferior to the noncriminal. Franz Joseph Gall studied the bumps and irregularities of the skulls of criminals and concluded that by examining the shape of a person's skull, one can measure behavior.

The body-type theories are based on the belief that there is an association between criminal behavior and body type. The difference and defectiveness theories are based on the concept that criminals are biochemically different from noncriminals. PMS and PMT have been considered as factors in violent personal crime by women. Chromosomal abnormality has also been considered as a factor in crime causation.

Review Questions

1. If the causes of criminal misconduct are in fact biologically related, then the concept of responsibility and choice becomes moot. Would it be cruel to punish a person for a crime for which he or she was not responsible?
2. Explain the differences between the concepts of free will and determinism.

3. What are some of the biological reasons given for crime causation? Do you agree with them?
4. Compare and contrast Ferri and Lombroso.

References

Bartol, C., Bartol, A. (2007). *Criminal behavior: A psychosocial approach* (8th ed.). Upper Saddle River, NJ: Prentice Hall.

Coser, L. (1971, Fall). The sociology of poverty. *Social Problems*, 13, 138–151.

Darwin, C. (1871). *Descent of man*. London: Murry.

Glueck, S., and Glueck, E. (1950). *Unraveling juvenile delinquency*. New York: Commonwealth Fund.

Gould, J. (1969). Auguste Comte. In T. Raison (ed.), *The founding fathers of social science*. Harmondsworth, England: Penguin, 214–219.

Hoffer, A. (1978). Some theoretical principles basic to orthomolecular psychiatric treatment. In L. J. Hippen (ed.), *Ecologic-Biochemical Approaches to Treatment of Delinquents and Criminals*. New York: Van Nostrand Reinhold.

Hooten, E. A. (1939). *The American criminal: An anthropological study*. Cambridge, MA: Harvard University Press.

Hunter, R. D., and Dantzker, M. L. (2002). *Crime and criminality: Causes and consequences*. Upper Saddle River, NJ: Prentice-Hall.

Kevles, B. H., and Kevles, D. J. (1997, October). Scapegoat biology. *Discovery*, pp. 58–64.

Kretschmer, E. (1925). *Physique and character*, W. J. H. Sprott, trans. London: Trubner.

Marsh, F. H., and Katz, J., eds. (1985). *Biology, crime and ethics*. Cincinnati, OH: Anderson.

Masters, R., and Roberson, C. (1990). *Inside criminology*. Englewood Cliffs, NJ: Prentice Hall.

Schlapp, M. G., and Smith, E. H. (1928). *The new criminology*. New York: Boni.

Sellin, T. (1972). Enrico Ferri. In H. Mannheim (ed.), *Pioneers in criminology* (2nd ed.). Montclair, NJ: Patterson Smith, 361–384.

Sheldon, W. H. (1949). *Varieties of delinquent youths*. New York: Harper.

Vold, G. B., and Bernard, T. J. (1986). *Theoretical criminology* (3rd ed.). New York: Oxford University.

Winkler, K. J. (1986, January 16). Criminals are born as well as made. *Chronicle of Higher Education*, p. 9.

Chapter 7

Exposure to Violence

Introduction

The Yale Child Study Center (2009) estimated that nearly 4 million children are victims of serious assault, and 9 million have witnessed a serious violent act. In this chapter, the effects of exposure to violence are explored. Much of the data used in this chapter were adapted from the August 2009 research report by Vuong, Silva, and Marchionna.

According to Garbarino (1995), when children are exposed to violence they suffer not only the immediate trauma of the incident but also creation of a "socially toxic" environment that tends to negatively affect children's normal development and their future well-being. Garbarino contended that children exposed to domestic violence are more likely than nonexposed children to be abused or neglected and more likely later to be in an abusive adult relationship, as either aggressor or victim. He noted that children encounter violence in their daily life—at home, at school, through the media, or on the streets of their neighborhoods.

Vuong, Silva, and Marchionna (2009) noted that there was extensive research on children who are direct victims of violence. Children who are exposed to violence suffer many of the same consequences. These studies have found that exposure at a young age results in short-term and long-term consequences, affecting children throughout their developmental phases and into adulthood. The researchers noted that such children are at increased risk for teen pregnancy, drug use, and mental health problems, and those children exposed to violence, directly abused, or neglected are more likely to be arrested as juveniles, as adults, and for violent crimes.

BOX 7.1 STUDY: VIOLENCE AT HOME HARMS CHILDREN'S BRAINS

According to an April 26, 2010, story published in the *Yomiuri Shimbun* ("Study: Violence at Home," 2010), research jointly conducted by Kumamoto University and Harvard University concluded that people who have witnessed domestic violence in childhood between parents are biologically affected. These people are likely to have a significantly smaller visual cortex later in life according to this research. The visual cortex of the brain processes information from the eyes.

The research lent credibility to a statement included in the federal Child Abuse Prevention, Adoption, and Family Services Act of 1988 that the emotional trauma of witnessing domestic violence can harm children's development and therefore constitutes a form of child abuse. In the research, the brains of individuals who were not physically abused but routinely saw a father severely physically abuse a mother when the subjects of the study were from 3 to 17 years old were compared with individuals who grew up in a family with no such domestic violence.

Images of the brains of those individuals involved were taken by magnetic resonance imaging. The imaging showed that the group who witnessed severe domestic violence had on average 20.5 percent less visual cortex in the right hemisphere of their brains than the other group. In addition, the blood flow in the right visual cortex of the group who witnessed domestic violence was 8.1 percent more than in the other subjects, showing that part of the brain was hyperactive, according to the study.

Juveniles as Victims or Criminals

A 2002 National Council on Crime and Delinquency (NCCD) study on teenage victimization concluded that the children exposed to violence or abused experience more problems in school, both with teachers and in their academic performance (Wordes and Nuñez, 2002). According to Wordes and Nuñez, the victimization of teenagers in America has gone largely unrecognized. Instead, in the context of crime and violence, our nation's young people are typically characterized as troublemakers, predators, and violent criminals rather than as victims. The researchers concluded that when victimization has been recognized, public attention has focused almost solely on large-scale incidents, such as school shootings. In addition, the victims of these tragic events represent only a fraction of the teens who become crime victims. The researchers contended that after years of focusing solely on juvenile offenders, it is time to shift our attention to the plight of juvenile victims.

According to Wordes and Nuñez (2002), teenagers are victimized at alarming rates at home, in school, and on the street, and teenagers are two times more likely than others to be victims of violent crime. The researchers noted that a national survey of high school students concluded that one in five teenagers reported that they were a victim of a violent crime in the past year. The researchers also pointed out that teenagers are more likely to be victims of property crimes than adults, although they do not often report it to the police.

The researchers noted that for most youth, school was a relatively safe haven, and that two-thirds of serious violent crimes committed against teenagers happened outside school property. Students who are expelled from school are victimized at three times the rate of those who are not expelled. Home is not always safe for adolescents according to the researchers. They noted that one-quarter of all substantiated cases of child abuse and neglect was for children between the ages of 12 and 17. They concluded that this means that there are approximately a quarter million substantiated child protective service cases involving teens. Moreover, teenagers are more likely to have a substantiated sexual abuse case than younger children.

Youth who are poor, African American, Hispanic, or American Indian are at the highest risk of victimization. As noted by the researchers (Wordes and Nuñez, 2002), African American teenagers are twice as likely to have a substantiated report of child maltreatment and are five times more likely to be killed by a gun than white teenagers. American Indian teenagers were more likely than any other group to be a victim of violent crime—49 percent higher than the rate for African Americans.

Wordes and Nuñez (2002) concluded from their study that abused teenagers show more problems in school, difficulty with teachers, and poor academic performance. Abuse is also a risk factor for teen pregnancy, drug use, and mental health problems. Young women with a history of sexual abuse show problems, including major depression, drug and alcohol addiction, teen pregnancy, prostitution, and suicide. According to Wordes and Nuñez, the data suggest that being a victim of a crime in the previous year is also related to becoming an offender.

The analysis (Glesmann, 2009) of the Adolescent Health Survey showed that of the youth who were violent offenders, only 5 percent were not victimized in the past year, and 54 percent were victimized in both years of the study. Even statistically controlling for other facts that are related to violent offending, victimization in the previous year was the strongest predictor. In addition, another 2009 NCCD study of risk factors leading to gang involvement found that living in a community with high levels of violence is a risk factor for later gang involvement (Glesmann, 2009).

Substance Abuse

According to Wordes and Nuñez (2002), research indicated a strong relationship between early exposure to violence and later substance abuse. They noted that children exposed to violence are three times more likely than their peers to abuse or become dependent on a large range of substances.

Community Violence

Wordes and Nuñez (2002) noted that community violence is generally defined as an act of interpersonal violence perpetrated by an individual not intimately related to the victim. This broad category encompasses property and weapons offenses, gangs and drugs, the sound of gunshots, and the presence of graffiti.

The researchers (Wordes and Nuñez, 2002) found that children exposed to community violence can also include those found or left at crime scenes. Communities at risk for violence exhibit such characteristics as unemployment, poverty, urbanization and population density, neighborhood decline (fewer positive social interactions, less involvement in community activities, less cohesiveness), and transiency. While some of these factors can be quantified (unemployment and poverty), others are more subjective (neighborhood decline).

Wordes and Nuñez (2002) also concluded that parents report only half the violence that their children report. Although community violence is difficult to measure, a few surveys did measure youth's perception of safety in their own communities. The researchers noted that a National Longitudinal Study of Adolescent Health reported that, in 1996, nearly 10 percent of youth in grades 7–12 had witnessed a shooting or stabbing of another person. Another national study found that 46 percent of the youth surveyed had changed their daily routines because of safety concerns. About 12 percent had changed their routes to and from school for the same reason.

School Violence

Wordes and Nuñez (2002) considered that school violence was a subset of community violence, and that it can range from something as serious as school shootings to something as simple as student perception of safety. More common incidents of school violence included bullying, victimization, fighting, weapons possession, teacher injury, and the availability and use of drugs or alcohol on campus. The research concluded that the tragedies of Columbine, Springfield, and Little Rock highlight the particular concern that, while schools are generally safe, these events have traumatic consequences, not only for those who were victims, but also for those who were present or even for those who were affiliated with the schools.

Considering the amount of time children spend at school and the influence of school on a child's life, Wordes and Nuñez (2002) opined that efforts should be made to create schools that are as safe as possible.

Domestic Violence

As noted by Wordes and Nuñez (2002), *domestic violence* is typically defined as violence between intimate partners. However, with regard to children, domestic violence can refer to those who have witnessed violence between their parents or caretakers and to those who are abused—physically or sexually—by their caretaker.

Neglect is often also included in this category. The researchers concluded that sexual abuse falls into two main categories, the first through noncontact, such as the exploitation of children in pornography or prostitution, the second through physical contact, such as intercourse. Children who have witnessed the arrest of a parent or caregiver or experienced the incarceration of a parent should also be included in this category.

Wordes and Nuñez (2002) concluded that studies of family violence are underdeveloped and often biased in scope, and that what is known and accepted is that abusive partners are also likely to be abusive parents; these parents are typically not biologically related to the victim, such as a stepparent. Researchers have also found that certain risk factors exist among abusers, such as lower socioeconomic status, experience of maltreatment during childhood, and greater levels of perceived individual stress. However, it is important to note, according to Wordes and Nuñez, that most individuals with said risk factors are not child abusers.

The researchers pointed out that the Bureau of Justice Statistics reported that 35 percent of households where domestic violence has occurred have children under age 12 living in them. They also noted that according to the older National Violence Against Women Survey and its contemporary, the National Crime Victimization Survey (Violence at home, 2010), reporting rates have increased in the past decade, from 30 percent to 60 percent; reasons for underreporting include a protection of privacy, followed by fear of reprisal. Data also show that partner violence often coincides with child maltreatment in the home.

Media Violence

Does violence in the media contribute to violent behavior by children? Wordes and Nuñez (2009), noted that children now have greater access to technology—television, movies, music, and video games—and that there is cause for concern about the amount of violence to which children are exposed at a young age. They referred to the reports by the Kaiser Family Foundation, which revealed that 99 percent of children live in homes with televisions, and that the average youth spends nearly six hours per day using some form of media, with three of those hours spent watching television. Seventy-seven percent of youth have a television in their bedroom, a situation that presumably makes parental monitoring of content more difficult.

Wordes and Nuñez (2002) noted that studies have found that violence in the media poses three threats. First, young children who are exposed to media violence become desensitized to acts of aggression and violence and perceive reality to be more violent than it actually is. Second, due to their inability to separate fiction from reality, young children begin to imitate the violent behaviors that they see. In fact, studies have found that children who see aggressive acts on television are more likely to imitate those actions in play or generally be more aggressive in their interactions. Third, children exposed to media violence are more likely to fear becoming a victim of such acts.

A research study by Huesmann, Moise-Titus, Podolski, and Eron (2003) found that children who watched many hours of violence on television when they were in elementary school tended also to show a higher level of aggressive behavior when they became teenagers. By observing these youngsters into adulthood, Huesmann et al. found that the ones who had watched a lot of TV violence when they were eight years old were more likely to be arrested and prosecuted for criminal acts as adults. Interestingly, the researchers concluded that being aggressive as a child did not predict watching more violent TV as a teenager, suggesting that TV watching may more often be a cause rather than a consequence of aggressive behavior.

It appears that a typical child in the United States watches 28 hours of TV weekly, seeing as many as 8,000 murders by the time he or she finishes elementary school at age 11; worse, the killers are depicted as getting away with the murders 75 percent of the time while showing no remorse or accountability. Such TV violence socialization may make children immune to brutality and aggression, while others become fearful of living in such a dangerous society.

According to the Web site of the American Psychological Association (APA) (2010, May 5), the research clearly showed that watching violent TV programs can lead to aggressive behavior. The APA passed a resolution in 1985 informing broadcasters and the public of the potential dangers that viewing violence on television can have for children (APA, 2004). In 1992, the APA Task Force on Television and Society published a report that further confirmed the link between TV violence and aggression.

To combat media violence, the U.S. Congress passed the Children's Television Act of 1990 (CTA), which outlined new regulations for commercial broadcast stations. As a result of the CTA, stations are required to air at least three hours of programming that furthers the education and informational needs of children 16 years and under in any respect, including children's intellectual/cognitive or social/emotional needs. The programs must be labeled with the designation E/I and have clearly stated, written educational objectives. The educational programs contain both direct and indirect messages fostering cooperation and compassion rather than aggression. Parents now have positive options when it comes to choosing TV programs for their children. Research on television and violence has also led to the development of content-based rating systems that allow parents to make judgments about the content of programs before allowing their children to watch them.

According to the APA (2004), besides warning of the harmful effects of violent media content, psychology has a strong history of bringing out the best in television. For example, Daniel R. Anderson, a professor of psychology at the University of Massachusetts, has worked with producers of children's programs like *Sesame Street* and *Captain Kangaroo* to help TV shows educate children.

Violent Music Lyrics

Anderson and other researchers (Anderson, Carnagey, and Eubanks, 2003) studied how violent music lyrics affect children and adults. In a study involving college students, they found that songs with violent lyrics increased aggression-related thoughts and emotions, and this effect was directly related to the violent content of the lyrics. One of their major conclusions was that when considering violent entertainment media, content matters.

Combating Violence in the Media

The research study by Wordes and Nuñez (2002) advocated engaging children in afterschool activities to reduce the amount of time they may spend watching television, unsupervised or otherwise. Given that the hours between school and evening (3 to 7 p.m.) are prime time for juvenile crimes, afterschool activities not only keep youth off the streets but also promote values and behaviors that work as protective factors, such as increased school achievement, adult success, and reduced levels of delinquency. The researchers noted that studies estimated that 10 million to 14 million children are left unsupervised after they leave school campuses. They noted that in the 1990s many federally funded afterschool programs were cut, leaving some 300,000–600,000 children without access to afterschool care. They concluded that reinvestment in such programs could greatly affect outcomes for youth.

Domestic Violence Home Visit Intervention Project

The Yale Child Study Center has established a Domestic Violence Home Visit Intervention (DVHVI) project. The project was designed to focus on the specific needs of children and families affected by domestic violence. The center developed the DVHVI project to address the complex and intertwined legal, psychological, and practical issues that confront many families who experience domestic violence. According to the center reports (Yale Child Study Center, 2009), children exposed to domestic violence are of particular concern because they are at very high risk of psychological and behavioral difficulties that are often overlooked by parents and professionals. The DVHVI goal is to interrupt the intergenerational cycle of violence by increasing families' safety and security, reducing children's repeat exposure to escalating episodes of violence, and increasing children's access to supportive services in the community. The project conducts a series of home visit outreaches by teams of police officers and domestic violence advocates to households in which an incident of domestic violence has been reported to the police. The general purposes of home visit follow-up are to

- assist in immediate safety planning;
- provide information regarding the criminal justice system and other available services;
- establish personal contact between families and local officers;
- enhance enforcement of domestic violence laws;
- increase parents' awareness of children's responses to potentially traumatic events; and
- facilitate connections between families and community services, including mental health assessment and treatment for affected children

An evaluation of the DVHVI project in 2006–2007 indicated that the program was a success (Yale Child Study Center, 2009).

Gang Resistance Education and Training Program

The Gang Resistance Education and Training (GREAT) program is a school-based, law enforcement officer-instructed, classroom curriculum. The primary objective of the program is prevention, and it is intended as an immunization against delinquency, youth violence, and gang membership. GREAT lessons focus on providing life skills to students to help them avoid delinquent behavior and violence to solve problems.

The GREAT program, previously administered by the Bureau of Alcohol, Tobacco, Firearms, and Explosives (ATF), is now administered by the Bureau of Justice Assistance (BJA), a component of the Office of Justice Programs (OJP), U.S. Department of Justice. Since its inception in 1991, over 8,000 law enforcement officers have been certified as GREAT instructors, and more than 4 million students have graduated from the GREAT program.

In calendar year 2009, the GREAT instructors of the Chicago Police Department were able to reach 600 youth between the ages of 9 and 14, and in some cases, instructors donated some of their time to ensure that the project would be successful.

Safe Start Centers*

In an attempt to reduce the effects of observing violence by children, the Safe Start Initiative was started on a national level by the Office of Juvenile Justice and Delinquency Prevention (OJJDP). The Safe Start Center is a national resource center designed to support the Safe Start Initiative on a national level. The goals of the center are as follows:

---

* Material for this section was taken from the Safe Start Web site at http://www.safestartcenter.org/pdf/ssc_fact-sheet.pdf (accessed April 26, 2010).

- To broaden the scope of knowledge and resources on hand for responding to the needs of children exposed to violence and their families
- To provide and disseminate information about the Safe Start Initiative and emerging practices and research concerning children exposed to violence
- To raise national awareness about issues concerning children exposed to violence

The goal of the Safe Start Initiative is to broaden the knowledge of and promote community investment in evidence-based strategies for reducing the impact of children's exposure to violence. Eleven demonstration grantees were funded to create a comprehensive service delivery system to improve the accessibility, delivery, and quality of services at any point of entry for children exposed to violence and their families. A process evaluation broadened our understanding of how communities can successfully implement policy and practice interventions to minimize the negative consequences of exposure to violence.

Fifteen Promising Practices Pilot Sites, funded in 2005, are focusing on implementing and measuring developmentally appropriate services for children exposed to violence within the context of the systems that serve them. A process and outcome evaluation of these grantees will broaden the understanding of the impact of specific intervention strategies on outcomes for children and families.

The centers work with national partners and a multidisciplinary group of experts to provide training and technical assistance to the 15 Promising Practices Pilot Sites, including

- Individualized and multisite consultation
- National conference calls to address issues of concern
- An up-to-date national database of consultants with specific technical and content expertise
- Active recruitment of expert consultants as well as matching services and effectiveness assessments

The center also works to develop publications about the Safe Start Initiative and innovations in the field of children's exposure to violence, including

- A bimonthly e-newsletter to raise awareness of available resources and make information readily available to Safe Start grantees and partners
- A quarterly topical bulletin to provide information promoting an improved understanding of children's exposure to violence and better access to quality care for children and their families
- Policy and practice briefs that provide practical clinical, administrative, training, and collaboration information
- Manuals and guidelines targeted to both specific systems and broad audiences
- A media kit to raise public awareness of the scope and impact of children's exposure to violence

In addition, the center convenes national and regional Safe Start meetings to foster a learning community and ensure the efficient sharing of knowledge and skills among grantees, national partners, and the general field. A regularly updated Web site provides information, resources, and notifications about new products. For information on Sate Start Programs in various areas of the country, see http://www.safestartcenter.org.

Teen Action Partnership

The Teen Action Partnership is a youth leadership initiative designed to get adolescent victims the help they need, to reduce the incidence of repeat victimization, and to develop youth leadership. This initiative, which was launched in early 2003 in four sites around the country, is supported by a grant from the U.S. Department of Justice Office of Community-Oriented Policing Services (COPS).

The National Center for Victims of Crime (NCVC; 2005) contends that the Teen Action Partnership gives youth—both victims and nonvictims—a unique opportunity to become resources to themselves and to their communities and empowers teenagers to address the problem of teen victimization in a meaningful and productive way. The elements of the Teen Action Partnership include the following:

- Youth partners use a process that includes assessment, advocacy, and outreach to peers and community leaders.
- Teens learn and teach others to address the needs of teen victims and prevent violence in their communities.
- Teens learn and teach others to address the needs of teen victims and prevent violence in their communities.

In 2010, groups of teens in four different sites around the country were

- Completing a community assessment focused on the local experience of teen victimization and the resources available to teen victims;
- Advocating for public policies that support teen victims;
- Conducting a peer outreach campaign to raise awareness of teen victimization; and
- Encouraging teen victims to get help.

The NCVC works directly with each of the four sites to provide the organizations with up-to-date information on the impact of crime on adolescence as well as training, troubleshooting, communication strategies, and technical assistance throughout the project. In all stages of the project, the youth hold leadership positions and work to effect positive change in their communities.

Child Sexual Abuse

The NCVC provides support and guidance on detecting and preventing criminal acts against juveniles. The material in this section on child sexual abuse was adapted from their Web site.

Child sexual abuse refers to any sexual contact with a child or teen. It includes many different acts. Some of these are touching the vagina, penis, or anus of a child; having a child touch the abuser's vagina, penis, or anus; putting an object, penis, or finger into the vagina or anus of a child; and showing a child pictures or movies of other people undressed or having sex. There are also other forms of child sexual abuse.

Sexual abuse can happen to boys or girls of any race, ethnicity, or economic background.

Sexual abuse is not a child's fault. The only person responsible for this kind of behavior is the abuser. People who sexually abuse children usually know the victims before making sexual contact. Abusers can be anyone, even someone the victim used to look up to, like, or trust, such as a neighbor, babysitter, friend, or member of the family or household.

Most of the time, because abusers are often older, bigger, or more powerful than the victims, children are afraid of what will happen if they do not cooperate with the abuse or if they tell someone. Sometimes, abusers will threaten or hurt victims in other ways to make them do what they want.

The age of children protected by child sexual abuse laws is different from state to state. In most states, sexual contact between an adult (18 years or older) and someone under 16 years old is child sexual abuse and is against the law, even if the abuser believes the young person agreed to the sexual activity. Children and young teens are protected from any sexual contact by adults and older teens because, when there is such a difference in power, sexual contact is harmful.

According to the NCVC, if you are a victim of child sexual abuse, you might

- Feel angry, sad, lonely, or depressed.
- Feel like you have no friends.
- Feel guilty, even though the abuse is not your fault.
- Want to hurt someone else or yourself.
- Feel like taking steps to defend yourself.
- Feel helpless to stop the abuser.
- Feel hopeless about whether anything can be done.
- Feel anxious all the time.
- Feel bad about yourself or your body.

According to the center, research suggests that child sexual abuse is common and highly underreported. Child sexual abuse has been reported up to 80,000 times a year.

Approximately one in three girls and one in seven boys are sexually abused during childhood.

The child should be advised that

■ Being sexually abused is not your fault.
■ Nothing about what you say, the way you look, or your behavior gives anyone the right to use or hurt you.
■ You have a right to ask for help.
■ If you are sexually abused, you may need medical care. Try to get to a safer place and call 911.
■ You should tell a trusted parent or adult as soon as possible.
■ Abuse is not a secret you have to keep.
■ You should keep telling until you get the help you need to feel safe.
■ You should tell a teacher, counselor, or principal at school if there is no one you can trust at home.
■ You can contact the police, a sexual assault or rape crisis counseling center, or child protective services for help.
■ If you need help finding someone to call, contact the National Crime Victim Helpline at 1-800-FYI-CALL (1-800-394-2255).

Extremely Violent Video Games

In the case of *Video Software Dealers Association v. Schwarzenegger* (2009), the state of California attempted to regulate the sale of violent video games to juveniles. The following excerpts taken from the U.S. Court of Appeals for the Ninth Circuit brief of the state attorney general provides some interesting commentary on the regulation of violent video games, as does the counter argument by the attorney for the software dealers. The U.S. Supreme Court decided in April 2010 to review the case.

From Attorney General Brown's Appellant Brief

> **Issue:** IN THE LIMITED CONTEXT OF THE SALE TO MINORS, VIDEO GAMES THAT ARE SO VIOLENT THEY APPEAL TO A DEVIANT OR MORBID INTEREST OF MINORS, ARE PATENTLY OFFENSIVE UNDER COMMUNITY STANDARDS, AND LACK ANY LITERARY, ARTISTIC, POLITICAL OR SCIENTIFIC VALUE FOR MINORS ARE NOT ENTITLED TO FIRST AMENDMENT PROTECTION.

Neither the Supreme Court nor this Court has addressed whether extremely violent material—material that, absent a sexual component, otherwise meets the established definition of obscenity—may be considered obscene as to minors. This appears to present a question of first impression for the Court, and its resolution deserves more analysis than the mere regurgitation of non-binding opinions from out-of-circuit courts offered by Plaintiffs. The State Defendants have presented this Court with a thoughtful, reasoned approach to analyzing the constitutionality of California's violent video game law that properly balances the rights of children and adults with the rights of the states and parents.

Argument:

The definition of "violent video game" established by California ensures, *ab initio*, that only material that is unworthy of protection as to minors will come within the parameters of the Act. *See* Civ. Code § 1746 (d)(1)(A) (hereafter the "Act"). Plaintiffs' concerns that children will be prohibited from purchasing video games that parallel "great literature" or track "Homeric epics in content and theme" are completely unfounded. Great literature surely has literary value for minors in all communities, which by definition exempts such games from the Act.

Notably, Plaintiffs fail to address or even acknowledge the fact that only a narrow subset of extremely violent video games is targeted by the Act. For example, the video tape included in the legislative record contains video clips of interactive play of the video game "Postal 2," as well as others. As is shown by multiple clips of actual game play, there exists a subset of extremely violent video games (Postal 2, in particular) that appear to have absolutely no storyline other than for the player to kill, maim, dismember, or assault as many other characters as possible for no apparent reason. Plaintiffs do not even attempt to explain how prohibiting children from purchasing these games will somehow prevent them from becoming "well-functioning, independent-minded adults and responsible citizens. ... (quoting *American Amusement Machine Ass'n v. Kendrick*, 244 F.3d 572, 576–77 (7th Cir. 2001)). Nor can they, as the Act allows children to continue to purchase video games where the violent content occurs in a context that is otherwise in line with community standards, is not patently offensive, or contains artistic, literary, or social value for minors.

Plaintiffs argue that the State Defendants fail to recognize the differing rationales underlying the regulation of sexual versus violent material. These rationales might differ as to adults, but the rationales for regulating sexually explicit material and violent material are exactly the same in the context of minors: Promoting "the well-being of [the state's] children" by helping parents protect them from "material [that] might be harmful." *Ginsberg v. State of New York*, 390 U.S. 629, 639 (1968).

The social interests sought to be protected by laws restricting children's access to sexually explicit material apply with equal force to extremely violent material. The Supreme Court has continuously embraced the premise that sexually explicit material has adverse effects upon children who, by their very nature, are intellectually and emotionally less mature than adults. *Bethel School District No. 403 v. Fraser*, 478 U.S. 675, 684 (1986) (noting that its prior cases "recognize the obvious concern on the part of parents, and school authorities acting *in loco parentis*, to protect children ... from exposure to sexually explicit, indecent, or lewd speech.") Yet in the context of sexually explicit material, there is a noticeable lack of scientific evidence supporting a causal nexus between a child's exposure to such material and any resulting physical or psychological harm. Indeed, it appears the Supreme Court has never required *any* empirical proof of harm when children are involved.

In stark contrast, as the record demonstrates, there is a large and continuously developing body of social science that supports California's concern that children who play extremely violent video games can become automatically aggressive, experience increased aggressive thoughts and behavior, engage in antisocial behavior, become desensitized to violence, and perform poorly in school. Nonetheless, in apparent disregard of this robust body of research, courts across the nation have given *less* First Amendment protection to sexually explicit material than to violent material. This archaic and irrational dichotomy can no longer be justified, if ever it was. First Amendment jurisprudence must acknowledge that extremely violent material can be *more* harmful to children than obscene or indecent sexually explicit material. Analyzing California's violent video game law under the variable obscenity standard set forth in *Ginsberg v. State of New York*, as described in Appellants' Opening Brief, will eliminate this unsupportable dichotomy and allow states to assist parents in protecting their children from the harmful effects of violent material to the same extent as sexually explicit material.

As Justice Frankfurter recognized over fifty-five years ago, "[c]hildren have a very special place in life which law should reflect. Legal theories and their phrasing in other cases readily lead to fallacious reasoning if uncritically transferred to determination of a State's duty towards children." *May v. Anderson*, 345 U.S. 528, 536 (1953) (Frankfurter, J., concurring). "Properly understood, then, the tradition of parental authority is not inconsistent with our tradition of individual liberty; rather, the former is one of the basic presuppositions of the latter. Legal restrictions on minors, especially those supportive of the parental role, may be important to the child's chances for the full growth and maturity that make eventual participation in a free society meaningful and rewarding." *Belloti v. Baird,* 443 U.S. 622, 638–39 (1979).

Here, the only games covered by the Act are, by definition, those with no redeeming value whatsoever for children. Whatever First Amendment value these games may possess for adults, such games are simply not worthy of constitutional protection when sold to children. There is no sound basis in logic or policy for treating violent material with no redeeming value for children any different from sexually explicit material. Therefore, the Act is properly reviewed under *Ginsberg v. State of New York,* which it unquestionably survives. *See* AOB at 20–22.

Plaintiffs blithely argue at several junctures that "numerous other Courts of Appeal and district courts have unanimously rejected governmental attempts to restrict video game expression based on its content. However, this statement over-simplifies the legal argument and mis-portrays the issue as judicially foreclosed. But the fact of the matter is that the cases cited by Plaintiffs have different evidentiary records, reflect different procedural postures, and address differing language in the particular statutes at issue.

For example, in reviewing a ruling on a preliminary injunction motion, the court in *American Amusement Machine Association v. Kendrick* stated that "[i]t is conceivable though unlikely that in a plenary trial the City can establish the legality of the ordinance. ... If the games used actors and simulated real death and mutilation convincingly, or if the games lacked any story line and were merely animated shooting galleries (as several of the games in the record appear to be), a more narrowly drawn ordinance might survive a constitutional challenge." 244 F.3d 572, 579–580 (7th Cir. 2001). In fact, neither the statute at issue in *Kendrick* nor in any other case relied upon by Plaintiffs is identical to the statute at issue here. *See id.* at p. 573 (describing statute); *Entertainment Merchants Association v. Henry,* No. CIV-06–675-C, 2007 U.S. Dist. LEXIS 69139 (W.D. Okla. Sept. 17, 2007) (same); *Entertainment Software Association v. Hatch,* 443 F. Supp. 2d 1065, 1067 (D. Minn. 2006) (same).

These differences are not inconsequential. For example, the language of the statute at issue in *Video Software Dealers Association v. Maleng,* was deemed too narrow because it only regulated video games in which the player killed, injured, maimed or otherwise caused physical harm to a human form who is depicted as a law enforcement officer. 325 F. Supp. 2d 1180, 1189–1190 (W.D. Wash. 2004). Even so, the Court in *Maleng* went on to note that a state "probably" could impose a restriction on the dissemination of video games to children under 18 if the games contained sexually explicit images and "maybe" if the games contained violent images, "such as torture or bondage, that appeal to the prurient interest of minors." Moreover, in *Interactive Digital Software Association v. St. Louis County,* there is no indication that the same evidence available to the California legislature was available to the legislating body in St. Louis County. 329 F.3d 954, 957, 959 (8th Cir. 2003) (St. Louis ordinance was passed in 2000, whereas here the Act was passed in 2005). Thus, contrary to Plaintiffs' statements, these cases do not describe any settled principles of law; rather, a close reading of the cases confirms that this is truly an unsettled area of the law that other courts have posited remains open to a narrow and carefully crafted legislative enactment.

A.   The Act Promotes a Compelling State Interest.

Plaintiffs argue that the Act cannot survive review under strict scrutiny because, as they bluntly put it, the State's interests in "preventing violent, aggressive, and antisocial behavior," and "preventing psychological or neurological harm" to children are "not compelling." ("But regardless of the emphasis, neither of these purported interests can save the Act … because the interests are not compelling. … ") Fortunately, both the court below and the Supreme Court flatly disagree with Plaintiffs' unfounded position. *Sable Communications of Cal., Inc. v. F.C.C.,* 492 U.S. 115, 126 (1989) ("We have recognized that there is a compelling interest in protecting the physical and psychological well-being of minors.")

B.   The State's Interests Are Promoted by the Act.

Plaintiffs' main argument appears to be that this Court should simply reject the body of social science relied upon by the Legislature because other courts have rejected similar evidence. Plaintiffs offer no independent analysis on the topic, but instead simply regurgitate the unsupported findings of other courts.

Notably, the court below found the States' evidence credible and acknowledged that exposing children to extreme violence can be harmful. The obstacle for the court below, however, was that in its opinion the evidence did not adequately single-out video games from other forms of violent media. *Ibid.* ("this court is not as doubtful as other courts have been as to the legislature's power to restrict the access of minors to violent video games or as skeptical of Dr. Anderson's conclusions."). But even assuming the social science concerning the unique harm caused by violent video games as compared to other media is still evolving, the Constitution allows the Legislature to address the harmful effects media violence has on children one phase at a time.

"Each medium of expression, of course, must be assessed for First Amendment purposes by standards suited to it, for each may present its own problems." *Southeastern Promotions, Ltd. v. Conrad,* 420 U.S. 546, 557 (1975). To this extent, the Supreme Court has consistently upheld a legislature's prerogative to deal with significant societal problems one aspect at a time. *See Erznoznik v. City of Jacksonville,* 422 U.S. 205, 215 (1975); *Williamson v. Lee Optical of Oklahoma,* 348 U.S. 483, 488–489 (1955). In *Williamson,* the Supreme Court recognized that "[e]vils in the same field may be of different dimensions and proportions, requiring different remedies. Or so the legislature may think. ... Or the reform may take one step at a time, addressing itself to the phase of the problem which seems most acute to the legislative mind. ... The legislature may select one phase of one field and apply a remedy there, neglecting the others." *Williamson,* 348 U.S. at 489.

Here, it may well be the case that all violent media that otherwise meet the definition for obscenity are harmful to children. It certainly does not follow, however, that the Constitution prohibits states from dealing with the problem one medium at a time. No rational public policy would be served by such a limitation. California must be allowed to address the serious problems associated with children's exposure to extremely violent material one medium at a time as their harmful effects are established.

C. The Act Advances the State's Interests through the Least Restrictive Means.

Plaintiffs essentially argue that constitutional principles are best served by allowing children to continue purchasing extremely violent video games because apparently some of the "new" gaming consoles include parental controls that allow parents to limit their child's access to some games based upon the games. This argument fails for multiple reasons.

First, nothing in the record establishes that these controls actually existed at the time the Act was passed into law. Secondly, Plaintiffs themselves acknowledge that the ESRB [Entertainment Software Rating Board] rating system is voluntary, and not all video game publishers submit their games to the ESRB for rating. Thus, for games receiving no ESRB rating, the console controls would apparently be useless. Allowing children to purchase these extremely violent video games on the dubious assumptions that (1) the children have also purchased "new" game consoles, (2) the new game consoles have parental controls allowing parents to restrict access to certain games, and (3) the games purchased by the children have been rated such that the console's parental control feature can have any meaning at all, cannot seriously be considered an effective alternative to simply restricting children's ability to purchase these games at the outset. And finally, any child with a computer or gaming console connected to the Internet can easily search the World Wide Web for instructions on how to bypass the parental control feature of any console. There is simply no less restrictive means that is *as effective* as the Act in achieving the compelling interests at stake.

The definition of "violent video game" contains two separate, independent clauses, either of which is severable from the Act. The Act's own severability clause provides as follows: "The provisions of this title are severable. If any provision of this title or its application is held to be invalid, that invalidity shall not affect other provisions or applications that can be given effect without the invalid provision or application." Civ. Code § 1746.5. Plaintiffs correctly acknowledge that this Court should look to state law to determine if a statutory provision is severable, but they fail to properly apply the test.

Under established California precedent, invalid portions of a statute may be severed from the valid portion where the invalid provisions are (1) grammatically, (2) functionally and (3) volitionally separable from the remaining statute. *See, e.g., Hotel Employees and Restaurant Employees International Union v. Davis*, 21 Cal. 4th 585, 613 (1999). A provision is grammatically separable if it is distinct and separate and can be removed as a whole without affecting the wording of any of the measure's other provisions. *Ibid.* A provision is functionally separable if it is not necessary to the measure's operation and purpose. *Ibid.* And a provision is volitionally separable if it is not of critical importance to the measure's enactment. See *Calfarm Ins. Co. v. Deukmejian*, 48 Cal. 3d 805, 822 (1989); *Sonoma County Organization of Public Employees v. County of Sonoma*, 23 Cal. 3d 296, 320 (1979); *Santa Barbara School Dist. v. Superior Court of Santa Barbara County*, 13 Cal. 3d 315, 331 (1975).

Contrary to plaintiffs' argument, severing the secondary definition from the Act is both grammatically and functionally possible, as the two definitions for "violent video game" are provided in the disjunctive by use of the term "either." Civ. Code § 1746 (d)(1). Thus, the secondary definition of "violent video game" can be deleted in its entirety, along with the conjunctive term "either," and the primary definition can independently exist without reference to the severed portion.

Moreover, the secondary definition of "violent video game" is volitionally severable. A provision is volitionally severable if it appears that the valid portions would have been adopted had the legislative body foreseen the partial invalidity of the statute. *Calfarm Ins. Co. v. Deukmejian, supra*, 48 Cal. 3d at 821–22. Here, there is no indication that the legislative intent behind the Act was an "all or nothing" approach; to the contrary, the fact that the Legislature included the express severability clause demonstrates it intended to retain as much of the Act as possible in the event some portion of it were to be found invalid. *See Santa Barbara School Dist. v. Superior Court of Santa Barbara County, supra,* 13 Cal. 3d at 331 (finding that the proponents of a proposition for desegregation would be happy to achieve at least some substantial portion of their purpose even if a portion was invalid and stating that a severability clause is not conclusive, but it "normally calls for sustaining the valid part of the enactment"); *Sonoma County Organization of Public Employees,* 23 Cal. 3d at 320 (holding that a statute containing a severability clause meets the requirements for severance because the unconstitutional portions of the statute could be mechanically severed).

Here, the unequivocal intent expressed in the Act is to restrict the ability of children to purchase extremely violent video games. The Act, as severed, accomplishes the Legislature's goal. Therefore, the secondary definition is properly severable from the Act.

Conclusion

For all of the foregoing reasons, the Act survives judicial review in all respects. Therefore, the district court's order granting summary judgment in favor of Plaintiffs was improper as a matter of law and should be reversed by this Court, and summary judgment on all causes of action in favor of the State Defendants should be granted. (2008 U.S. 9th Cir. Briefs 16620; 2008 U.S. 9th Cir. Briefs LEXIS 427)

Counterstatement of Facts Filed by Video Software Dealers

A. The Act.

The Act imposes a civil penalty of up to $ 1,000 on any person who "sell[s] or rent[s] a video game that has been labeled as a violent video game to a minor." Cal. Civ. Code § 1746.1(a). A "violent video game" is defined by the Act as one "in which the range of options available to a player includes killing, maiming, dismembering, or sexually assaulting an image of a human being, if those acts are depicted" in a manner that meets one of two sets of criteria. Id. § 1746(d)(1). The first set of criteria—the only portion defended by the State on appeal—requires that the depictions be such that "[a] reasonable person, considering the game as a whole, would find appeals to a deviant or morbid interest of minors," be "patently offensive to prevailing standards in the community as to what is suitable for minors," and "cause[] the game, as a whole, to lack serious literary, artistic, political, or scientific value for minors." Under a second provision, which the State now concedes is unconstitutional but argues is severable, a game is restricted if the actions depicted enable "the player to virtually inflict serious injury upon images of human beings or characters with substantially human characteristics in a manner which is especially heinous, cruel, or depraved in that it involves torture or serious physical abuse to the victim."

The Act's "violent" video game ban purportedly serves two purposes: "preventing violent, aggressive, and antisocial behavior" and "preventing psychological or neurological harm to minors who play violent video games." Furthermore, the Act purports to make "findings" that "[e]xposing minors to depictions of violence in video games" makes them "more likely to experience feelings of aggression, to experience a reduction of activity in the frontal lobes of the brain, and to exhibit violent antisocial or aggressive behavior," and that "[e]ven minors who do not commit acts of violence suffer psychological harm from prolonged exposure to violent video games."

In addition to imposing substantial penalties on persons who sell or rent "violent" video games to minors, the Act imposes an additional, content-based burden on video games. The Act provides that "[e]ach violent video game that is imported into or distributed in California for retail sale shall be labeled with a solid white '18' outlined in black. The '18' shall have dimensions of no less than 2 inches by 2 inches" and must be placed on the face of the video game package. Cal. Civ. Code § 1746.2. Failure to label a "violent" video game subjects a manufacturer, distributor or importer to a $ 1,000 penalty.

B. Plaintiffs and the Nature of Video Games.

Plaintiffs are associations of companies that create, publish, distribute, sell and/or rent video games, including games that may be regulated as "violent video games" under the Act. In this facial challenge, Plaintiffs also assert the rights of willing listeners.

Video games are a modern form of artistic expression. Like motion pictures and television programs, video games tell stories and entertain audiences through the use of complex pictures, sounds, and text. These games frequently contain storylines and character development as richly detailed as (and sometimes based on) books and movies. Like great literature, these games often involve themes such as good versus evil, triumph over adversity, struggle against corrupt powers, and quest for adventure.

Indeed, the games submitted into evidence by Plaintiffs—which may potentially be restricted by the Act based on their depictions of violence—demonstrate the expressive features of video games. For example, both Resident Evil 4 and Tom Clancy's Rainbow Six contain detailed plots and battles of good against evil, and each parallels movies (Resident Evil) or a book (Rainbow Six) that minors in California are legally able to obtain without restriction. These games also contain depictions of violence; Resident Evil 4, for example, allows the main character to "kill" images of zombies or mutants. Another game, God of War, provides a storyline drawn from Greek mythology. That game follows the adventures and travails of Kratos, a Spartan warrior, in his efforts to kill Ares, the God of War, in a complex quest that takes him through ancient Athens and Hades.

C. *The Video Game Industry's Voluntary Rating System.*

Like other popular media, including motion pictures, television, and music, the video game industry has adopted a voluntary and widely used rating system for video games. That system—which the Federal Trade Commission ("FTC") has called the "most comprehensive" of industry-wide media rating systems—is implemented by the ESRB, a self-regulatory body that assigns independent ratings and descriptions for video game content. The ESRB gives one of six age-specific ratings to each game it rates: EC (Early Childhood); E (Everyone); E10+ (Everyone 10 and older); T (Teen); M (Mature); and AO (Adults Only). ER 95–96. The ESRB also assigns content descriptors to each game, such as "Crude Humor," "Language," "Suggestive Themes," "Cartoon Violence," and "Sexual Violence," among over two dozen others.

The purpose of the ESRB system is to provide easily understood information about games to consumers and parents to empower them to make informed choices about the games they may buy, rent, or play. Like the movie rating system, the ESRB system is entirely voluntary; nonetheless, essentially all video game publishers submit their games for rating. Similarly, video game retailers throughout the nation are part of a widespread and voluntary effort to educate consumers about the ESRB system and to implement a store-by-store policy of restricting the sale of "M" games to individuals under age 17.

D. *The District Court's Decisions.*

The district court issued two opinions, one granting a preliminary injunction against enforcement of the Act and one granting summary judgment for the Plaintiffs, denying summary judgment for the Defendants, and entering a final injunction against the Act.

In its decision granting the Plaintiffs' motion for a preliminary injunction, the district court recognized that video games are "protected by the First Amendment", and that "[c]hildren 'are entitled to a significant measure of First Amendment protection.'" Erznoznik v. City of Jacksonville, 422 U.S. 205, 212 (1975). The Court then considered and rejected the Defendants' argument that the deferential standard of review under Ginsberg v. New York, 390 U.S. 629 (1968), should be extended beyond restrictions on sexual speech to minors and applied in this case. Indeed, responding to Defendants' suggestion that "a state could regulate a minor's access to games about embezzling, bomb building, and shoplifting, without violating the First Amendment, if a causal connection with harm to children could be established," the court sharply disagreed, noting that "[n]o court has previously endorsed such a limited view of minors' First Amendment right[s]." Instead, the court concluded, consistent with all other courts to consider similar laws, that Act is subject to strict scrutiny under the First Amendment, and that the Act was unlikely to survive strict scrutiny.

On summary judgment, the court reiterated that video games are expression protected under the First Amendment and that the Act is subject to strict scrutiny. After deciding that the State had at least some compelling interest supporting the Act, the court concluded nevertheless that the Act was unconstitutional. The district court first held that the Act's second definition of "violent video game" in § 1746(d)(1)(B) was too broad because it contained "no exception for material for some redeeming value" and "could literally apply to some classic literature if put in the form of a video game." The court next held that the three-pronged definition of "violent video game" under § 1746(d)(1)(A), although more narrow, was still unconstitutionally broad. As the court noted, the Act does not distinguish between the age of the minor purchasing or renting the game, but "[i]n light of the fact that, upon turning eighteen, one can vote and fight in a war, a showing needs to be made that an individual nearing the age of majority needs to be shielded from uncensored speech to the same extent as an early adolescent." Moreover, the court found the term "image of a human being" to be insufficiently narrow because it is "not limited to what appears to be an actual living human being."

Second, the district court held that the State had failed to demonstrate that plausible, less restrictive alternatives would be ineffective to achieve the State's goals. In particular, the court held that the State failed to demonstrate that "industry labeling standards, either alone or combined with technological controls that enable parents to limit which games their children play" inadequately protect the State's interest.

Third, the court held that the State could not show that the Act furthered the State's purported interests because the State's "evidence does not establish the required nexus between the legislative concerns about the well-being of minors and the restrictions on speech required by the Act." In particular, the court concluded that "there has been no showing that violent video games as defined in the Act, in the absence of other violent media, cause injury to children," that "the evidence does not establish that video games … are any more harmful than violent television, movies, internet sites or other speech-related exposures," and that "[t]here has also been no detailed study to differentiate between the effects of violent videos [games] on minors of different ages." Finally, addressing the labeling requirement, the court concluded that it need not resolve the parties' dispute over the level of scrutiny to apply in light of the court's holding that the Act is unconstitutional.

Summary of Argument

The district court correctly held that the Act violates the First Amendment on its face and must be permanently enjoined. In so holding, the district court joined the numerous other Courts of Appeal and district courts that have unanimously rejected governmental attempts to restrict video game expression based on its content.

The Act's content-based restriction on protected speech plainly violates the First Amendment. The State's principal argument that deferential scrutiny should apply under the First Amendment—merely because the State disapproves of the message conveyed to minors by certain speech—is seriously flawed and has been rejected by every court to have considered the issue. No court has ever extended the lesser scrutiny afforded under Ginsberg v. New York, 390 U.S. 629 (1968), beyond the realm of sexual speech to minors, and indeed, doing so would blatantly infringe on minors' long-recognized free speech rights. Moreover, the State concedes for the first time on appeal that the second of the Act's two independent definitions of violent video games goes too far under even its eviscerated view of the First Amendment. Because that second definition is not severable under California law, its conceded invalidity provides another basis for affirming the district court's judgment to enjoin enforcement of the Act.

Apparently recognizing the weaknesses of its baseless argument that lesser scrutiny under the First Amendment should apply, the State argues, alternatively, that the Act satisfies strict scrutiny. But the State has not met, and cannot meet, the demands of strict scrutiny, for at least three reasons. First, the State has identified no compelling interest that the Act furthers. The State identifies two interests that the Act supports—"preventing violent, aggressive, and antisocial behavior" and "preventing psychological or neurological harm to minors who play violent video games." While preventing violence and psychological harm are compelling interests at a general level, the State has no compelling basis for using censorship to accomplish these goals. The State's asserted concern for preventing violent behavior cannot possibly meet the stringent standard established in Brandenburg v. Ohio, 395 U.S. 444, 447 (1969)—a standard that the State does not even try to satisfy. Absent compliance with Brandenburg, the government may not restrict expression based on its content in order to affect the behavior of the listener. Yet that is precisely what the State's concern with alleged "psychological harm" amounts to: a claim that violent content affects minors' behavior and thoughts in ways that the State deems undesirable. As numerous courts have found, that is nothing more than a form of thought control that is foreign to the First Amendment.

Second, the evidence submitted by the State does not come close to constituting sufficient evidence of harm that would justify the Act's restrictions on speech. None of the studies the State has submitted as evidence establishes a causal relationship between depictions of media violence and adverse effects on minors. Nor do the studies show that violent video games pose any sort of unique "harm" to minors not caused by other violent media to which minors are regularly exposed. Indeed, the State's proffered evidence is riddled with caveats, fails to address studies reaching contrary conclusions, and has been unequivocally rejected by other courts that reviewed it. Here, the State has failed to meet its burden of providing "substantial evidence" in support of its asserted interests.

Third, the Act is not narrowly tailored to address the State's asserted interests and the State has not met its burden of showing that the Act is the least speech-restrictive means of addressing those interests. The Act singles out video games for regulation without addressing other forms of media violence that the State itself contends are harmful to minors. Thus, the State has not shown that the Act's speech restriction will in fact materially alleviate the "harm" that the State has identified—exposure of minors to violence in the media. Further, as the district court held below, the State failed to meet its burden of showing that other less-speech-restrictive alternatives would not be sufficient to address the State's concerns by empowering parents to make informed decisions about what media their children watch or play. What the State mischaracterizes as an "effort to assist parents," is in fact outright censorship of protected speech based on the ill-founded assumption that parents are unable to supervise the activities of their own children.

In addition to failing strict scrutiny, contrary to the district court's suggestion otherwise, the Act should be held unconstitutional on the independent ground that the Act's definition of a "violent video game" is unconstitutionally vague and does not come close to providing sufficient notice of lawful conduct. And finally, particularly given the Act's other constitutional infirmities, the Act's labeling requirement is clearly unconstitutional, as the district court correctly held.

If you were sitting on the U.S. Supreme Court as a Justice, how would you rule on the issue?

Review Questions

1. What steps may be taken to reduce exposure to violence for children?
2. Should there be more restrictions on the media?
3. What types of programs should be developed to reduce such exposure?

References

American Psychological Association. (2004). Violence in the media—psychologists help protect children from harmful effects. Retrieved January 21, 2010, from http://www.apa.org/research/action/protect.aspx.

Anderson, C. A., Carnagey, N. L., and Eubanks, J. (2003). Exposure to violent media: The effects of songs with violent lyrics on aggressive thoughts and feelings. *Journal of Personality and Social Psychology*, 84(5), 960–971.

Child Abuse Prevention and Treatment Act (Public Law 93-247, 42 U.S.C. § 5106).

Garbarino, J. (1995). *Raising children in a socially toxic environment.* San Francisco: Jossey-Bass.

Glesmann, C. (2009). *Youth in gangs: Who is at risk?* Oakland, CA: National Council on Crime and Delinquency.

Huesmann, L. R., Moise-Titus, J., Podolski, C. L., and Eron, L. D. (2003). Longitudinal relations between children's exposure to TV violence and their aggressive and violent behavior in young adulthood: 1977–1992. *Developmental Psychology*, 39(2), 201–221.

National Center for the Victims of Crime. (2005). Teen Action Partnership. Retrieved January 21, 2010, from http://www.ncvc.org/tvp/main.aspx?dbID=DB_TeenActionPartnership788.

Video Software Dealers Association v. Schwarzenegger, 556 F.3d 950 (9th Cir. Cal. 2009) Writ of certiorari granted by U.S. Supreme Court (on April 30, 2010), 130 S. Ct. 2398 (U.S. 2010).

Vuong, L., Silva, F., and Marchionna, S. (2009, August). *Children exposed to violence.* Oakland, CA: National Council on Crime and Delinquency.

Wordes, M., and Nuñez, M. (2002). *Our vulnerable teenagers: Their victimization, its consequences, and directions for prevention and intervention.* Oakland, CA: National Council on Crime and Delinquency.

Yale Child Study Center. (2009). Domestic Violence Home Visit Intervention. Retrieved January 21, 2010, from http://childstudycenter.yale.edu/ research/trauma.html.

Study: Violence at home harms children's brains. (2010, April 26). *Yomiuri Shimbun.* Retrieved April 26, 2010, from http://www.yomiuri.co.jp/dy/national/20100426TDY02T02.htm.

Chapter 8

Violent Crimes

Introduction

This chapter introduces the more popular violent crimes against individuals. Any discussion of violent crimes will naturally start with a discussion of the most violent murder. The definitions of what conduct constitutes a specific crime varies with each state, but generally the definitions are similar; in this chapter, the most common ones are used and discussed.

Murder

While the killing of another human being has been recognized for centuries as prohibited conduct, the exact nature of the crime was not clearly defined during early historical times. The English common law established three forms of homicide: justifiable homicide, excusable homicide, and criminal homicide. All three of these homicides involve the killing of another human being. The distinction between them involves the circumstances surrounding the killing.

Justifiable homicide involves killing under circumstances sanctioned by the sovereign. Killing during war or acting as a executor for the state are examples of commission of justifiable homicide. In this form of homicide, the person doing the killing does not harbor any evil intent and acts under "color of law."

Excusable homicide occurs when one kills another by mistake or in self-defense. When one kills another as a result of an unprovoked attack, the

135

law would deem this to be an act of self-defense, and thus the killing is "excused." If a person were driving a car in a neighborhood at 10 miles per hour and struck and killed a child who darted out from behind a bush, the law may hold that the person was not at fault; therefore, the killing was excusable homicide.

Criminal homicide is a killing involving unlawful conduct and evil intent on the part of the killer. Criminal homicide is not sanctioned by the state and is considered one of the most serious types of crimes in our society.

Homicide as a common law crime was created by English judges rather than the English legislature (Wallace and Roberson, 2008). The early common law decisions have in some instances been translated into statutes in many of our states. These statutes have broken down the crime of homicide into graded levels—murder, voluntary and involuntary manslaughter, and negligent manslaughter. The most serious type of homicide is murder. Anyone who has watched a television show believes that he or she understands what is involved in murder. However, the laws surrounding murder can be confusing and complex. A specific set of circumstances is required to establish the elements of murder.

Murder is the most serious of the homicide classifications. According to the Federal Bureau of Investigation (FBI), there is one murder committed in the United States every 26 minutes (Report to the Nation on Crime and Justice, 2006). These murders range from killings stemming from arguments with family or acquaintances to deaths that occur as a result of simply not following the rules of the road when driving a car. Since early times, there has been controversy over the definition, classification, and types of murder. The following discussion of the elements of murder attempts to clarify this controversy.

Murder Defined

Murder is the purposeful, knowing, or reckless unlawful killing of another human being. The crime of murder can be divided into two basic elements:

1. **The defendant must have acted with the necessary specific intent to kill or engage in conduct so outrageous that the specific intent to kill will be inferred.** Courts and scholars have debated over the years on the proper name to use when describing the intent or mens rea necessary for murder (LaFave and Scott, 1986, p. 528–545). The term *malice aforethought* was at one time the favored term when describing the defendant's intent in a murder case. Many states have moved away from using malice aforethought and have substituted other terms to define the necessary specific intent. For example, Pennsylvania uses the terms *poison, lying in wait, willful, deliberate,* or *premeditated* to establish the necessary specific

intent. New York uses terms such as *with the intent to cause the death of another* and *a depraved indifference to human life*, or the person *recklessly engages* in conduct causing a great risk of death (Wallace and Roberson, 2008).

Contrary to popular television shows, murderers seldom announce their state of mind before or during the commission of the crime. Courts are therefore required to review the facts of the case to determine if the defendant exhibited, via his or her actions, the necessary intent for murder. By whatever term or name it is called, the mens rea necessary for murder is a specific intent to kill or conduct so outrageous that the specific intent to kill will be inferred.

2. **The defendant's conduct must have caused the death of another human being.** This element requires a death as a result of the defendant's acts or failure to act. Any behavior by the defendant will suffice. This element also includes the term *another human being*. This term presumes a living person. Similarly, the definition of murder precludes suicide since that is the taking of one's own life.

Many states continue to use the term *malice aforethought* to encompass the terms intentionally, knowingly, or recklessly. When someone kills another in a premeditated or reckless way, the courts and society must examine the killing to determine how serious or heinous the act was. This determination assists in defining the degree of murder.

Degrees of Murder

In early English common law, there were no degrees of murder. However, America developed the "first-degree" and "second-degree" concept of murder in Pennsylvania as early as 1794. This law contained a preamble that explained the rationale behind establishing different degrees of murder. The statute stated: "And whereas the several offenses, which are included under the general denomination of murder, differ so greatly from each other in the degree of their atrociousness, that it is unjust to involve them in the same punishment" [see Pennsylvania Laws of 1794 Chapter 257, Section 1 and 2 (1794)].

The two forms or degrees of murder are based on the seriousness of the type of homicide. First-degree murder is normally classified as a killing that is premeditated. This type of killing occurs when it is determined the defendant had time to reflect on the act and form the intent to kill (*State v. Snowden*, 1957). Examples of premeditated murders include those in which the defendant carries out the killing using explosives, by lying in wait to ambush the victim, using poison to accomplish the homicide, or by torturing the victim.

Most states have simple second-degree murder statutes that hold all other murders are murders of the second degree. The establishment of degrees of murder is an effort on the part of society to divide this type of homicide into two classifications. The classification of murder into degrees assists us in determining the seriousness of this crime.

Voluntary Manslaughter

Voluntary manslaughter is the second most serious form of homicide. While it requires the same type of intent that is necessary for murder, the crime is "downgraded" to voluntary manslaughter if there was a factual pattern that provoked the defendant into killing a person. This provocation does not excuse the defendant's acts; rather, society has made a determination that some facts inflame the passions of a reasonable person to the point that the person will react by killing the instigator. This killing, while intended, is not in the same class as murder and therefore should be treated differently.

Defined

Voluntary manslaughter can be defined as the intentional and unlawful killing of another person in response to adequate provocation. It is composed of three elements:

1. **The defendant must have acted with the same intent required for the crime of murder (express or implied intent to kill).** Voluntary manslaughter is an intentional killing of another. However, a majority of states downgrade this killing from murder to manslaughter based on the fact that the defendant was provoked into killing the victim.

    To reduce murder to voluntary manslaughter, the provocation must be of such a nature as to cause a reasonable person to kill. Yet, reasonable people, no matter what the provocation, do not kill. The law recognizes this fact by holding that one who kills on provocation is guilty of manslaughter, and one who acts in a reasonable manner in killing another, such as in self-defense, is not guilty of any crime.

2. **There must be adequate provocation for the defendant's actions.** For the defendant to claim adequate provocation, two requirements must be satisfied:

    a. The provocation must be adequate.

    b. The killing must be in the heat of passion. The provocation must be so extreme that the defendant acted in a murderous rage. The defendant's passion must be sudden and with no cooling off period.

3. **The defendant's conduct must have caused the death of another human being.** The traditional view requires a causal relationship between the defendant's act and another's death.

The Model Penal Code does away with use of the term *voluntary* or *involuntary* manslaughter. It defines *manslaughter* as

1. § Unlawful killing of another human being that was
2. (a) Committed in a reckless manner, or
   (b) Committed under the influence of extreme mental or emotional disturbance for which there is a reasonable explanation or excuse.

The basis on which this section of the code was founded was that the pattern of statutory treatment of manslaughter by the states was substantially deficient for failing to confront the major policy questions raised by this offense (*People v. Velez*, 1983). New York has accepted the Model Penal Code View in its definition of manslaughter of the first degree [see New York Statutes, Penal Law Section 125.20 subsection 2 and Section 125.25 (a)].

A majority of states as well as the federal government still retain use of the concept of voluntary manslaughter. Voluntary manslaughter is based on the concept that a killing that would ordinarily be classified as murder may be downgraded to voluntary manslaughter if there exists adequate provocation. While the Model Penal Code has eliminated the term *voluntary manslaughter*, a majority of states still retain this classification of homicide, which is based on the concept of provocation. Adequate provocation requires the defendant be provoked, that the provocation be so grievous that the defendant acted in the heat of passion and without the rage cooling off. While voluntary manslaughter requires intentional acts as part of the killing, the next form of homicide only requires an act that results in a death.

Involuntary Manslaughter

Involuntary manslaughter is one of the most confusing forms of homicide in that this crime involves the death of another person under factual situations that do not establish a wicked and depraved mind. Rather, in some cases the death resulted from activity that many persons in society engage in on a daily basis—drinking and driving, speeding in a school zone, cleaning a handgun, or playing with a weapon without checking to ensure that it is unloaded.

Involuntary manslaughter is the unintentional killing of another human being caused during the commission of an unlawful act not amounting to a felony or as the result of criminal negligence. The crime of involuntary manslaughter can be divided into three elements:

1. **The killing of another human being was unintentional.** The defendant need not intend to kill the victim to be found guilty of involuntary manslaughter. The defendant needs only to have the general intent to commit the act or acts that caused the death.

2. **Death occurred as a result of an unlawful act or the defendant's criminal negligence.** If the defendant commits a misdemeanor and death results, he or she may be charged with involuntary manslaughter. This type of unlawful act is sometimes referred to as the "misdemeanor manslaughter doctrine."

The most common form of misdemeanor is a traffic offense; however, other misdemeanors will meet this requirement. For example, a simple battery may suffice. An unintentional killing caused by any criminally negligent act of the defendant is involuntary manslaughter. The courts require more than simple "civil negligence." The criminal negligence standard involves a high and unreasonable risk of death to another.

The handling of firearms calls for a higher degree of care than normal, and criminal negligence will be found in the unintended killing by the defendant when the defendant was handling or using a weapon. The Model Penal Code deals with these situations under negligent manslaughter, which is discussed in the next section.

In addition to the causal link between the defendant's act and the death, some courts require a close connection between the time and place of the act and the death (*People v. Mulcahy*, 1925). Plus, for the defendant's conduct to be unlawful, it is not necessary that the defendant know that some law forbids this conduct (*People v. Nelson*, 1955). There is no requirement that the defendant have any specific intent to violate the law that makes his or her conduct unlawful.

3. **The defendant's unlawful act or negligence caused the death.** The defendant may violate a statute or act in a criminally negligent manner, but unless his or her conduct causes the victim's death, the courts will not hold the defendant criminally liable. For example, a person who is required to have a license to perform services might perform those services, and the victim might die. Unless the failure to obtain a license was the activity that caused the death, the courts will not hold the defendant liable (*People v. Penny*, 1955).

The federal system defines *involuntary manslaughter* as the killing during the commission of an unlawful act not amounting to a felony or killing that results from the commission of a lawful act without due caution. Title 18 U.S.C. 1112 defines *involuntary manslaughter* as

> (a) Manslaughter is the unlawful killing of a human being without malice. It is of two kinds:
>
> ...
>
> Involuntary—In the commission of an unlawful act not amounting to a felony, or in the commission in an unlawful manner, or without due caution and circumspection, of a lawful act which might produce death.

A majority of the states still retain the involuntary manslaughter classification. These states define this crime in much the same terms as the federal government.

Involuntary manslaughter is the unintended killing of another person. The law will hold the defendant accountable in any one of two situations: (1) a death resulted when the defendant was committing an unlawful act, not amounting to a felony, or (2) the defendant acted with criminal negligence that caused the death of another.

Negligent Manslaughter

Negligent manslaughter is a relatively "new" form of homicide. It is based on the Model Penal Code position that voluntary and involuntary manslaughter are difficult concepts to apply in some instances. As a result, the drafters of the Model Penal Code established the concept of the crime of negligent manslaughter.

Negligent manslaughter is the unintentional killing of another human being caused by the negligence of the defendant. The crime of negligent manslaughter is composed of three elements:

1. **The killing of another human being was unintentional.** Similar to involuntary manslaughter, the defendant does not have to intend to kill another person. The death of the person may be unintentional.
2. **The death resulted from a negligent act by the defendant.** The courts usually require "gross negligence." This is a higher standard than mere "civil negligence" but does not reach the level of recklessness necessary for voluntary manslaughter.

   In states, such as California, that have adopted a separate vehicular manslaughter statute, mere negligence may be sufficient to charge a defendant with vehicular manslaughter. Criminal negligence involves the failure of the defendant to perceive the risk in a situation in which the offender has a legal duty of awareness.
3. **The defendant's negligence caused the death.** This is the traditional causation requirement. The negligent act or actions of the defendant must cause the death of the victim.

A majority of the states and the federal government still retain the voluntary/involuntary classification. However, many of these states use criminal negligence as a ground for conviction under their involuntary manslaughter statutes.

Robbery

Robbery is one of the most serious forms of theft-related crimes in America. It is included as one of four major violent crimes grouped together by the FBI for purposes of comparison. Stores, both large and small, have been the target of armed robberies. Daily news reports cover the drama of bank and armored car robberies. It is no wonder that the average citizen is frightened by the prospect of facing a street mugger. Statistics validate this fear. Fifty-five percent of all robberies take place during the evening and early morning hours. Approximately one in every three involves injury to the victim. Seventeen percent occur at or near the victim's home, and 10 percent occur in a parking lot or garage. Less than 1 percent of the victims suffered no monetary loss. Over 28 percent lost less than $50, and at the other extreme, 18 percent were robbed of $500 or more.

Typology of Robbers

There have been numerous studies and reports concerning the crime of robbery. These range from statistical analysis of the crime to attempts to classify robbery by patterns. One classic typology was conducted by McClintock and Gibson (Wallace and Roberson, 2008), who categorized robberies into five distinct areas:

Robbery of persons who control money or goods. This category includes robberies of commercial establishments such as jewelry stores, banks, and offices.

Robbery in an open area. These robberies include street mugging, purse snatches, and other attacks on streets, in parking lots, and in open garages.

Robbery in private residences. These robberies normally occur after the offender has broken into the victim's home.

Robbery by a short-term acquaintance. This classification includes robbery that occurs after a chance encounter. A meeting at a party, a bar, or after a brief sexual encounter can lead to examples of this type of robbery.

Robbery by a long-term acquaintance. This type of robbery is relatively rare but does occur on a regular basis. This robbery may include the robbery from persons who have been romantically involved with the offender for a short period of time.

Another well-known typology was conducted by Conklin (1972). He classified robberies by identifying the type of offender rather than the location of the robbery. Conklin classified robberies into four major categories:

Professional robber. The professional robber is a career criminal. This is a way of life with these offenders. They plan and execute these robberies carefully. They operate in groups with specific tasks assigned to each member. They may plan and carry out three to four major robberies in any given year.

Opportunist robber. This is the most common type of robber. They do not specialize in robbery. These offenders will commit all types of larceny offenses, with robbery just one of the many crimes they commit. They normally do not plan out their crime but act when the opportunity presents itself.

Addict robber. These offenders are addicted to a controlled substance and rob to support their habit. However, most drug abusers are interested in quick and safe crimes and will commit burglary or other theft-related crimes before turning to robbery. The addict robber does not plan the robbery in the same detail as the professional robber but is more cautious than the opportunist robber.

Alcoholic robber. These offenders have little interest in planning their offenses. They engage in robberies to support their addiction. Many of them commit the crime while intoxicated, and as a result they are caught more often than the other classes.

These and other scholars have attempted to classify various aspects of the crime of the robbery in an effort to explain why or how it occurs. This information assists society in understanding this dangerous and personal crime. Robbery is a personal crime in that the victim comes into contact with the offender for a period of time necessary to cause fear or fright. How long a period of contact and the level of fear necessary to constitute robbery is explained under the discussion of the elements of robbery.

Robbery Defined

Robbery is the theft of property from the person or immediate presence of another by use of force or fear. The crime of robbery has four distinct elements:

1. **Theft of Property.** This element of robbery is similar to larceny. One of the distinctions between larceny and robbery is that many larceny statutes establish a value that determines whether the theft will be treated as a misdemeanor or felony. This is not the case when dealing with robbery. The amount of the item taken is immaterial to establishing the seriousness of the crime. It will be considered robbery if the mugger on the street demands and receives $1 or $5,000.

    The offender must intend to keep the property. Thus, robbery is a specific intent crime. Similar to larceny, there must be specific intent to deprive the owner of the property. In robbery, this is fairly easy to prove by looking at the defendant's words, actions, or both. The defendant does not have to retain the property for any length of time to establish this intent. For example, if an offender pulls a gun on a citizen, demands the money, and then flees the scene with the money, the fact that a police officer arrests the offender one block from the scene does not allow the defendant to claim that he did not intend to keep the money. The courts will infer the specific intent to keep the property.

The property may be anything or of any value. An empty wallet is property for purposes of robbery. If a victim were required to part with the wallet, this element is complete. It does not matter that the fair market value of the wallet may be $2. The reason the legislatures and courts have taken this position is based on a combination of the second and third element of the crime: Robbery is a personal crime involving danger to the victim.

2. **Taking.** The taking of the property must be from the "person or immediate presence" of another. The term *immediate presence* is broadly interpreted to include any place within sight or hearing or even smell. In one famous case, a cow was stolen from a large herd of cattle that was scattered for a mile or more on a plain. The herd was being watched by a cowboy. The court held that the taking of the cow was from the immediate presence of the cowboy.

3. **From the person or presence of another.** Someone may commit a burglary, and the victim will not find out until he or she discovers the property is missing from his or her home or business. Robbery requires the property to be taken from the person or from that person's immediate presence. The term *presence of another* means simply that the offender must take property that he or she does not own.

   This element of robbery does not require that the victim physically have possession of the item that is taken. The property does not have to be attached to the victim by a string, belt, or other item. It is sufficient if the victim has control over the item. For example, if the victim were sitting on a park bench with a package next to him or her and the offender approached the victim, pulled a gun, and stated, "I'm taking your package, don't try to stop me," a robbery has been committed even though the victim was not holding on to the package at the time the offense occurred. If a person has physical control over property and is prevented from stopping the crime because of force or fear exerted by the actions of the offender, this element has been satisfied. A different problem arises if the victim has control over the property but is unaware that the offender has taken it. This issue is addressed in the final element of the crime.

4. **By use of force or fear.** The traditional robbery occurs when the offender confronts the victim, brandishes a weapon of some sort, and demands money. This is clearly an act of placing the victim in fear of his or her safety. The second situation arises when the robber physically assaults the victim; the victim surrenders his or her property or is prevented from resisting as a result of the assault.

There are other situations that are not so clear as related to this element of the crime. Is a pickpocket guilty of robbery? The offender has removed property from the person of another. However, the victim is unaware of the act; therefore, the final element of robbery—force or fear—is missing. Accordingly, a pickpocket is guilty of larceny, not robbery. What if force is added to the situation?

Is the mugger who approaches from behind and snatches an old lady's purse from her hand quickly without giving her a chance to resist guilty of robbery? There is the removal of property from the presence of another and force is used to accomplish the crime. The courts are divided on this issue, with some holding that since the victim was unaware of the act until after it was completed, the final element of robbery is missing, and the crime is larceny. The rationale for this position is that the victim was not touched or placed in fear of bodily harm. Other states specifically include this type of act as robbery. The better position is that since the victim may be harmed as the purse is jerked from her possession, the rationale for robbery—that of specific harm to the victim during a taking of property—has been satisfied, and this type of act should fall under the definition of robbery.

The force or fear necessary for the commission of robbery is a complex factual determination. Questions such as where the property is located, when the victim became aware of the crime, and whether there was physical force or intimidation used must be answered when addressing this element. Robbery is both a dangerous and a personal crime. It is a combination of larceny and assault that is considered to be of such a distinctive nature that the drafters of the Model Penal Code set it apart from other theft crimes by including the offense as a separate article in the code.

The drafters of the Model Penal Code examined the history of the crime of robbery and pointed out that the average citizen is especially frightened of the violent petty thief who operates in the streets and alleys of almost every city. The ordinary citizen may become angry at surreptitious larceny, embezzlement, or fraud, but the specter of a street mugger committing a robbery late at night on a deserted street raises terror in the minds of almost everyone.

The Model Penal Code modernizes the common law rules regarding robbery by punishing the act as a crime even if the robber does not obtain anything of value. In addition, the code makes it a crime to lawfully obtain property, then use force or fear to prevent the owner from reclaiming it. At the same time, the code retains the essence of the common law crime—that of a theft committed by force or fear.

Sex Offenses

The discussion of sex offenses is a necessity in any examination of crimes against persons. This section is not intended to cause anyone displeasure or discomfort. For some students, this will be their first exposure to physical acts that are not considered normal or even talked about in polite company. Some of the acts discussed in this section will show a twisted and sick mind. Sex crimes or offenses are repulsive to modern society, and they range from violent and gross to simply a seamy side of modern-day life.

Many of these crimes, while they involve acts that could be classified as having sexual connotations, are from many experts' points of view nothing more than violent acts of aggression against women.

Rape

Rape is one of the most feared, misunderstood, and repulsive crimes in the United States. Many Americans have unrealistic images of rapists. They believe a rapist is some sort of low-life animal who prowls the night and looks like a Neanderthal with a sloping brow and beady eyes. A rapist looks just like the neighborhood boy or man who delivers the morning paper. He can be anywhere and strike at anytime. While many scholars have researched the issue, no one has yet come forward with a single acceptable reason why men engage in the crime of rape.

There is no known cause or genetic factor that predisposes some men to engage in this type of assaultive sexual behavior. However, there have been several theories that have been advanced in an attempt to explain the reasons why certain persons carry out these acts against women.

Donald Symons (1979) suggested that man's biological sex drive is behind his aggressive assault. Rape is viewed as an instinctive drive associated with the need of perpetuating the species. Symons' theory holds that men still have this primitive sex drive that mandates they have sex with as many women as possible. His position holds that rape is intertwined with sexuality as well as violence.

Gebhard (1965) set forth the position that rapists are suffering from psychotic tendencies or have sadistic feelings toward women. In addition, Groth suggested that every rapist exhibits anger, power, and sadism. These two scholars accepted the psychological explanation for the cause of rape.

Russell (1975), in her book *The Politics of Rape*, set forth the theory that rape is part of the masculine qualities accepted in U.S. society. Russell's position was that, in our society, young boys are taught to be aggressive and dominant. Men learn to separate their sexual desire from other intimate feelings, such as love and respect. Rape is viewed as a form of domination over women.

There are numerous other theories of why men engage is this assaultive behavior toward women. At present, there does not appear to be one generally accepted cause for this crime. Most authorities agree that rape is a violent crime, it is a crime involving the sexual organs of both the offender and the victim, and it is a crime that subjects the women to psychological duress and pain. The crime of rape may appear at first glance to be a relatively simple crime with two basic elements; however, these elements contain numerous complex issues that raise both legal and emotional questions.

Rape is the unlawful act of sexual intercourse with another person against that person's will by force, fear, or trick. The crime of rape has two elements: unlawful sexual intercourse and commission by use of force, fear, or trick.

Regarding unlawful sexual intercourse, this element is specifically gender neutral in its approach. Traditional common law and early statutes authorized prosecution of rape against a man. Early courts and legislators took the position that a man cannot be raped either by another man or by a female. In fact, many of the existing statutes hold to this position. Michigan is an example of a state with a more progressive statute that defines rape in gender-neutral language. To assume that men can rape women and not to accept the possibility that a woman can rape a man is to perpetrate a position that women are the weaker sex and naturally submissive to the demands of men.

For purposes of rape, sexual intercourse requires penetration of the penis into the vagina. Penetration does not have to result in a completed act of sexual intercourse. There is no requirement for ejaculation or emission by the male for the crime to have been complete.

In early court cases, the prior sexual history of the victim was admitted. There was a variety of theories on which the victim could be cross-examined regarding her previous sexual activity: To show that since she had intercourse with another person, she was more likely to have consented to intercourse with the defendant, to illustrate that she was a person of loose morals and therefore would have intercourse with anyone including the defendant. Modern-day statutes prevent introduction of this kind of evidence. These statues are normally called rape shield laws and prohibit the defendant or his attorney from questioning the victim regarding her previous sexual activity or introducing other evidence surrounding her past sexual practices.

Closely related to the victim's past sexual history, but separate from it, is the issue of consent. This is one of the most complex and emotional issues in the crime of rape. The classic defense in most rape cases is that the victim consented to sexual intercourse. Of course, defendants do not raise this issue if there has been physical force involved or the victim was underage and therefore incapable of granting consent. However, many rapes involve the use of threats or slight force, which results in overcoming the victim's initial resistance. In these cases, the defendant will argue that the victim consented; therefore, it was not rape but consensual sexual activity between adults. Tied to the issue of consent is the position of society that minors cannot knowingly give consent to certain acts. One of these acts is sexual intercourse. Issues regarding intercourse with minors, unconscious persons, and incompetents are discussed in more detail in the following section.

Committed by use of force, fear, or trick. There are three distinct situations that are covered by this element of the crime of rape. It may occur as the result of force that overcomes the victim's resistance; the victim may be placed in a situation in which she fears for her safety and therefore submits to the act; or the victim may be tricked and become incapable of giving consent.

In the first situation, the defendant utilizes brute force to require the victim to submit to the sexual acts. This force may take the form of a physical beating with fists, clubs, or other objects. The victim is left battered as a result of the defendant's acts. There are physical marks on her body as a result of the violent assault by the perpetrator. She may receive bruises, her clothing may be ripped from her body, and she may be in a state of physical and emotional shock as a result of her encounter.

The second situation is similar to the first but occurs when the victim no longer resists the attacker's advances as a result of fear for her safety. This fear may be caused by the defendant's brandishing of a weapon, whether it be a knife, gun, or club. In these situations, the victim may comply with the attacker's demands and not have any marks on her as a result of the incident.

Authorities in the field are split regarding the actual percentage of rapes involving nonstrangers. Some believe the actual number of "acquaintance rapes" is low in comparison to violent rapes by strangers. Others accept the Department of Justice statistics regarding the percentage of rapes by nonstrangers and attribute the low numbers to a reluctance on the part of the victim to report these types of sexual advances.

The third situation involves the defendant "tricking" the victim. This is a broad category that includes sex with minors and incompetents as well as use of alcohol or drugs to render the victim incapable of giving informed consent. As briefly discussed, our society has determined that persons under a certain age cannot legally give consent for purposes of engaging in sexual intercourse. The common law held consensual intercourse with a minor under the age of 10 was rape. In modern society, the general rule is that when a female reaches the age of 18, she is considered an adult and capable of entering into binding contracts and giving consent for purposes of engaging in lawful sexual intercourse. This issue does not normally arise, however, at this age. Consent becomes important when the defendant engages in sexual intercourse with a minor between the ages of 3 and 16. There are numerous incidents of child sexual abuse in which the defendant has engaged in a course of sexual intercourse with a minor over a period of years. Since the victim cannot legally agree to intercourse, the defendant may be charged with rape. There are wide variations among the states regarding the age at which a minor can give consent. Many jurisdictions have special statutes that prohibit sexual relations with young children. Some of these statutes call this type of sexual intercourse *statutory rape*, and some impose penalties as severe as those for forcible rape for this type of conduct.

A person who is classified as mentally incompetent cannot legally give consent to sexual relations. When a person takes advantage of these types of victims and has intercourse, the law allows him to be charged with rape. The issue with this type of situation is defining what constitutes mental incompetence. States have approached this issue in a variety of ways: Some states hold a person to be incompetent if she is incapable of expressing any judgment on the matter. Other states impose a requirement that the woman did not have the ability to comprehend the moral nature of the act. A third group of states addressed the issue of incompetence by asking if the women had the capacity to understand the character and probable consequences of sexual intercourse. The first approach is too restrictive and would only protect those women suffering from an extreme form of mental retardation. The second alternative is vague in that the courts would have to examine the victim's moral values. The last approach seems to allow the most latitude and protect both the defendant and victim. The drafters of the Model Penal Code have adopted this approach with a slight variation that requires the defendant to know that the victim is suffering from a mental condition that renders her incapable of appraising the nature of her conduct.

The third category involves tricking the victim by causing her to use alcohol or drugs to the point that she cannot legally consent to the act or she is rendered unconscious as a result of her ingestion of liquor or drugs. In these cases, the victim may be unconscious or so impaired that she cannot consent to the act of sexual intercourse. The test in this area is similar to the approach used when dealing with incompetent victims.

The states and courts have adopted various laws regarding the crime of rape. At present, there is no single definition that is accepted by all the jurisdictions.

Rape is more than a simple violent assault that ends when the perpetrator finishes his or her physical act. It can have long-term psychological effects on its victims. These consequences include rape trauma syndrome, acute stress disorder (ASD), and post-traumatic stress disorder (PTSD).

Rape trauma syndrome is a type of PTSD. The essential feature of this disorder is the development of characteristic symptoms after the sexual assault that are usually beyond the range of ordinary human experience. Often, the victim will have recurrent painful memories of the incident or recurring dreams or nightmares in which the incident is reexperienced. Diminished responsiveness to the external world, called *psychic numbing,* usually starts after the rape. A victim may feel detached from others and complain that she has lost the ability to become interested in activities that were previously meaningful to her—particularly those associated with intimacy, tenderness, and sexuality.

ASD is acute stress that is experienced in the immediate aftermath of a traumatic event. The characteristic feature of ASD is the development of anxiety, dissociative symptoms, and other manifestations that occur within *one month* after exposure to the traumatic event. To receive a diagnosis of ASD, the victim must have experienced, witnessed, or be confronted with an event that involved actual or threatened death, serious injury, or a threat to the physical safety of the victim or others. In addition, the victim's response to such a condition must involve intense fear, helplessness, or horror. This diagnosis requires that the victim experience several of the symptoms of PTSD, and that he or she must experience three of five PTSD dissociative symptoms during or immediately after the traumatic incident.

The dissociative symptoms are derealization, depersonalization, dissociative amnesia, subjective sense of numbing, and reduction in awareness of surrounding. In the event these symptoms last longer than 30 days, the victim may be suffering from PTSD.

PTSD was first identified when some Vietnam veterans began experiencing flashbacks of events that occurred during combat. PTSD is defined as the development of characteristic symptoms following a psychologically distressing event that is outside the range of usual human experience. Traumatic events include, but are not limited to, military combat, violent personal assault, kidnapping, being taken hostage, terrorist attack, torture, incarceration as a prisoner of war, natural or man-made disasters, severe automobile accidents, or diagnosis with a life-threatening illness. The characteristic symptoms involved require that the person experience, witness, or be confronted with an event or events that involved actual or threatened death or serious injury or a threat to the physical integrity of self or others, and the person's response involved intense fear, helplessness, or horror.

The symptoms the victim may experience include reexperiencing the traumatic event, avoidance of stimuli associated with the event, numbing of general responsiveness, and increased agitation.

Sodomy

The ancient city of Sodom was allegedly destroyed by God because of its residents' unspeakable sexual acts. The term *sodomy* was derived from this biblical description of a city and its citizens who engaged in certain erotic sexual acts. In early England, this act was considered so vile that the famous legal commentator Blackstone refused to name it. He referred to the act as "the infamous crime against nature." This early revulsion continued in America, and some statutes still refer to the crime by the term coined by Blackstone. One state charges sodomy as "the abominable and detestable crime against nature."

Similar to rape, the definition and elements of sodomy include the requirement that force or fear be used to overcome resistance. While numerous states have modified their earlier position regarding acts between consenting adults, some states still punish the act whether it is homosexual or heterosexual in nature. These states do not require any physical coercion be used by the perpetrator for the statute to apply. In other words, some states punish sodomy even if it is a consensual act among consenting adults in the privacy of their own bedroom.

Sodomy is the unlawful sexual penetration of the anus of one person by the penis of another committed by use of force or fear. The crime of sodomy can be divided into three basic elements:

1. **Unlawful sexual penetration by the penis of one person.** At one time in England, it was required that there not only be penetration but also an emission or ejaculation for the crime to be complete. However, the modern view is that any penetration by the penis of a person is sufficient to establish this element of the crime. The crime is complete on any penetration.
2. **With the anus of another.** Early English law punished the crime if the act was with an animal or another human. However, American statutes have divided these acts into two separate crimes, and to be convicted of the crime of sodomy, the offender must penetrate another human's anal cavity. The crime as written applies to both female and male partners.

3. **By use of force or fear.** Similar to the crime of rape, knowing voluntary consent is a defense to the crime of sodomy. Thus, sodomy between consenting adults would not be a crime. This is the case whether the act is homosexual or heterosexual in nature. The same type or amount of force or imposition of fear that is required in rape is necessary in sodomy.

Assaultive Crimes

Assault and battery are frequently considered as the same offense, although they are separate and distinct offenses. A battery consists of the unjustified offensive touching of another. Assault is either an attempted or threatened battery. The critical difference between assault and battery is that battery requires an actual or constructive touching of the person. In some aggravated assault crimes, the "assaults" actually refer to batteries. For example, the crime of assault causing serious bodily injury is actually a battery rather than an assault.

Battery

Battery is the unlawful, willful, and offensive touching of the person of another. Battery has three distinct elements:

1. The willful and unlawful
2. Use of force or violence, and
3. Against the person of another.

The unjustified offensive touching is the *actus reus* of the crime of battery. In most states, no actual bodily injury is necessary to constitute battery. The Model Penal Code, however, requires at least a slight bodily injury to constitute the crime of battery. It is not necessary that the victim actually fear physical harm as the result of the touching. For example, the offensive touching of the breasts or kissing of a woman may be a battery.

In many cases, it is unclear regarding whether the touching should be considered as offensive. For example, a hug or kiss from an elderly aunt may be offensive to the young child but certainly not be of the criminal type. The test generally used is whether a reasonable person would consider the touching offensive.

It is immaterial how the offender caused the offensive touching. For example, it can be the firing of a weapon or hitting with the fist. There is no requirement that the touching actually touch the person; a constructive touching is sufficient. In one famous case, the accused was convicted of battery when he hit the horse that the victim was riding. In another case, a defendant was convicted of battery when he convinced a six-year-old girl to touch his sexual organs.

Consent may be a defense to battery as long as the contact is not "unlawful." For example, a person may consent to being kissed and fondled, and the consent would be a defense to a battery charge. Participation in sporting events is a common example of consent to battery; that is, the quarterback of a football team cannot claim he was unlawfully struck by the charging linebacker. If, however, the contact is unlawful, consent is no defense (e.g., a person cannot legally consent to being shot with a pistol, and a minor cannot legally consent to sexual contact).

Assault

An assault is an attempt to injure the person of another or an intent to frighten without actual injury. Assault, "attempted" battery type, has three distinct elements:

1. An unlawful attempt
2. With apparent present ability
3. To commit an injury to the person of another.

Assault, "threatened" battery type, has three distinct elements:

1. A threat
2. With apparent present ability
3. To commit an injury to the person of another.

There are two standard types of assault: (1) the attempted battery and (2) placing a person in fear of a battery by menacing behavior. In several states, like California, the second type of behavior is not an assault. In those states, assault is only an attempted battery. Since an assault is in many cases an attempted battery, a defendant may be convicted of an assault even though a battery was actually committed.

In most states, the courts have extended battery liability not only for intentional conduct but also for those situations in which the defendant acted in a criminally negligent fashion. Normally, criminal negligence is conduct that the accused knew or should have known would result in harm to others. Several states have limited battery liability to situations in which the accused acted in a willful, wanton, or reckless manner.

The doctrine of transferred intent is applied to those cases when the offender intended to injure one person and by mistake or accident injures another. Thus, if one intends to strike another but instead accidentally harms a different person, the intent to injure is transferred to the actual victim. The intent may still be used to justify an assault on the intended victim. For example, D shoots at X intending to kill her. He misses and hits V. D is guilty of assault on X and battery on V. The battery of V is based on the doctrine of transferred attempt.

Summary

Definitions of Typical Violence Offenses

Murder and nonnegligent manslaughter: The willful (nonnegligent) killing of one human being by another.

Negligent manslaughter: The killing of another person through negligence.

Forcible rape: The carnal knowledge of a person, forcibly or against that person's will or not forcibly or against the person's will if the victim is incapable of giving consent because of his or her temporary or permanent mental or physical incapacity.

Forcible sodomy: Oral or anal sexual intercourse with another person, forcibly or against that person's will or not forcible or against the person's will if the victim is incapable of giving consent because of his or her youth or because of his or her temporary or permanent mental or physical incapacity.

Sexual assault with an object: To use an object or instrument to unlawfully penetrate, however slightly, the genital or anal opening of the body of another person forcibly or against that person's will or not forcibly or against the person's will if the victim is incapable of giving consent because of his or her youth or because of his or her temporary or permanent mental or physical incapacity.

Forcible fondling: The touching of the private body parts of another person for the purpose of sexual gratification forcibly or against that person's will or not forcibly or against the person's will if the victim is incapable of giving consent because of his or her youth or because of his or her temporary or permanent mental or physical incapacity.

Aggravated assault: An unlawful attack by one person on another in which the offender uses a weapon or displays it in a threatening manner or the victim suffers obvious severe or aggravated bodily injury involving apparent broken bones, loss of teeth, possible internal injury, severe laceration, or loss of consciousness. This also includes assault with disease (as in cases when the offender is aware that he or she is infected with a deadly disease and deliberately attempts to inflict the disease by biting, spitting, etc.).

Simple assault: An unlawful physical attack by one person on another if neither the offender displays a weapon nor the victim suffers obvious severe or aggravated bodily injury involving apparent broken bones, loss of teeth, possible internal injury, severe laceration, or loss of consciousness.

Intimidation: To unlawfully place another person in reasonable fear of bodily harm through the use of threatening words or other conduct but without displaying a weapon or subjecting the victim to actual physical attack.

Kidnapping: The unlawful seizure, transportation, or detention of a person against his or her will or of a minor without the consent of his or her custodial parent(s) or legal guardian.

Review Questions

1. How does a prosecutor prove intent in murder cases? Can the prosecutor rely simply on statements made by the perpetrator?
2. Why should heat of passion be accepted as a mitigating circumstance in voluntary manslaughter cases?
3. Why is rape considered by many as a crime of power rather than a sexual offense?

References

American Law Institute. (2002). Model Penal Code. Chicago: American Law Institute.

Conklin, J. (1972). *Robbery and the criminal justice system.* New York: Lippincott.

Gebhard, P. (1965). *Sex offenders: An analysis of types.* New York: Harper and Row.

Groth, N. (1979). *Why men rape?* New York: Plenum Press.

LaFave, W., and Scott, A. (1986). *Criminal law.* St. Paul, MO: West.

New York Statutes. (2004). Penal Law Sections 125.20 and 125.25.

Pennsylvania Laws of 1794. (1794). Chapter 257, Sections 1 and 2.

People v. Mulcahy. (1925) 318 Ill. 332 (Ill. 1925).

People v. Nelson. (1955). 131 Cal.App.2d 571.

People v. Penny, 44 Cal. 2d 861, 285 P.2d 926, 929 (Cal. 1955).

Russell, D. (1975). *The politics of rape.* New York: Stein and Day.

State v. Snowden, 313 P 2d 706 (Idaho 1957).

Symons, D. (1979). *The evolution of human sexuality.* London: Oxford University Press.

U.S. Code Title 18 Section 1112 (2009).

U.S. Department of Justice, BJS. (2006). *Report to the nation on crime.* Washington, DC: Government Printing Office.

Wallace, H., and Roberson, C. (2008). *Principles of criminal law* (4th ed.). Boston: Pearson.

Chapter 9

Gangs and Violence

Introduction

> Once found principally in large cities, violent street gangs now affect public safety, community image, and quality of life in communities of all sizes in urban, suburban, and rural areas. No region of the United States is untouched by gangs. Gangs affect society at all levels, causing heightened fears for safety, violence, and economic costs.

> **U.S. Bureau of Justice Assistance, 2005, p. 2**

Gangs are becoming more widespread, and gang-related violence is increasing. Federal, state, and local criminal justice professionals face a number of distinct challenges when dealing with gangs. One of the first challenges is to agree on what constitutes a gang. There is continuing controversy regarding the definition of the term gang. One authority defines gang as any group of people who band together for criminal activity or who commit crime as a group. Various local or municipal jurisdictions have developed their own definition of what constitutes a gang. Many states have statutory definitions of gangs, and these vary from state to state.

One scholar has suggested that we identify gangs based on certain common traits. These features include (1) formal organizational structure, (2) identifiable leadership, (3) a territory, (4) recurrent interaction, and (5) engaging in serious or violent behavior (Missouri's Task Force on Gangs and Youth Violence, 2010)

BOX 9.1   GANGS IN LOS ANGELES

In Los Angeles County, law enforcement officials are aware of more than 1,300 street gangs with over 150,000 members. In the city of Los Angeles alone, there are over 400 separate gangs and an estimated 39,000 gang members ("City of Los Angeles, "Gang Reduction Strategy"; U.S. Bureau of Justice Assistance, 2007).

Gangs account for approximately 43 percent of all homicides in Los Angeles County. In 2004, of the 1,038 homicides, 454 were gang related (City of Los Angeles Criminal Justice Center, 2005).

Los Angeles has long been recognized as the epicenter of gang activity nationwide. Other recent estimates indicated approximately 1,350 street gangs, with as many as 175,000 members in the seven-county area of responsibility (San Luis Obispo, Santa Barbara, Ventura, Los Angeles, Riverside, San Bernardino, and Orange) of the Federal Bureau of Investigation (FBI) in Los Angeles. Many gangs have a nationwide presence, such as the Bloods, the Crips, Mara Salvatrucha (MS-13), and 18th.

A second controversy concerns the number of gangs and the number of serious crimes committed by them. At present, there is no national reporting system regarding the number of gangs. Since there is no reliable reporting system regarding gangs, it is hard to estimate the number of serious crimes committed by members. However, most law enforcement agencies agree that gang violence continues to grow.

Some gangs form along ethnic or racial lines. Many gangs identify themselves by a name derived from a street or neighborhood where they live, a rock band they like, or a cult they follow. Examples of gangs formed along ethnic lines include the following:

■ Asian (Vietnamese, Hmong, Thai, Japanese, or Chinese): Cheap Boys, Natoma Boys, Wah Ching, Lady Rascals (female), and Southside Scissors (female)
■ African American: Crips, Bloods
■ Hispanic: White Fence, Los Vatos Locos, Midnight Pearls (female)
■ White (white supremacists, satanic, punk): Skinheads, Stoners

Another type of gang is known as a tagging crew. Tagging crews are individuals known as "taggers" who join together for the sole purpose of placing their names or slogans in visible places. While taggers can be individuals with no gang affiliation, recent trends in Southern California indicate that more and more taggers belong to street gangs.

Gangs use graffiti (i.e., drawings or writings scratched on a wall or other surface) to identify themselves and their territory and, in some instances, to communicate messages. The graffiti may include a gang member's name, the member's nickname, a declaration of loyalty, a memorial to a slain gang member, threats, challenges, and warnings to rival gang members. Gang graffiti is most commonly found on neighborhood walls, fences, and mailboxes. Some gangs purposefully destroy property to leave their trademark graffiti behind. Abandoned houses are also a favored target for graffiti; however, any building can be a target.

The graffiti of various gangs can be generally identified by their "signatures." Hispanic gang graffiti is often written in blocked letters and is very stylized. Some Asian gangs are now mimicking the blocked Hispanic style of graffiti. African American and white gang graffiti tends to be similar to each other and to use a simple crude style. However, the white gang graffiti may include Nazi symbols and other graphically violent drawings.

Acts of Violence by Gangs

Gangs remain the primary distributors of drugs throughout the United States (National Gang Threat Assessment, U.S. Bureau of Justice Assistance, 2005.) Gangs are employing an increased level of sophistication in the planning and execution of criminal acts, especially against law enforcement officers (U.S. Bureau of Justice Assistance, 2005).

Victims of Gang Violence

Gang members were more likely to victimize younger persons than older persons. Younger victims of violence were more likely than older victims to believe the perpetrator was a gang member. Urban victims were more likely than suburban or rural victims to identify offenders as gang members. Hispanics were more likely than non-Hispanics to be victims of violent crimes committed by gang members. Hispanic victims of violence identified the offenders as gang members at a higher rate than non-Hispanic victims and blacks at a higher rate than whites (Harrell, 2005). According to the *Supplementary Homicide Reports* of the FBI, each year between 1993 and 2003 from 5 percent to 7 percent of all homicides and from 8 percent to 10 percent of homicides committed with a firearm were gang related (Harrell, 2005).

Regional Trends in Gangs

As noted in the *National Gang Threat Assessment* (U.S. Bureau of Justice Assistance, 2005), while general trends were apparent across the nation, each region also noted specific trends affecting their communities.

Northeast

- Neighborhood or homegrown gangs and hybrid gangs are being seen with increasing frequency.
- A growth of gangs within Hispanic immigrant communities has occurred, bringing increased violence and crime to many communities.
- The frequency of incidents of gang-related violence and drug trafficking on Indian reservations has increased.
- Gang members display a lack of respect for their community and for law enforcement.
- This region is particularly vulnerable to drug distribution by gangs because of the compact nature of the region and the well-developed transportation infrastructure.
- Gangs are reported to be most frequently involved in crimes relating to vandalism and graffiti, firearm possession, assault, and homicide.

South

- Mara Salvatrucha (MS-13) is one of the newest threats to the region, especially in Washington, D.C., Virginia, and the surrounding areas.
- The growth of gangs within the Hispanic community has brought increased levels of violence and crime to the region.
- Communities are noting increases in graffiti and tagging.
- Neighborhood or homegrown gangs are reported throughout the region.
- Gangs in this region are most likely to be involved in the distribution and sale of marijuana and cocaine.

Midwest

- Gang activity around schools and college campuses has increased.
- Gangs are concealing their affiliations and colors to hide from law enforcement.
- Gangs are substantially involved in both the wholesale and street-level distribution of drugs in this region.
- Gangs are increasingly cooperating with each other to facilitate crime and drug trafficking.
- Gang and drug activity in Indian country has increased.
- Indian country is being affected by the high level of drug trafficking. Hispanic street gangs are reportedly using Native Americans to transport narcotics onto reservations.

West

- Gangs are employing an increased level of sophistication in the planning and execution of criminal acts, especially against law enforcement officers.

- Street gangs are frequently involved in the distribution of both marijuana and methamphetamine.
- The number of cases of identity and credit card theft perpetrated by gang members has increased.
- Reports indicated an increased use of firearms by gang members.
- Approximately three-quarters of respondents to this survey reported moderate-to-high involvement of gangs in the street-level distribution of drugs.

More than 90 percent of respondents in this region reported some level of gang involvement in vandalism and graffiti.

Characteristics of Gangs

Gangs, drugs, and violence are continuing problems in our society. However, not all gangs engage in drug dealing, and all gangs do not consist of juveniles or former prison inmates. Gangs are as varied as any other facet of our modern society. Although gangs appear to be more highly structured than other delinquent groups, they vary from region to region. It is impossible to examine all the various gangs that exist today; however, we can list some of the more common characteristics of most gangs: diversity, change, concentration, gang structure, social contexts, family, schools, organized crime, and prisons.

- Diversity. There is a great deal of variability in gangs, gang activity, and gang problems. Gangs vary by ethnic makeup, involvement in violent crimes, drug-related activities, age of members, and organizational stability.
- Change. Gangs evolve due to a number of factors, including demographic shifts, economic conditions, and other influences.
- Gang problems are concentrated. A small percentage of gang members accounts for most of the harm done by their gangs. More than 60 percent of crimes are committed at a few particularly dangerous locations, with crime rates much higher in neighborhoods in which most potential offenders live or visit.

Gang structure. Although gangs appear to be more highly organized than simple delinquent groups, there are wide differences between different gangs. Some gangs base their membership on geographic areas such as neighborhoods, while others only admit members of a certain age span. Some gangs are part of a larger alliance known as nations. Estimates of gang size range from four members to thousands in a gang or a nation.

Gangs have different types of members. There are as many different types of memberships as there are gangs; however, two classes appear to be common to most gangs: core members, including gang leaders and regular members, and wannabees, who are those that desire to join the gang or who are new members in the gang.

Most authorities agree that male gang members are almost exclusively responsible for gang-related crime, including violent offenses. About 5 percent of gang crimes appear to be committed by females. Male gang members outnumber female members by 20 to 1; however, many gangs have female auxiliaries or affiliates.

Gang socialization differs by age, context, and situation. Reasons for joining gangs include a need for recognition, status, safety, power, excitement, and new experiences. Youth raised under extreme social deprivation are drawn to gangs. Gang affiliation may be viewed as an expected socialization process in certain communities in which they are viewed as embodying such values as honor, loyalty, and fellowship. The gang may be seen as part of the family and contributing to the development of the clan.

- Social contexts. Rapid urban development, lack of community identity, increasing poverty, and social isolation contribute to institutional failures and the development of gangs. The interplay of social disorganization and the lack of access to legitimate resources contribute to deviant behavior. Families, schools, politics, organized crime, and prisons have an impact on gang development.
- Family. Family disorganization, such as single-parent families, does not by itself lead children into gangs. A variety of other factors must accompany a weak or disorganized family structure to produce a youth who becomes involved in gangs. These factors include the availability of a peer group that does not support the family and school.
- Schools. A gang member is likely to be a youth who has done poorly in school and has little identification with school staff. The member does not like school and uses it for gang-related activities instead of academic-related learning. Few schools directly address gang-related problems. Gang-related violence usually does not erupt in schools, although gang recruiting may occur on the school grounds. Schools that have strong leadership and more concerned learning environments usually have lower rates of gang problems.
- Organized crime. Greater competition among various criminal organizations, the relative increase in older youth and adults in gangs, and the expanded street-level drug market have contributed to the integration of violence and organized gang activity. Many youth gangs have become subunits of organized crime for purposes of drug distribution, car theft, extortion, and burglary.

Prisons. Prison gangs and street gangs are interdependent. The prison or training school may be regarded as facilitating and responding to gang problems. In most states, prison gangs are outgrowths of street gangs, but there is some evidence that prison gangs may emigrate to the streets. Prison incarceration has led to increased gang cohesion and membership recruitment in many institutions.

Several factors seem to motivate youth to leave gangs: (1) growing up and getting smarter, (2) fear of injury, (3) serving time in prison, (4) a girlfriend or marriage, (5) a job, (6) drug dealing, (7) concern for youth, (8) interest in politics, (9) religion, and (10) the assistance of an adult (U.S. Bureau of Justice, 2005). In some cases, the departure from a gang was accompanied by a complete break with gang peers and departure from the neighborhood. In most cases, it simply involved a lack of involvement in criminal activity.

Communities are responding to gang problems by mobilizing neighborhoods; increasing social interaction, especially with youth; increasing economic opportunities, such as special schools and job programs; and more active law enforcement responses, including gang suppression units. Gang violence is a serious problem that will not simply disappear as the gang members grow older. Society must be willing to pay the price to deal with the conditions that draw youth to gangs. Only by identifying those conditions and responding to them can we hope to address this serious form of violence.

Prison Gangs

The material for this section was taken from the *National Gang Threat Assessment* (U.S. Bureau of Justice Assistance, 2005). Prison gangs pose a significant threat to correctional officials across the country. The rise of gang crime and the incarceration of thousands of gang members during the 1980s perpetuated the issue of gang membership in prisons. Inmate gangs thrive on violence, extortion, and a range of illicit activity involving drugs, gambling, and prostitution. The need of inmates to form associations for self-protection creates an environment ripe for recruiting and controlling gang members. Compounding this problem, many inmates are incarcerated near their communities, where gang members continue to have significant influence. Frequently, prison gang members continue to affiliate with one another and commit criminal acts once released into the community.

While little information about the presence and composition of gangs in prisons is available, a 2002 survey commissioned by the National Major Gang Task Force (U.S. Bureau of Justice, 2005) revealed details about gangs and security threat groups (STGs) in U.S. prisons and jails.

- Prison and jail officials identified more than 1,600 STGs, comprising 113,627 inmates, in their jurisdictions.
- An average of 13.4 percent of all inmates per prison system and 15.6 percent of all inmates per jail system were estimated to be involved in STGs.
- The median numbers of inmates estimated to be involved in STGs per prison and jail system were 1,575 and 300, respectively.

■ The most frequently identified STGs in both prison and jail settings included the Crips, Bloods, Gangster Disciples, Latin Kings, and Aryan Brotherhood. The Mexican Mafia, La Nuestra Familia, the Black Guerilla Family, and the Texas Syndicate have also been identified in earlier studies as dominant prison gangs.

■ Both prisons and jails reported substantially more STG-related incidents of violence against inmates than against staff members. Likewise, in both prisons and jails, approximately one-third of all violent incidents were STG related, whether directed against staff or inmates.

■ State correctional systems in California, Colorado, New Jersey, Texas, and Wisconsin, as well as in the Federal Bureau of Prisons, have the highest number of STG-involved inmates; correctional systems in Hawaii, New Mexico, and Wisconsin have the highest percentage of STG-involved inmates.

■ Incarcerating gang members has done little to disrupt their activities and, in many ways, has augmented their growth and power inside prisons.

■ High-ranking gang members exert increased control and discipline over their street gangs from prison.

■ Prison gangs have hierarchical structures based on power and ranks and are organized to survive leadership changes. This structure insulates gang leaders from direct involvement in criminal activity and, ultimately, prosecution.

■ Many inmates who have not been previously exposed to gangs are recruited and, after serving their sentences, allied with the gang outside the prison walls.

■ The Mexican Mafia (La Eme) controls many of the Hispanic gangs in Southern California by imposing a street tax on drug sales.

■ A Latin Kings leader responsible for an entire network of gang members across Illinois used his cell phone to organize an elaborate drug ring and order hits. He was indicted in 1997 for running the drug-dealing operation from behind prison walls.

■ Latin Kings members are known for their control over correctional officers and routinely order hits on those who fail to cooperate with them.

Female Gangs

The material for this section was taken from the *National Gang Threat Assessment* (U.S. Bureau of Justice Assistance, 2005). Young women continue to take active roles in gangs. Although the number of female gangs is increasing, street gangs are still predominantly made up of males. All-female gangs continue to be an anomaly as most female gang members tend to be affiliated with male gangs. The responsibilities of females in gangs are evolving. While they continue to assume the traditionally subordinate functions of providing emotional, physical, and sexual support to male gang members, females are taking more active roles in gangs as some female gang members have graduated from affiliate status to membership.

This elevation in status also involves an elevation in risk. Females now assist in the movement of drugs and weapons for male gang members and gather intelligence from rival gangs. Others are committing drug sales, robberies, assaults, and drive-by shootings on behalf of male gang members. Respondents to the *National Gang Threat Assessment Survey* (U.S. Bureau of Justice Assistance, 2005) reported that female gang members in their jurisdictions most often

- Assist male gang members in committing crimes;
- Carry drugs and weapons and provide safe houses for contraband;
- Commit assaults and larcenies and intimidate other female students in schools;
- Engage in prostitution; and
- Engage in drug sales, vandalism, and credit card and identity theft.

Although female gang members can be just as violent as their male counterparts, violence committed by female gang members is still relatively low compared to that of male gang members. One Chicago-based study found that although females in gangs may fight as much as males, they use weapons less frequently and are less likely to kill (Hagedorn, 1999).

A large number of fights and assaults involving female gang members occur within the school setting. Some females commit violent crimes to gain status and prove themselves worthy of the gang. However, male gang members rarely grant women the same power or status as men in the gang. There have also been numerous reports of females sexually exploited by males within the gang. Female gang members are often "sexed in" (rather than "jumped in") to the gang, an initiation ritual that involves sex with several gang members, often for an extended period of time (Hagedorn, 1999).

Although female gang membership in male-dominated gangs is increasing, the prevalence of predominantly female gangs continues to be a rare phenomenon. The data from the *National Gang Threat Assessment* (U.S. Bureau of Justice Assistance, 2005) revealed that 10 percent of law enforcement agencies are now reporting exclusively female gangs.

Female gang members are generally more inclined to commit property crimes and drug offenses, and most of their assaults and fights occur within a school setting and without weapons. Although female gang members commit relatively little violent crime, violence among girls in gangs is on the rise, and law enforcement agencies are concerned about their increasing brutality and their roles as weapons providers.

Review Questions

1. Why do youth join gangs?
2. What steps can law enforcement take to reduce gang violence?
3. Explain the changing role of females in relation to gang involvement.

4. Why does gang membership appear to be increasing?
5. Explain the issues involved with gangs in prisons.

References

City of Los Angeles Criminal Justice Center. (2005). *Review of homicide crime statistics*. Los Angeles: State of California.

Hagedorn, J. M. (1999, February). Girl gangs: Are girls getting more violent? *Streetwise*, 8(2), 39–43.

Harrell, E. (2005, June). *Violence by gang members, 1993–2003*. NCJ 208875. Washington, DC: BJS.

Missouri's Task Force on Gangs and Youth Violence. (2010). Why youths join gangs. Retrieved April 24, 2010, from http://www.commpartnership.org/gangtaskforce/.

U.S. Bureau of Justice Assistance. (2005). *National gang threat assessment*. Washington, DC: Government Printing Office.

U.S. Bureau of Justice Assistance. (2007). *Annual report to Congress: Creating a safer America*. Washington, DC: U.S. Bureau of Justice Assistance.

U.S. Bureau of Justice. (2007). *City of Los Angeles, gang reduction strategy*. Washington, DC: U.S. Bureau of Justice.

Chapter 10

Hate Crimes

Introduction

Hate violence has a long history in the United States. However, some sources are suggesting that it has increased in the recent past. Accurately measuring the number of hate crimes committed is extremely difficult, and it was only with the passage of the federal Hate Crime Statistics Act of 1990 that statistics were kept on this crime. In addition, two other factors contribute to the lack of meaningful statistics in this area: the lack of training by law enforcement, which causes many officers to fail to recognize incidents of racial violence, and the natural reluctance on the part of many victims of hate crimes to report such incidents to law enforcement agencies.

History of the Hate Crime Acts

Congress enacted the Hate Crime Statistics Act of 1990 in response to mounting national concern over crimes motivated by bias. The act directs the attorney general to collect data "about crimes that manifest evidence of prejudice based on race, religion, sexual orientation, or ethnicity" (Section 1a). The U.S. attorney general delegated the responsibility for developing and implementing a hate crime data collection program to the director of the Federal Bureau of Investigation (FBI), who assigned the task to the Uniform Crime Report (UCR) program. In September 1994, Congress passed the Violent Crime Control and Law Enforcement Act, which amended the Hate Crime Statistics Act to include both physical and mental disabilities. The UCR program began collecting statistics on offenses motivated by bias against physical and mental disabilities in January 1997. The Church Arson Act of 1996 mandated that hate crime data collection become a permanent part of the UCR program.

Hate Crimes Defined

A hate crime is targeted criminal activity, usually motivated by prejudice based on perceived personal characteristics of the victims. These motivations may include race, religion, ethnicity, and sexual orientation. Hate crimes are not limited to individual activity; many organizations have been labeled as "hate groups," with their group objectives and activities promoting prejudicial behavior and even organized criminal activity targeting groups of citizens.

FBI Guidelines

The FBI Hate/Bias Motivation Guidelines to law enforcement agencies for determining what constitutes a hate crime are as follows:

- Because of the difficulty of ascertaining the offender's subjective motivation, bias is to be reported *only* if the investigation reveals sufficient objective evidence of biased motivation to meet a probable cause-type standard.
- Bias is a preformed negative opinion or attitude toward a group of people based on race, religion, ethnic/national origin, sexual orientation, or disability.
- A hate crime is a criminal offense committed against a person or property and is motivated by the offender's bias against race, religion, ethnic/national origin, sexual orientation, or disability.

Examples of Hate Crimes

- Murder motivated by hate based on gender, race, color, religion, nationality, country of origin, disability, gender, or sexual orientation is a "special circumstances" crime eligible for punishment including death or life in prison without parole.
- Use of force, threats, or destruction of property that interferes with another's exercise of civil rights is a misdemeanor.
- Committing a crime with the intent of interfering with another's exercise of civil rights is a felony.
- Violation of a civil order protecting the exercise of civil rights is a misdemeanor.
- Committing a felony motivated based on the victim's race, color, religion, nationality, country of origin, ancestry, disability, or sexual orientation is eligible for an enhanced prison sentence.

- Vandalism of a place of worship is a felony.
- Committing acts of terrorism, such as burning a cross, on private property is a misdemeanor.
- Committing acts of religious terrorism is a felony.
- Use of explosives in an act of terrorism in special places, such as churches, health facilities, etc., is a felony.
- Absent a threat of violence, speech alone does not constitute a hate crime. (Napa Valley Criminal Justice Training Center, 2009)

State Hate Crime Laws

All states have some form of hate crime laws. For example, the Texas Hate Crimes Act, Chapter 411.046 of the Texas Government Code, defines hate crimes as crimes that are motivated by prejudice, hatred, or advocacy of violence, including, but not limited to, incidents for which statistics are or were kept under Public Law 101-275 (the Federal Hate Crimes Statistics Act). The state law further defines hate crimes as crimes that manifest evidence of prejudice based on race, religion, sexual orientation, ethnicity, and, added in 1997, disability.

Issues in Collecting Data on Hate Crimes

The guidelines for hate crime data collection consider the fact that hate crimes are not separate, distinct crimes but are traditional offenses motivated by the offender's bias. Because of this issue, the developers decided that hate crime data could be derived by capturing the additional element of bias in those offenses already reported to the UCR program. Attaching the collection of hate crime statistics to the established UCR data collection procedures, they concluded, would fulfill the directives of the Hate Crime Statistics Act without placing an undue additional reporting burden on law enforcement and in time would develop a substantial body of data about the nature and frequency of bias crimes occurring throughout the nation. As a result, the law enforcement agencies that participate in the national hate crime program collect details about an offender's bias motivation associated with the following offense types: murder and nonnegligent manslaughter, forcible rape, aggravated assault, simple assault, intimidation, robbery, burglary, larceny-theft, motor vehicle theft, arson, and destruction, damage, or vandalism of property. The law enforcement agencies participating in the National Incident-Based Reporting System also collect data on additional bias-motivated crimes against persons or crimes against property (e.g., fraud) and publish these crimes as "other."

Trends in Hate Crimes

Hate crime tends to be increasing in some areas and decreasing in others. California provides a good snapshot of the trends in hate crimes.

Hate Crime Changes in California from 2007

- Anti-homosexual hate crime events increased 77.2 percent from 57 in 2006 to 101 in 2007.
- Anti-white hate crime events increased 14.1 percent from 64 in 2006 to 73 in 2007.
- Anti-black hate crime events increased 15.3 percent from 432 in 2006 to 498 in 2007.
- Anti-Jewish hate crime events increased 3.9 percent from 129 in 2006 to 134 in 2007.
- Hate crime events decreased 2.0 percent from 1,426 in 2007 to 1,397 in 2008.
- Hate crime offenses decreased 4.9 percent from 1,931 in 2007 to 1,837 in 2008.
- The number of victims of reported hate crimes decreased 3.7 percent from 1,764 in 2007 to 1,698 in 2008.
- The number of suspects of reported hate crimes decreased 9.5 percent from 1,627 in 2007 to 1,473 in 2008.
- Anti-gay hate crime events increased 16.7 percent from 132 in 2007 to 154 in 2008.
- Anti-black hate crime events decreased 8.2 percent from 498 in 2007 to 457 in 2008.
- Anti-Hispanic hate crime events decreased 8.1 percent from 160 in 2007 to 147 in 2008.
- Anti-Jewish hate crime events increased 37.3 percent from 134 in 2007 to 184 in 2008. (Napa Valley Criminal Justice Training Center, 2009)

National Hate Crime Statistics

Data for this section were taken from the *Report on Hate Crime Statistics* (FBI, 2007).

Single-Bias Incidents

An analysis of the 7,621 single-bias incidents reported in 2007 revealed the following:

- 50.8 percent were racially motivated.
- 18.4 percent were motivated by religious bias.
- 16.6 percent resulted from sexual-orientation bias.
- 13.2 percent stemmed from ethnicity/national origin bias.
- 1.0 percent were prompted by disability bias.

Offenses by Bias Motivation within Incidents

Of the 8,999 single-bias hate crime offenses reported in the above incidents:

- 52.5 percent stemmed from racial bias.
- 16.4 percent resulted from religious bias.
- 16.2 percent were motivated by sexual-orientation bias.
- 14.0 percent were prompted by ethnicity/national origin bias.
- 0.9 percent resulted from biases against disabilities. (Based on Table 1 [all table referrals in this quotation are to the original document].)

Racial Bias

In 2007, law enforcement agencies reported that 4,724 single-bias hate crime offenses were racially motivated. Of these offenses:

- 69.3 percent were motivated by anti-black bias.
- 18.4 percent stemmed from anti-white bias.
- 6.0 percent were a result of bias against groups of individuals consisting of more than one race (anti-multiple races, group).
- 4.6 percent resulted from anti-Asian/Pacific Islander bias.
- 1.6 percent were motivated by anti-American Indian/Alaskan Native bias. (Based on Table 1.)

Religious Bias

Hate crimes motivated by religious bias accounted for 1,477 offenses reported by law enforcement. A breakdown of the bias motivation of religious-biased offenses showed:

- 68.4 percent were anti-Jewish.
- 9.5 percent were anti-other religion.
- 9.0 percent were anti-Islamic.
- 4.4 percent were anti-Catholic.
- 4.3 percent were anti-multiple religions, group.
- 4.0 percent were anti-Protestant.
- 0.4 percent were anti-Atheism/Agnosticism/etc. (Based on Table 1.)

Sexual-Orientation Bias

In 2007, law enforcement agencies reported 1,460 hate crime offenses based on sexual-orientation bias. Of these offenses:

- 59.2 percent were classified as anti-male homosexual bias.
- 24.8 percent were reported as anti-homosexual bias.
- 12.6 percent were prompted by an anti-female homosexual bias.
- 1.8 percent were the result of an anti-heterosexual bias.
- 1.6 percent were classified as anti-bisexual bias. (Based on Table 1.)

Ethnicity/National Origin Bias

Of the single-bias incidents, 1,256 offenses were committed based on the perceived ethnicity or national origin of the victim. Of these offenses:

- 61.7 percent were anti-Hispanic bias.
- 38.3 percent were anti-other ethnicity/national origin bias. (Based on Table 1.)

Disability Bias

There were 82 reported hate crime offenses committed based on disability bias. Of these:

- 62 offenses were classified as anti-mental disability.
- 20 offenses were reported as anti-physical disability.

In 2004, of the 9,528 victims of hate crimes, 9,514 victims were involved in a single-bias incident. More than half of that number (53.8 percent) were victims of racial prejudice. Of those, 67.9 percent were victimized because of antiblack attitudes, and 20.1 percent were targets of antiwhite sentiments. Data for this section were based on the FBI (2005) Uniform Crime Report: Crime in the United States.

Victims of religious intolerance made up 16.7 percent of the victims of incidents involving a single bias. Of those, 67.8 percent were victims of anti-Jewish bias, and 12.7 percent were targets of anti-Islamic bias.

Of the total number of victims of single-bias incidents, 15.6 percent were attacked because of a sexual orientation bias. The majority of those victims, 60.9 percent, were the objects of antimale homosexual attitudes on the part of the offenders.

Every 23.1 Seconds One Violent Crime
Every 32.6 minutes One Murder
Every 5.6 minutes One Forcible Rape
Every 1.3 minutes One Robbery
Every 36.9 seconds One Aggravated Assault (FBI, 2007)

Of the victims in single-bias incidents, 13.2 percent were targeted because of the offenders' ethnicity/national orientation bias. Of those, 51.5 percent were marked because of the perpetrators' anti-Hispanic views.

Less than 1 percent of the total victims of crimes motivated by a single bias were targets of an antidisability bias. Of the 73 victims of this type of bias, 49 were the subjects of a bias against a mental disability. Fourteen of the total 9,528 victims of hate crimes were the objects of multiple biases on the part of the offenders.

Acts of racial violence reflect a racial prejudice or interpersonal hostility that is based on the view that different cultures do not merit treatment as equals or that they deserve blame for various problems within society. Many minority cultures are viewed in a certain manner. These stereotypes are race-based generalizations about a person's behavior or character that are typically not substantiated with scientific data. This stereotyping may act as a trigger to violence with different cultures. Stereotyping does not cause violence; however, physical violence is easier to perform on a dehumanized victim. Attackers may believe that the minority is "invading their turf." This may occur when a minority family moves into a traditional neighborhood that has not had any previous experience with that particular culture. Attackers may also claim that minority cultures are taking jobs that rightfully belong to "real Americans." These and other rationalizations deny minority cultures status as accepted citizens.

Persons of color and certain religious groups have traditionally been the target of hate crimes. These groups have been victimized on both a national and an international scale. They continue to be victimized today. For example, in New York (FBI, 2008), 30 percent of all bias incidents were committed against African Americans, and another 30 percent were perpetrated against Jews. In Los Angeles in that same year, the majority of racial incidents were against African Americans, and more than 90 percent of religiously motivated incidents were against Jews. The arson of African American churches is but another example of the continuing victimization of persons of color.

Disabled persons are also victims of hate or bias crimes. As the number of disabled persons in our nation has increased, so has the number of hate crimes and abuse against these individuals. Some perpetrators seek disabled victims because their disability makes them "easy prey" for these type of offenders. An example is a developed disabled women who may have an intellectual ability of a 7-year-old child and may be sexually assaulted by a caretaker. A disabled person is one who has a physical or mental impairment that substantially limits one or more of the major life activities of that individual, that person has a record of such impairment, or that person is regarded as having such an impairment. Major life activities include such activities as walking, seeing, hearing, speaking, breathing, learning, and working.

Antigay and antilesbian violence became a national issue with the murders of San Francisco mayor George Moscone and city supervisor Harvey Milk. Their deaths became symbols of both the strength of the homosexual community as well as the hostility that is directed at them. Attacks against gays infected with HIV/AIDS have increased in the last several years.

Women also have been the subject of hate or bias crimes. They continue to be targets of violence because of their gender. Many states include gender as a classification within their hate crime statutes.

Legal Aspects of Hate Crimes

Prosecuting a perpetrator for violation of a hate crime raises several emotional and constitutional issues. The First Amendment prohibits the federal government and the states from enacting any law that unduly regulates a person's freedom of expression. However, from the founding of our nation, the Supreme Court has held that such freedom of expression is not unlimited. There are situations in which conduct or other activities while expressing beliefs or thoughts are outside the scope of the First Amendment protection.

Hate crimes deal with both the expression of beliefs and action. The expression of beliefs reflects hatred or loathing toward a certain group, while the action is criminal in nature. Thus, crafting a criminal statute that regulates hate crimes is no easy task.

In 1992, the Supreme Court struck down a local hate crime ordinance in St. Paul, Minnesota, that criminalized the use of hate symbols, such as the burning of a cross, on the grounds that it violated an individual's right to freedom of expression (*R.A.V. v. City of St. Paul, 1992*).

In *Wisconsin v. Mitchell* (1993), the U.S. Supreme Court unanimously upheld the constitutionality of the hate crime statute of Wisconsin, which increased penalties for crimes motivated by hate or bias. Todd Mitchell was a 19-year-old black male who was outraged over a scene in the film *Mississippi Burning*, which depicted a young black child being attacked by a white racist. On seeing a 14-year-old white male, Mitchell asked his companions if they wanted to get that white boy. They attacked him, leaving the victim comatose for four days with possible brain damage. Mitchell was convicted of aggravated battery, and the sentence was doubled from two to four years after it was proven that he had intentionally selected his victim based on race. Mitchell challenged the constitutionality of the hate crime enhancement statute, claiming it violated the First Amendment freedom of expression.

The U.S. Supreme Court upheld the statute, stating bias or hate crimes were valid for three main reasons:

1. While the government cannot punish an individual's abstract beliefs, it can punish a vast array of depraved motives for crime, including selecting a crime victim based on race, religion, color, disability, sexual orientation, national origin, or ancestry.
2. Hate crimes do not punish thoughts; rather, they address the greater individual and societal harms caused by bias-related offenses in that they are more likely to provoke retaliatory crimes, inflict distinct emotional harms on their victims, and incite community unrest.
3. Hate crime penalty enhancement laws do not punish people because they express their views.

As this discussion indicates, laws prohibiting certain conduct will be considered constitutionally valid. Nonthreatening, bigoted expression is still protected as long as it does not evolve into bias-motivated action. When such beliefs are the basis for hate or bias crimes, professionals in the field should be able to identify them.

Identifying Hate Crimes

To identify hate or bias crimes, we must first define these offenses. Recognizing bias crimes involves an evaluation of a number of factors. There is no generally accepted, foolproof list of indicators whether the offense is motivated by bias or hate of a particular group. However, the Office for Victims of Crime has identified seven general categories that should be examined when evaluating criminal acts. These factors include cultural differences, written or oral comments, use of symbols, representation of organized hate groups, prior hate crimes, victim or witness perceptions, and lack of other motive. Depending on the situation, one of these factors by itself may strongly indicate that the offense may be classified as a bias or hate crime. On the other hand, several of these indicators may not present conclusive evidence that the crime was motivated by hate or bias. Each case should be evaluated on its own merits.

Racial, ethnic, gender, and cultural differences. Is the victim of a different culture than the offender? Investigators may not be able to establish this fact from the victim. They may have to look for other indicators that point to any cultural differences between the victim and the offender. These other factors include the cultural diversity of a number of locations, including the place of attack or the victim's home or workplace. Inquiry should be made regarding whether the victim was engaged in activities that represent or promote his or her group, such as a gay rights march. Did the incident occur on a date that has a special significance to certain cultures, such as Martin Luther King's birthday? Even if the victim is not a member of any recognized cultural or ethnic minority, he or she may have supported such a group, and the attack may be in reprisal for that activity. Finally, questions must be asked about whether there is a history of violence between the victim's culture and any other group.

Written or oral comments or gestures. Inquiry should be made regarding whether the attackers made any comments or gestures before, during, or immediately after the attack. These comments might refer to the victim's race, sex, or gender. Likewise, the attackers may make certain gestures, such as indicating affiliation with another group.

Drawings, markings, symbols, and graffiti. Care should be taken to look for any drawings or symbols that might indicate membership in a group. These may be on the victim's house, place of work, house of worship, or where the attack occurred.

Representations of organized hate groups. Sometimes, hate groups will call members of the media and take credit for a bombing, burning, or other act of violence. They may also leave a trademark at the scene of the crime. For example, a burning cross may be found outside the victim's home.

Previous existence of bias or hate crime incidents. Did the incident occur in a location where previous hate crimes have occurred? If there have been a series of crimes involving victims of the same culture or the incidents occurred in the same location that is frequented by members of a specific culture, those facts may indicate that the crimes are motivated by hate or bias. Interview the victim to determine if he or she received previous harassing mail or phone calls based on an affiliation or membership in a group.

Victim/witness perception. The victim should be questioned to determine if he or she perceived the crime as motivated by bias. This may not always be accurate, but the victim's input in this area is always critical.

Lack of other motives. If there is no other motive for the incident and the victim is a member of a minority culture, the fact that it may be motivated by bias or hatred of that group should always be considered.

The presence or absence of these factors does not establish the existence of a hate-related crime. In fact, there are several caveats that must be exercised when evaluating these crimes. These caveats might appropriately be called false-positive factors. These factors include the following:

Requirement for a case-by-case assessment. Each crime must be evaluated on its own merits. The existence or nonexistence of bias or hate as the motivation for the offense must be evaluated in light of all the facts and circumstances surrounding the crime.

Misleading facts. Care must be taken not to rush to judgment in what appears to be a hate crime. There may be other facts that negate this first impression. For example, the victim may tell the officers that the perpetrator used a racial epithet during the assault. Further investigation may reveal that the victim and the offender were both of the same race or culture.

Feigned facts and hoaxes. Some offenders may leave hate symbols in an effort to give the false impression that the offense was motivated by bias or hatred when in fact it was simply an ordinary crime. Other perpetrators may leave symbols or signs of certain groups as a hoax or to mislead investigators.

There are occasions when determining whether the offense is really a hate crime may be difficult. Even if police officers cannot prove that the offense was a hate crime, the victim may believe that hate or bias was in fact the motivation. The effect of such crime on victims is unique and in many cases more devastating than other crimes because of the psychological impact on the victim.

The victim must live with the realization that the crime was not a random act of violence; rather, the victim was targeted or selected for victimization based on beliefs, race, culture, religion, or sexual preference. Bias crimes are "message crimes" that send a message of terror to the victim because the victim is different from the majority of other Americans. Some victims of bias crimes may not have any personal community support systems. They may have recently arrived in the United States and have not developed a support base within the general community or their specific culture. Other victims may fear discovery of their status and therefore decline to report suspected hate crimes. This aspect of this type of victimization is especially true for closeted gays and lesbians, undocumented aliens, and those who suffer from other disabilities, such as HIV/AIDS infection.

Bias crimes also have an impact on the victim's immediate community and culture. Such crimes increase tension with the minority community and raise the specter of retaliation by members of that community. As a result of these factors, bias or hate crimes pose special problems for victim service professionals.

Typology of Offenders

Understanding more about those who commit hate crimes allows victim service professionals to help the victim understand some of the dynamics involved in this type of crime. Although research is still under development in this area, Levin and McDevitt (1993) established three categories of offenders: thrill-seeking offenders, reactive offenders, and mission offenders.

The thrill-seeking offenders are generally groups of teenagers who are not otherwise associated with any other formal hate group. They engage in these acts for a variety of reasons, including an attempt to gain a psychological or social thrill or rush, a desire to be accepted by others, or a desire to be able to brag about the act later. Almost any member of a minority group may be a target of these groups. They generally operate outside their own area or neighborhood and actively look for targets of opportunity. Since these attacks are random and usually fail to follow any pattern, it is often difficult to identify the perpetrators of these types of hate crimes.

The reactive offenders have a sense of entitlement concerning their rights or lifestyle that does not extend to the victim. They usually do not belong to any organized hate group but may associate with one to mitigate a perceived threat to their way of life. When a victim acts in such a manner that it causes these offenders to feel that their lifestyle is threatened, they may react with violence. They will commit hate crimes to send a message to the victim or the victim's community that will cause the victim to stop whatever action is threatening the perpetrator's rights or lifestyle. These crimes normally occur within the offender's own community, school, or place of work. Examples of these types of hate crimes include burning crosses at a minority member's new home in a predominantly white neighborhood, beating a minority person who takes a job in a traditionally white occupation, and other acts of violence directed at maintaining the status quo.

The mission-oriented offenders may suffer from a mental illness, including psychosis. They may experience hallucinations, withdrawal, and impaired ability to reason. These offenders may believe they have received instructions from a higher deity to rid the world of this "evil." They typically have a sense of urgency about their objectives and believe that they must act before it is too late. The victim is usually a member of a group that is targeted for elimination. These perpetrators will look for a victim in the victim's own neighborhood. An example of this type of offender was Marc Lepine, who killed 14 women at the University of Montreal, stating that he hated all feminists.

Sapp, Holden, and Wiggins (1993) developed a typology of hate offenders based on their ideology. They believed that ideology is used by hate groups to serve as a symbolic set of ideas that provides the group with a perceived social legitimacy. Ideology is a way of thinking used by a group to express its beliefs and social values. Sapp classified hate groups into three basic categories: Christian conservatism, based on the identity movement; white racial supremacy; and patriotism and survival.

Christian conservatism based on the identity movement uses passages in the scripture identifying certain groups as superior to others and the notion that a nation, rather than being a geographic, political, or economic entity, is a culture grouped according to bloodlines and shared history. Racial identity thus becomes the basis for national identity.

These groups may adopt a postmillennium view that holds that the second coming of Christ cannot happen until Christians purge the earth of sin and establish the Holy Land. As Gale pointed out, this is potentially a blueprint for genocide in that it allows these groups to cleanse the Holy Land of "sinners." Therefore, mass murders of "inferiors" and those who oppose the groups and their churches are mandated.

White racial supremacy groups also include racial purity proponents. Racial purity is concerned with the purity of the Aryan race or God's children. Refugees, illegal aliens, legal immigrants, Jews, blacks, Hispanics, Asians, and non-Christians are all considered a threat to white racial purity theorists. The Ku Klux Klan is an example of a white supremacy group. Its founding fathers stated that its purpose was the maintenance of the supremacy of the white race in the republic since that race is superior to all other races.

Patriotism and survival groups have come to the attention of the general public because of incidents in Idaho and Montana involving various members of militia groups. These groups offer an attractive ideology to some conservative groups in America. They point out the economic troubles, including unemployment, and blame these problems on refugees and other nonwhite groups. They argue that special interests control the government and decry the moral bankruptcy of our leaders.

These groups blame lax courts for encouraging criminals. They target the media because they believe the media glorify criminals and are responsible for the total breakdown of morals in America. Some of these groups use quotations from the Constitution as a basis for their beliefs and argue that they are no longer subject to the laws of the United States.

Bias and hate crimes do not just happen; they are motivated by a variety of feelings, beliefs, and emotions. The result is intimidation of the individual as well as his or her community. Criminal justice professionals must understand these crimes and their impact to properly respond to these offenses.

Review Questions

1. Should individuals convicted of committing a hate crime receive more severe punishment than if the crime was not hate motivated?
2. Should the lack of bias be considered in sentencing a defendant?
3. What can be done to reduce hate crimes?

References

FBI. (2002). *Hate/Bias motivation guidelines*. Washington, DC: DoJ.

Federal Bureau of Investigation. (2005). *Uniform crime report: Crime in the United States, 2004*. Washington, DC: Department of Justice.

FBI. (2007). *Report on hate crime statistics*. Washington, DC: DoJ.

Federal Bureau of Investigation. (2008). *Uniform crime report: Crime in the United States, 2007*. Washington, DC: Government Printing Office.

Gale, T. (2004). *Genocide*. Wadsworth, CA: Cengage.

Levin, J., and McDevitt, J. (1993). *The rising tide of bigotry and bloodshed*. New York: Plenum.

Napa Valley Criminal Justice Training Center. (2009). Bias and hate crimes victims' guide. Retrieved April 23, 2010, from http://www.nvccjtc.org/nvchatecrimes.html.

R.A.V. v. City of St. Paul, 112 S.Ct. 2538 (1992).

Sapp, A. D., Holden, R. N., and Wiggins, M. E. (1993). Value and belief systems of right-wing extremists. In R. J. Kelly (ed.), *Bias crimes: American law enforcement and legal responses.* Reading, UK: Office of the International Criminal Justice Administration, 131–152.

Texas Hate Crime Act, Texas Statutes. (2001). Section 411.046.

U.S. Church Arson Prevention Act of 1996. 18 U.S. Code 241.

U.S. Hate Crime Statistics Act. (1990). 28 USC 534.

U.S. Violent Crime Control and Law Enforcement Act. (1994). 28 USC 994.

Wisconsin v. Mitchell, 113 S.Ct. 2194 (1993).

Chapter 11

Shame and Violence

Introduction

Chapter 3 introduced several correlates that appear to be strongly associated with violence. We began the discussion by first exploring the concept of values and the immense preoccupation with material possessions. In addition, we explored the effects of poverty, alcohol abuse, neglect, and low levels of education. Especially, when considered as components of a cyclical pattern, each variable contributes to the possibility of one engaging in violence as a means to reduce unpleasant emotion.

In this chapter, an additional variable is brought forward that was intentionally withheld in Chapter 3. The depth and breadth of shame deserves specific attention to make every attempt to capture the salience of its ability to contribute to violent behaviors. In Chapter 3, we used the word *correlates* to describe the relationship between each of the variables individually and collectively with violence. This is because none of the variables has the capacity to cause violence. This is precisely because shame causes violence (Gilligan, 1996, 2001; Lewis, 1995; Scheff and Retzinger, 2001). In essence, each of the correlates, especially as a collective group, has a strong potential to result in feelings of shame. Not all individuals who experience shame will engage in violence; however, for violence to occur shame is present.

What Is Shame?

Shame is a concept that describes one's global assessment of self as negative and results in extremely painful feelings (Hanser and Mire, 2010). As noted by Fosha

(2000), "Shame is a quintessential aversive affect and plays a major role in the development of pathology" (p. 113). The use of the concept "global assessment" is critical in describing the emotion of shame. When one experiences shame and then internalizes the shame, the result is a feeling of complete and utter inadequacy. This feeling of totality is precisely what makes shame such a robust causal factor of violence. It is also what delineates shame from guilt. Guilt is a feeling commonly associated with doing something "wrong." Guilt is about behavior (M. Young, personal communication, April 30, 2010). The feelings of guilt, however, are not generalized to the total self. Someone who feels guilty about a particular action or lack of action may experience a motivation toward corrective action. Shame is much more profound and is a result of experiencing rejection following some expression of one's true self. Shame is about self not behavior (M. Young, personal communication, April 30, 2010). In essence, shame is a feeling of worthlessness as a result of being judged as inadequate. A person's recent expression captures the true meaning of shame: "When the guy confronted me, I was caught off guard. I was not anticipating him doing that. I wasn't ready. He wanted to fight with me but at that moment I was afraid. I backed down and just left. I am a coward, and everyone who was there believes I am a coward."

What Are the Origins of Shame?

The attempt to answer what the origins of shame are comprehensively is truly a daunting task. It is necessary, however, to make a concerted effort to support the relationship between shame and violence. For our purposes, we concentrate on two primary areas in which shame is capable of being embedded in human beings:

1. One's family of origin or primary caregivers
2. Society at large

First, according to Lewis (1995), one experiences shame as a result of having some knowledge. Knowledge in this sense is related to several factors that must be accepted as valid measures of one's performance. Lewis proposed three factors are of prominence:

1. Knowledge of standards, rules, and goals
2. One's own behavior in regard to these rules
3. Knowledge of oneself

Knowledge of standards, rules, and goals begins to be implemented as soon as one enters into and begins the process of interacting with primary caregivers. It is through our caregivers that we learn what is right and wrong, acceptable modes of behavior, and differences between circumstances and appropriate responses to each. In essence, it is at this stage of development that one learns how to interact and conduct oneself within social networks. An important note regarding rules and standards is that some will be emphasized with greater intensity than others. The importance of this lies in the fact that shame will be most likely to result in association with those rules and standards that were transmitted from caregivers as most important.

Gilligan (1996) supported this postulate with information gleaned through his extensive conversations with inmates regarding their reasoning underlying past violent encounters. Overwhelmingly, he noted that responses centered around the concept of respect. This same concept provided the foundation for much of the information provided by Anderson (1999) in his seminal work regarding the code of the street. What, then, is the connection among shame, respect, and violence? In other words, why is it that respect is so centrally embedded within the cognitive framework of violent offenders? The short answer is that from a very early age, they were taught that the one "thing" no one can take from you is your self-respect— your dignity, your honor as a person. We may not have money, and we may not have the material "things" that other people have, but we are still human, and just because others have those things does not mean that they are better than us. So, do not ever, ever let someone make you feel as though he or she is better than you; never let anyone disrespect you.

Intense shame will result when one's behavior is not in accordance with one's knowledge of standards and rules from which they should operate. The example of the young man who felt as though he was a coward for not engaging in the fistfight also applies here. This young man had been taught that it is not acceptable to allow someone to disrespect him or put him in a position of inferiority. And, the knowledge of himself as a unique person, separate from others, provided the foundation for which the shame could be internalized. He was not feeling guilt for his behavior; he was feeling shame for being a coward.

Within this context, violence is a means (buffer) to protect the very core of one's self, that which caregivers have assured is most critical. With this message firmly intact, it can no longer be any surprise that some people will engage in violence to protect their innermost core. This is why, as we discuss in the next section, shame is so powerful. An animal caught in a trap will sacrifice body parts to survive. The animal will gnaw through its own legs to detach them from their core. Similarly, a human will sacrifice all, including freedom, to protect his or her respect, dignity, and honor—the origins of life. Without respect and dignity, a person is no longer viable.

Why Shame Is So Powerful

First, consider the Hindu origins of the word *shame*. It means "to hide" (M. Young, personal communication, April 30, 2010). As such, shame is capable of producing profound pain for those who have internalized shame to the degree that it becomes autonomous with oneself (M. Young, personal communication, April 30, 2010). In other words, internalized shame provides the basis for one to interpret or transform most stimuli, even neutral stimuli, into a shaming event that results in emotional pain from which we seek shelter.

Shame is so powerful because it serves as the precise mode through which one accepts and takes ownership of painful and extremely toxic messages:

1. You do not fit in.
2. You do not belong.
3. You are not worthy.
4. You are pathetic.
5. You make me sick.

Once owned and internalized, these messages destroy the very essence of what it is to be a human being. These messages render it largely impossible for one to feel:

1. A sense of connection to others
2. A sense of worth
3. A sense of something to offer (M. Young, personal communication, April 30, 2010)

Consider the analogy provided by Elliot and Elliot (2010). "A motor needs what is called a load—some work to do. Otherwise, it spins and spins and quickly burns itself out. With a load, the motor is fulfilled, so to speak" (p. 3). A person needs a sense of connection, a sense of worth, something to offer and ultimately a sense of respect, or like the motor, he, too, will burn out.

How Shame Is Directly Related to Violence

For some, violence serves as the buffer to shame. It is an attempt, albeit dysfunctional, to stave off "burning up" (Elliot and Elliot, 2006). The act of violence absorbs the shock and pain produced by shame and at least temporarily provides a small surface from which one is able to feel some relief from the intense emotional pain. For individuals who have internalized shame, violence can be viewed as an adaptive response.

Shame and Empathy

Lewis (1995) noted that people who are more prone to experiencing shame or who are in fact experiencing shame are much less able to feel empathy. This is an important observation because it directly affects one's reactions to certain situations or stimuli. Empathy is commonly thought of as one's ability to experience the feelings, thoughts, or attitudes of another. In many circumstances, the presentation of stimuli is a result of one feeling stress due to a perceived need to achieve some psychological state or a particular task. The presentation of this stimulus is experienced as aversive when the receiver of the stimuli feels threatened in his or her ability to follow through with or conform to the motivations of the presenter and carry out the task that is presented. An example may help to illuminate the relationship between shame and empathy and in some cases violence.

Consider a case of interpersonal violence between two young males on a neighborhood street corner. One of the young men (Mark) looks at another (Billy) with a menacing, "hard," look in which the eye contact is held longer than what is socially appropriate or acceptable among young men in a constant struggle for respect.

Mark has just been chided by his friends for not being tough enough. In fact, they have never seen him perform in a fight and question his ability to physically handle himself and subsequently protect them if they needed it. For Mark, shame is experienced as a result of not being unconditionally accepted by his peers. In essence, they are saying: "Your worth to us is completely dependent on your ability to perform in a fistfight. If you cannot fight, we do not want you around us. In fact, if you cannot fight just being around us becomes a liability. Others will single you out based on this weakness, and if we do not stand up for you, then the group as a whole is compromised and will lead to further acts of aggression by other groups. Therefore, if you are going to be a part of "Us," we need to know that you are capable." For a young man trying desperately to fit in, this is an extremely stressful situation. If Mark simply says, "I do not want to fight with anyone," he is labeled as weak, scared, and worthless and immediately discarded. For many young men, this is not an option as it would result in a complete destruction of self (shame). When this is the case, the only option is to prove oneself.

The problem, however, is that Billy is operating from the same rules and standards. In Billy's world, he cannot allow someone to "get over" on him and disrespect him. To do so would be to go against everything that he has been taught by his family and peers (society). For Billy, the only way to keep his "self" intact (and not experience debilitating shame) is to stand up squarely and directly to any threat posed by someone trying to disrespect him. In Billy's world, to ignore this overt and blatant act of aggression would be analogous to holding a sign saying "I am a coward."

The result is one that is all too common—violence as a result of two young men locked in a deadly cycle through which both are trying to achieve status, recognition, acceptance, and approval, the antithesis of shame. Mark and Billy are both willing to endure extreme physical violence to avoid shame. Their very survival is at stake. In some cases, death may even be the ultimate response. After the initial physical battle (or in some cases during), the combatant defeated (or in the process of being defeated) may feel that he has no other choice but to produce a weapon and kill the other in a last and final attempt to save credibility and worth and ultimately avoid shame.

How does empathy relate to this example? It is one variable that has the ability to moderate feelings of shame and is a result of understanding the motivations of another. Could Mark have avoided this circumstance? Yes, maybe if he understood the origins of why the group was demanding that he prove himself he could have felt empathy for them and walked away. He could have understood that the appearance of toughness was a means of survival and not necessarily a direct reflection of the true character of each individual. With such understanding, Mark may have chosen to simply seek out another group with different values. Billy also could have avoided the circumstance if he had the capacity to understand the true motivations of Mark. Mark's true motivation was to be accepted, and Billy happened to be the person through which he could achieve this acceptance. It was not personal; they may not have ever seen or spoken to each other previously. If Billy were able to frame these connections cognitively, he may have been able to feel empathy, which would have provided the foundation to walk away free of shame.

Of course, this example is sanitized and certainly constructed well outside modern realism. We understand this fully. To try to present such information to a group of adolescents vying for respect and admiration and expecting them to fully understand and embrace the postulates would be naïve at best. In essence, it would be like trying to train a group of deer not to engage in high, bounding leaps (a show of strength and health meant to communicate that they would be a difficult target) when confronted by predators. It would not make sense and may even exacerbate the problem. Many of these responses and actions are not only learned but also may have at least some grounding in instinct.

The same connection between shame and empathy is also applicable to incidents of interpersonal violence between spouses or partners. In essence, one engages in some action to reduce or avoid feeling shame, and the result is that the other is put in a position in which the perception is that a direct response is necessary to avoid being shamed. Being shamed equates to losing status within the relationship and ultimately the loss of control. For someone prone to shame, this is an unacceptable circumstance. Ultimately, the fear is that, "If I do not maintain control and dominance, my spouse [partner] will do something that could be so damaging that I may not survive."

This phenomenon plays itself out when one partner kills another after a long and tumultuous relationship. Often, the final straw is when one files for divorce or takes some overt and direct action to terminate the relationship. For the person who perpetrates the murder, the shame of losing the relationship (ultimately the shame of not being good enough to keep the spouse or partner from leaving) is so overwhelming that the only way to preserve one's self is to destroy the source of the shame. Again, there are no remnants of empathy because the actions of the other result in a dire condition in which one does not feel equipped to cope.

How Shame Is Related to the Correlates in Chapter 3

First, shame is related to each of the correlates in Chapter 3, and where there is violence, there is shame. The difficulty in articulating the connections, however, is because shame is both a contributor to and a result of each. The relationship between the variables is best thought of as cyclical and circular in nature and therefore does not have precise start and end points. It would be possible to pinpoint start and end points for an individual, but our goal in this is much broader and meant to show how the current construction of modern society affects all people and both contributes to and results in shame and for some, those who have internalized shame, contributes to the devastating phenomenon of violence.

Arguably, the most problematic construct within modern society is the preoccupation with material possessions as a reflection of success. Plainly stated, not all can achieve or reach a predetermined threshold for success in a system that is predicated on some having more than others. This aspect of modern society has the potential to induce shame. This potential is greatest among those considered to be the poorest of the poor. Those living below the poverty line are most susceptible to internalizing shame and resorting to violence to ease the pain.

The cycle continues as these individuals have children (Figure 11.1). Individuals who have internalized shame spend much of their emotional energy

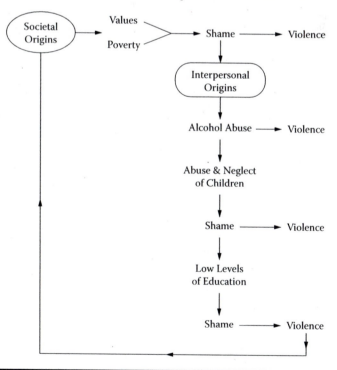

Figure 11.1

in an attempt to buffer the pain. Alcohol use and abuse is common, and with precious little emotional energy to spare, their children are often neglected and sometimes abused. Abuse and trauma initiate the process of embedding shame into these children. A child grows up believing that if he or she were somehow better, more worthy, or more important, he or she would not be the recipient of such harsh treatment.

At this point, the immense burden of severe emotional pain (shame) is now shared by the children of their abusers. Many children who have internalized the concept of shame will become disruptive, unruly, and violent. Each of these behaviors serves as a buffer in an attempt to minimize or dull the razor-sharp edge of shame. Similar to their parents or caregivers, they have little emotional energy with which to engage in more meaningful activities. They first have to survive psychologically and emotionally. Often, these children become labeled and outcasts.

A child suffering the effects of shame has little energy to devote to one method society says produces the best chance of success: school and their education. A child who moves into adolescence and young adulthood without a sufficient education is now poised, and in perfect position, to begin the cycle anew, a deadly cycle that often results in violence and death as one struggles to survive. Figure 11.1 is a graphic display of the relationship between shame and violence.

Conclusion

Shame is intricately connected to violence. It causes violence. If violence occurs, shame is present. Especially in conjunction with valuing material possessions, poverty, alcohol abuse, neglect and trauma, and low levels of education, shame provides the final toxin needed to ignite violent encounters. As noted by Gilligan (2001), if we want to prevent violence, we must learn not to shame people.

Review Questions

1. Discuss the concept of shame. How would you describe shame to someone who has never heard of the concept?
2. Discuss the connection among shame, values, poverty, alcohol abuse, neglect, and low levels of education.
3. Identify and discuss the purpose of interpersonal violence. In violence, what is the underlying problem that is attempting to be addressed?
4. Why is shame the ultimate toxin capable of producing violence?

References

Anderson, E. (1999). *Code of the street: Decency, violence, and the moral life of the inner city.* New York: Norton.

Elliot, J., and Elliot, K. (2006). *Disarming the inner critic.* Lafayette, LA: Anthetics Press.

Elliot, J., and Elliot, K. (2010). Skills for creating your own soulmate relationship [msg 4]. Message posted to love letters. http://www.soulmateskills.org.

Fosha, D. (2000). *The transforming power of affect.* New York: Basic Books.

Gilligan, J. (1996). *Violence: Reflections on a national epidemic.* New York: Vintage Books.

Gilligan, J. (2001). *Preventing violence.* New York: Thames and Hudson.

Hanser, R. D., and Mire, S. M. (2010). *Correctional counseling.* Upper Saddle River, NJ: Prentice Hall.

Lewis, M. (1995). *Shame: The exposed self.* New York: Free Press.

Scheff, T. J., and Retzinger, S. M. (2001). *Emotions and violence: Shame and rage in destructive conflicts.* Lincoln, NE: iUniverse.

Young, M. (2010). Personal Communication. April 30, 2010.

Chapter 12

Controlling Violence by the Use of Punishment

Introduction

A popular answer to the question of how to control violence is to "lock them up." In the United States, we confine a larger percentage of the population than almost all other countries, yet it has not kept our nation safe. In this chapter, we briefly examine punishment to provide a better understanding of its concepts and principles. Frequently, we hear comments that the prison system fails to prevent future crime. This is a fact that cannot be established. There is no way to clearly establish if the present correctional system promotes or reduces violent crime.

Beginning of Legal Punishments

In primitive societies, the remedy for wrongs done to one's person or property was personal retaliation against the wrongdoer. Unlike modern society, in the early primitive societies personal retaliation was encouraged. From the concept of personal retaliation developed "blood feuds." A blood feud occurred when the victim's family or tribe took revenge on the offender's family or tribe. Often, blood feuds escalated and resulted in continuing vendettas between families or tribes. In many cases, for religious reasons individuals were expected to avenge the death of kin.

The duty of retaliation was imposed by universal practice on the victim or, in case of death, the nearest male relative.

To lessen the costly and damaging vendettas, the custom of accepting money or property in place of blood vengeance developed. At first, the acceptance of payments instead of blood vengeance was not compulsory. The victim's family was still free to choose whatever form of vengeance they wished. Often, the relative power of the families or tribes decided the use of payments or blood vengeance.

The acceptance of money or property as atonement for wrongs became known as *les salica* or *wergeld*. This practice is still used in some Middle Eastern countries. The amount of payment was based on the rank or position of the victim. This tradition of accepting money for property damages was the beginning of the development of a system of criminal law.

One problem with the acceptance of payment as complete satisfaction for the wrong was the concept that punishment of an individual wrongdoer should also include some religious aspects. To many, crime was also a sin against the church and, later, the state. Accordingly, there developed the concept that punishment in the form of wergeld (payment to the victim) should also be supplemented with *friedensgeld* (payment to the church or later to the crown).

Fines and other forms of punishment replaced personal retaliation as tribal leaders began to exert their authority during the negotiations or proceedings concerning the damages caused by the wrongs committed. The wrongdoers were not required to attend the proceedings. If, however, they failed to follow the recommendations of the tribal leaders, they were banished or exiled and thus considered "outlaws."

Since criminal law requires an element of public action against the wrongdoer, the banishment or pronouncement of outlawry was the first criminal punishment imposed by society (Kocourek and Wigmore, 1915). Many present-day researchers consider the development of this custom as the beginning of criminal law as we know it today. Subsequent legal codes and punishments for different crimes have either stressed or refined the vengeance principle. The concept that a society expresses its vengeance within a system of rules was present in the ethics of primitive societies.

The two earliest codes involving criminal punishments were the Sumerian and Hammurabic codes. The punishment phases of these codes contained the concept of personal vengeance. The listed punishments in the codes were harsh, and in many cases, the victim or the victim's nearest relative was personally allowed to inflict punishment. Permitted punishments included mutilation, whipping, or forced labor. At first, the punishments were applied almost exclusively to slaves and bond servants and indicated a base or servile mentality toward those punished. Later, they were extended to all offenders.

The use of penal servitude also developed. Penal servitude involved the use of hard labor as punishment. It was generally reserved for the lower classes of citizens. Penal servitude included the loss of citizenship and liberty (i.e., civil death). With civil death, the offender's property was confiscated in the name of the state, and an offender's wife was declared a widow. Later, the use of penal servitude by the Romans was encouraged by the need for workers to perform hard labor.

The fact that early punishments were considered synonymous with slavery is indicated by the practice of shaving the heads of those punished as a "mark of slavery." Other marks of slavery used on punished wrongdoers included the branding on the forehead or use of a heavy metal collar that could not be easily removed.

The Greek code, Code of Draco, used the same penalties for both citizens and slaves and incorporated many of the concepts used in primitive societies (e.g., vengeance, outlawry, and blood feuds). Apparently, the Greeks were the first society to allow any citizen to prosecute an offender on behalf of the victim. This practice appears to indicate that public interest and protection of society had accepted the concept that crimes affected not only the victim but also society in general.

Punishment of Socrates

Socrates was charged in 399 BC with the offense of impiety (corrupting young minds and believing in new gods). He was tried before a jury of 500 members. The trial lasted only one day. He was found guilty by a margin of 30 jurors. The prosecution proposed the death penalty. Socrates had a right to propose an alternative penalty. He stated:

> Shall I [propose] imprisonment? And why should I spend my days in prison, and be the slave of the magistrates? Or shall the penalty be a fine and imprisonment until the fine is paid? There is the same objection. I should have to lie in prison, for money I have none, and cannot pay. And if I say exile, I must indeed be blinded by the love of life, if I am so irrational as to expect that when you, who are my own citizens, cannot endure my discourses and arguments, and have found them so grievous and odious that you will have no more of them, that others are likely to endure them. [as quoted by Masters and Roberson, 1985, p. 123].

The jury condemned him to death. He committed compulsory suicide by drinking poison, the Athenian method of execution.

Middle Ages

During the Middle Ages, rapid changes were made in the social structure of societies. In addition, the growing influence of the church on everyday life helped create a divided system of justice. The offender in committing a crime also committed a sin. Accordingly, he or she had two debts to pay—one to the victim and one to the church. Trials by ordeal were used by the churches as substitutes for trials. In a trial by ordeal, the accused was subjected to dangerous or painful tests in the belief that God would protect the innocent, and the guilty would suffer agonies and die. The brutality of the trial by ordeal ensured that most would die and thus be considered guilty. The practice of trial by ordeal was not abolished until about 1215.

It was also during the Middle Ages that the churches expanded the concept of crime to include new prohibited areas. This concept is still present in our modern-day codes. Sexual offenses were among the new areas now covered by law. Sex offenses, which include either public or "unnatural" acts, received horrible punishments. Heresy and witchcraft were also included in the new prohibited areas of conduct. The church inflicted cruel punishments and justified the punishments as necessary to save the unfortunate sinners. For example, the zealous movement to stamp out heresy resulted in the Inquisition. The Inquisition was a tribunal established by the church with broad powers to use for the suppression of heresy. The Inquisition searched out offenders rather than waiting for charges to be brought against them (Swain, 1931).

The Holy Inquisition

The word *inquisition* means an inquiry. In one sense, all modern courts of law are inquisitions. The Holy Inquisition was a court set up by the Church of Rome to inquire into cases of heresy. It was later extended to cover crimes of witchcraft and ecclesiastical offenses committed by members of the church. The idea of a court of inquiry into religious offenses was of early origin. For example, Jews found guilty by an inquisition of deserting their faith were sentenced to be stoned to death. The Holy Inquisition flourished in all European countries, but its barbarities were the greatest in Spain and the Spanish dominions. The sentences of the court were generally pronounced on Sunday in a church and consisted of burning, scourging, imprisonment, penances, humiliation, or fines.

Whipping was the usual method of punishing persons for minor offenses. Whipping was inflicted on women while kneeling and on men while lying on the ground. Generally, the victims were stripped to the waist and the blows inflicted on their backs (Swain, 1931).

Purpose of Criminal Sanctions

In discussing the purpose of criminal sanctions, various ideologies are presented. For purposes of this chapter, *ideology* refers to the belief system adopted by a group and consists of assumptions and values. The *assumptions* are beliefs about the way the world is constituted, organized, and operates. *Values*, however, are beliefs about what is moral and desirable (Durham, 1994). There are numerous methods to classify ideologies. Three popular classifications based on political theories that influence our corrections system are conservative, liberal, and radical.

The conservative ideology tends to accept the concept that human beings are rational, possess free will, and voluntarily commit criminal misconduct. Accordingly, criminals should be held accountable for the actions. Punishment should be imposed to inflict suffering on the criminal because the suffering is deserved, and it will deter future crime. The punishment imposed should fit the crime. This ideology, because of its view on the causes of human behavior, generally does not accept the concept of rehabilitation as an attractive objective of punishment.

The liberal ideology tends to view human behavior as greatly influenced by social circumstances, including one's upbringing, material affluence, education, peer relationships, and so on. Accordingly, human behavior is more than a simple product of free choice. All of the social influences are important factors in shaping our conduct. Viewing criminal behavior as a product of both social circumstances and individual actions, liberals are more likely to support rehabilitation as the proper purpose of criminal punishment. Most liberals tend to be receptive to a wider range of aims for criminal punishment, including deterrence.

The radical ideology rejects both the conservative and liberal ideologies. According to this ideology, crime is a natural consequence of our social system. According to the radicals, fundamental changes in the socioeconomic basis of society are required to control crime.

The ultimate purpose of criminal sanctions is generally considered to be the maintenance of our social order. Packer (1968) contended that the two major goals of criminal sanctions are to inflict suffering on the wrongdoers and the prevention of crime.

Dawson (1969) saw the major purpose of the criminal justice system as the identification in a legally acceptable manner of those persons who should be subjected to control and treatment in the correctional process. According to Dawson, if the correction system does not properly perform its task, the entire criminal justice system suffers. An inefficient or unfair correctional process can nullify the courts, prosecutors, and police alike. Conversely, the manner in which the other agencies involved perform their tasks has an important impact on the success of the process; thus, a person who has been unfairly dealt with prior to conviction is a poor subject for rehabilitation.

The four popular goals of criminal sanctions are retribution, deterrence, incapacitation, and rehabilitation. From the 1940s to the 1980s, rehabilitation was considered by most as the primary goal of our system. Since the 1980s, retribution has received popular support. Each of these four commonly accepted goals is discussed in this chapter.

Justification of Punishment

The problem of punishment causes constant, anguished reassessment, not only because we keep speculating on what the effective consequences of crime should be, but also because there is a confusion of the ends and means. We are still far from the answer to the ultimate questions (Schafer, 1969): What is the right punishment? On what grounds do we punish others?

Retribution

Retribution generally means "getting even." Retribution is based on the ideology that the criminal is an enemy of society and deserves severe punishment for willfully breaking its rules. Retribution is often mistaken as revenge. There are, however, important differences between the two. Both retribution and revenge are primarily concerned with punishing the offender, and neither is overly concerned with the impact of the punishment on the offender's future behavior or behavior of others. Unlike revenge, however, retribution attempts to match the severity of the punishment to the seriousness of the crime. Revenge acts on passion, whereas retribution follows specific rules regarding the types and amounts of punishment that may be inflicted. The biblical response of an "eye for an eye " is a retributive response to punishment. While the eye-for-eye concept is often cited as an excuse to use harsh punishment, it is less harsh than revenge-based punishment, which does not rule out punishment by "two eyes for an eye."

Sir James Stephen, an English judge, expressed the retributive view by stating that "the punishment of criminals was simply a desirable expression of the hatred and fear aroused in the community by criminal acts" (as reported by Packer, 1968, p. 18). This line of reasoning conveys the message that punishment is justifiable because it provides an orderly outlet for emotions that if denied may express themselves in socially less-acceptable ways. Another justification under the retribution ideology is that only through suffering punishment can the criminal expiate his or her sin. In one manner, retribution treats all crimes as if they were financial transactions. You got something or did something; therefore, you must give equivalent value (suffering).

Retribution is also referred to as "just desserts." The just desserts movement reflects the retribution viewpoint and provides a justifiable rationale for support of the death penalty. This viewpoint has its roots in a societal need for retribution. It can be traced back to the individual need for retaliation and vengeance. The transfer of the vengeance motive from the individual to the state has been justified based on theories involving theological, aesthetic, and expiatory views. According to the theological view, retaliation fulfills the religious need to punish the sinner. Under the aesthetic view, punishment helps reestablish a sense of harmony through requital and thus solves the social discord created by the crime. The expiatory view is that guilt must be washed away (cleansed) through suffering. There is even a utilitarian view that punishment is the means of achieving beneficial and social consequences through the application of a specific form and degree of punishment deemed most appropriate to the particular offender after careful, individualized study of the offender (Johnson, 1974).

Deterrence

Deterrence is a punishment viewpoint that focuses on future outcomes rather than past misconduct. It is also based on the theory that creating a fear of future punishments will deter crime. It is based on the belief that punishments have a deterrent effect. There is substantial debate regarding the validity of this concept. Specific deterrence is specifically aimed at the offender, whereas general deterrence works on others who might consider similar acts. According to this viewpoint, the fear of future suffering motivates individuals to avoid involvement in criminal misconduct. This concept assumes that the criminal is a rational being who will weight the consequences of his or her criminal actions before deciding to commit them.

One of the problems with deterrence is determining the appropriate magnitude and nature of punishment to be imposed to deter future criminal misconduct. For example, an individual who commits a serious crime and then feels badly about the act may need only slight punishment to achieve deterrent effects, whereas a professional shoplifter may need severe fear-producing punishments to prevent future shoplifting.

Often, increases in crime rates and high rates of recidivism are used to cast doubt that the deterrence approach is effective. Recidivism may cast some doubt on the efficacy of specific deterrence, but it says nothing about the effect of general deterrence. In addition, unless we know what the crime rate or rates of recidivism would be if we did not attempt to deter criminal misconduct, the assertions are unfounded. Are we certain that the rates would not be higher had we not attempted to deter criminals?

Incapacitation

At least while the prisoner is in confinement, the prisoner is unlikely to commit crimes on innocent persons outside prison. To this extent, confinement clearly helps reduce criminal behavior except for crimes committed in prison. Under this viewpoint, there is no hope for the individual as far as rehabilitation is concerned; therefore, the only solution is to incapacitate the offender.

Wolfgang's famous study of crime in Philadelphia indicated that while chronic offenders constituted only 23 percent of the offenders in the study, they committed over 61 percent of all the violent crimes (Zawitz, 1983). Accordingly, the supporters of the incapacitation viewpoint contend that incapacitating the 23 percent would have prevented 61 percent of the future violent crimes. This approach has often been labeled the "nothing-else-works" approach to corrections. According to this viewpoint, we should make maximum effective use of the scarce prison cells to protect society from the depredations of such dangerous and repetitive offenders. This approach is present in the "three strikes and you're out" statute of California.

There are two variations in the incapacitative viewpoint. *Collective incapacitation* refers to sanctions imposed on offenders without regard to their personal characteristics, such as all violent offenders. *Selective incapacitation* refers to incapacitation of certain groups of individuals who have been identified as high-risk offenders, such as robbers with a history of drug use. Under selective incapacitation, offenders with certain characteristics or history would receive longer prison terms than others convicted of the same crime. The purpose of incapacitation is to prevent future crimes, and the moral concerns associated with retribution are not as important as the reduction of future victimization (Durham, 1994). As Packer (1968) stated: "Incapacitation is a mode of punishment that uses the fact that a person has committed a crime as a basis for predicting that he will commit future crimes" (p. 63). Packer also stated that the logic of the incapacitative position is that until the offender stops being a danger, we will continue to restrain the offender. Accordingly, he contended that, pushed to its logical conclusion, offenses that are regarded as relatively trivial may be punished by imprisonment for life.

Rehabilitation

The rehabilitation approach is that punishment should be directed toward correcting the offender. This approach is also considered the "treatment" approach. This approach considers the criminal misconduct as a manifestation of a pathology that can be handled by some form of therapeutic activity. While this viewpoint may consider the offender as "sick," it is not the same as the medical approach. Under the rehabilitation viewpoint, we need to teach offenders to recognize the undesirability of their criminal behavior and to make significant efforts to rid themselves of that behavior.

The main difference between the rehabilitation approach and the retribution approach is that under the rehabilitation approach the offenders are assigned to programs designed to prepare them for readjustment or reintegration into the community, whereas the latter approach is more concerned with the punishment aspects of the sentence. Packer (1968) saw two major objections to making rehabilitation the primary justification for punishment. First, we do not know how to rehabilitate offenders. Second, we know little about who is likely to commit crimes and less about what makes them apt to do so. As long as we are ignorant in these matters, Packer (1968, p. 53) contended that punishment in the name of rehabilitation is gratuitous cruelty.

Purposes of Punishment

English Statement of Purposes

The United States is not the only country that has had problems determining the proper purposes of punishment. It appears that most other countries have the same problem. An examination of the English Statement of Purposes indicates that the English have similar problems. The English Prison Service has approximately 43,000 prisoners confined. The service declares that it "serves the public by keeping in custody those committed by the courts," and that its duty is to "look after them with humanity and help them lead law-abiding and useful lives in custody and after release." The purposes are divided into a series of goals:

- To keep prisoners in custody
- To maintain order, control, discipline, and a safe environment
- To provide decent conditions for prisoners and meet their needs, including health care
- To provide positive regimes that help prisoners address their offending behavior
- To allow prisoners as full and responsible a life as possible
- To help prisoners prepare for their return to the community [as reported by Masters and Roberson, 1985, p. 73]

Guiding Principles

Certain principles are used in guiding the decision regarding the proper disposition of a person convicted of criminal behavior. The principles are simple, yet subject to interpretation according to the philosophy of the individuals involved (Morris and Rothman, 1995). The generally accepted principles include the following:

Parsimony. The least-restrictive sanction necessary to achieve the defined purposes should be imposed. The debate regarding this principle centers on the purpose of criminal sanctions.

Dangerousness. This principle examines whether the likelihood of future criminality should be considered. The controversy on this point is whether we should use predictions of future misconduct as a basis for present criminal sanctions. There are numerous studies that indicated that predictions of dangerousness are unreliable. The studies indicated that we tend to overpredict future dangerousness in individuals. There are also the philosophical and due process concerns of punishing a person for conduct not yet committed (Morris, 1974).

Just desserts. Any sanction imposed should not be greater than that which is deserved by the last crime, or series of crimes, for which the defendant is being sentenced (Jeffery, 1973).

Social Purposes of Punishment

C. Ray Jeffery (1973), a noted criminologist, contended that the more glaring defect in most analyses of punishments is that the analyses view punishments always in the context of what it means to the individual offender and never in terms of what it means to society. The purpose of punishment, according to Jeffery, should be to establish social disapproval of the act. To him, the use of punishment by society is not as important in terms of whether it reforms the individual as in terms of what it does for society. He also contended that punishment serves an important social function in that it creates social solidarity and reenforces social norms.

Review Questions

1. Explain how the concept of blood feuds developed.
2. Discuss the functions and purpose of the Holy Inquisition.
3. Compare and contrast the three political ideologies regarding punishment.
4. Compare and contrast the rehabilitation and deterrence approaches to punishment.
5. How did the concept of punishment change during the Middle Ages?
6. Explain the various rationales for criminal sanctions.
7. List four popular goals of criminal sanctions.
8. Differentiate between specific and general deterrence.
9. Explain the differences between incapacitation and rehabilitation.

References

Dawson, R. O. (1969). *Sentencing: The decision as to type, length, and conditions of sentence.* Boston: Little, Brown.

Durham, A. M., III. (1994). *Crisis and reform: Current issues in American punishment.* Boston: Little, Brown.

Jeffery, C. R. (1973). The historical development of criminology. In H. Mannheim (ed.), *Pioneers in criminology* (2nd ed., p. 487). Montclair, NJ: Patterson Smith.

Johnson, E. H. (1974). Crime, correction, and society. Homewood, IL: Dorsey Press.

Kocourek, A., and Wigmore, J. (1915). *Evolution of law* (Vol. 2). Boston: Little, Brown.

Morris, N. (1974). *The future of imprisonment.* Chicago: University of Chicago Press.

Morris, N., and Rothman, D. J. (1995). As reported. In N. Morris and D. J. Rothman (eds.), *The Oxford history of the prison* (p. xi). New York: Oxford University Press.

Packer, H. L. (1968). *The limits of criminal sanction.* Stanford, CA: Stanford University Press.

Schafer, S. (1969). *Theories in criminology.* New York: Random House.

Swain, J. (1931). *The pleasures of the torture chamber.* New York: Dorset Press.

Zawitz, M. W., ed. (1983). *Report to the nation on crime and justice.* Washington, DC: Bureau of Justice Statistics, U.S. Government Printing Office.

Chapter 13

Victimology and Violence

Introduction

Society has long debated the role of a victim in violent crimes. Often, this debate has become a victim-blaming exercise. This chapter introduces victimology concepts. One question that should be considered is why a criminal chooses to commit a violent crime against one person rather than another person—why the rapist chooses one victim and not another. This question, however, is not intended to excuse the criminal from the consequences of his or her violent crime.

A complete and accurate understanding of the concepts inherent in victimology can only be attained by a review of the development of law, its history, philosophy, and development. Modern criminal law is the result of a long evolution of laws attempting to deal with deviant behavior in society (Wallace, 1997).

Early civilizations accorded victims many more rights than we did until the birth of the victims' rights movement in the United States. Early laws were known as primitive law, which was a system of rules in preliterate societies. These rules or regulations represent the foundation on which the modern legal system is built. Primitive laws typically contained three characteristics: (1) Acts that injured others were considered private wrongs; (2) the injured party was entitled to take action against the wrongdoer; and (3) this action usually amounted to in-kind retaliation. These types of laws encouraged blood feuds and revenge as the preferred method of making the victim whole.

As society matured, we learned the art of reading and writing. One result of this evolution was the development of written codes of conduct. The Code of Ur-Nammu dates back to the twenty-first century BC. Many of these codes treated certain wrongs, such as theft or assault, as private wrongs, with the injured party the victim rather than the state (Maine, 1905).

Code of Hammurabi

The Code of Hammurabi is considered one of the first known attempts to establish a written code of conduct. King Hammurabi ruled Babylon at approximately 2000 BC. He was the sixth king of the First Dynasty of Babylonia and ruled for about 55 years. Babylon, during that period of time, was a commercial center for most of the known and civilized world. Since its fortune was in trade and other business ventures, the Code of Hammurabi provided a basis for order and certainty. The code established rules regarding theft, sexual relationships, and interpersonal violence. It was intended to replace blood feuds with a system sanctioned by the state (Schafer, 1968).

The Code of Hammurabi was divided into five sections:

- A penal or code of laws
- A manual of instruction for judges, police officers, and witnesses
- A handbook of rights and duties of husbands, wives, and children
- A set of regulations establishing wages and prices
- A code of ethics for merchants, doctors, and officials (Masters and Roberson, 1985)

The code established certain obligations and objectives for the citizens of Babylon to follow. These included the following:

- An assertion of the power of the state. This was the beginning of state-administrated punishment. The blood feuds that had previously occurred between private citizens were barred under the code.
- Protection of the weaker from the stronger. Widows were to be protected from those who might exploit them, elder parents were protected from sons who would disown them, and lesser officials were protected from higher ones.
- Restoration of equity between the offender and the victim. The victim was to be made as whole as possible, and in turn, he or she forgave vengeance against the offender.

Of noteworthy importance in the code was its concern for the rights of victims (Gordon, 1957). In reality, this code may have been the first "victims' rights statute" in history. However, as will be seen, we as a society began to neglect victims in our rush to punish the offender, with the result that concern with victims' rights would not resurface until the present century (Mueller and Cooper, 1974).

Other Early Codes and Laws

Another important milestone in the development of American law was early Roman law. Roman law was derived from the Twelve Tables, written about 450 BC.

These laws existed for centuries as unwritten law. However, they applied only to the ruling patrician class of citizens. A protest by the plebeian class, the workers and artisans of Rome, caused commerce to come to a standstill. These workers wanted the law to apply to all citizens of Rome (Mueller, 1955). As a result, the laws were inscribed on 12 wooden tablets and prominently displayed in the forum for all to see and follow. These tables were a collection of basic rules relating to conduct of the family, religion, and economic life.

Early Roman legions conquered England in the middle of the first century. Roman law, customs, and language were forced on the English people during the next three centuries of Roman rule.

Emperor Justinian I codified the Roman laws into a set of writings. The Justinian Code, as these writings became known, distinguished between two major types of laws—public laws and private laws. Public laws dealt with the organization and administration of the republic. Private laws addressed issues such as contracts; possession and other property rights; the legal status of various persons, such as slaves, husbands, wives, and so on; and injuries to citizens. It contained elements of both our civil and criminal laws and influenced Western legal theory into the Middle Ages.

Prior to the Norman Conquest of 1066, the legal system in England was decentralized. There was little written law except for those regarding crimes against society. As a society, we had moved away from the teaching of the Code of Hammurabi, and crimes during this period were again viewed as personal wrongs. Compensation was paid to the victim or the victim's family for the offense. If the perpetrator failed to make payments, the victim's family could seek revenge, resulting in a blood feud. For the most part, during this period criminal law was designed to provide equity to what was considered a private dispute.

The Norman Conquest under William the Conqueror established royal administrators who rode circuit to render justice. These royal judges would use local custom and rules of conduct as a guide in rendering their judgment. This system, known as *stare decisis* (Latin for the phrase "to stand by the decided law"), would have far-reaching effects on modern American criminal law.

The next major development in the history of law was the acknowledgment of the existence of common law. Early English common law forms the basis for much of our present-day legal system. Common law is a traditional body of unwritten legal precedents created by court decisions during the Middle Ages in England. During this period of time, when cases were heard, judges would start their deliberations from past decisions that were as closely related as possible to the case under consideration. In the eleventh century, King Edward the Confessor proclaimed that common law was the law of the land. Court decisions were finally recorded

and made available to lawyers, who could then use them to plead their cases. Th
concept is one of the most important aspects of today's modern American law.

Victimization

Victimology is a relatively new concept in the United States. It is a study that
resides in a number of different academic disciplines across the nation. Some courses
that focus on victimology are offered in sociology, social work, criminology, and
even psychology. At the same time that academic institutions are awakening to
the necessity of offering courses in victimology, the victims' movement continues
to gain strength and momentum across America. While there is some interaction
between these two forces, there is still a great deal that they can learn from each
other (Wallace and Roberson 2010).

Victimology is the study of the victim, the offender, and society. This definition can encompass both the research or scientific aspects of the discipline and the
practical aspects of providing services to victims of crime. This combined definition
allows for a wide-ranging examination of various issues affecting victims of crime.
From its inception in the 1940s to the present, victimology has been an interdisciplinary approach to violence and its effect on victims.

Mendelsohn's Theory of Victimization

Benjamin Mendelsohn (1963) was a practicing attorney. In the course of prepar-
ing a case for trial, he would conduct in-depth interviews of victims, witnesses,
and bystanders. He would use a questionnaire that was couched in simple language and contained more than 300 questions concerning the branches of criminology and associated sciences. The questionnaire was given to the accused and
all others who had knowledge of the crime. Based on these studies, Mendelsohn
came to the conclusion that there was usually a strong interpersonal relationship between the offender and the victim. In an effort to further clarify these
relationships, he developed a typology of victims and their contribution to the
criminal act (Schafer, 1968). This classification ranged from the completely
innocent victim to the imaginary victim. Mendelsohn classified victims into six
distinct categories:

1. The completely innocent victim: This victim may be a child or completely
   unconscious person.
2. The victim with minor guilt: This victim might be a woman who induces a
   miscarriage and dies as a result.
3. The victim who is as guilty as the offender: Those who assist others in committing crimes fall within this classification.

4. The victim more guilty than the offender: These are persons who provoke others to commit a crime.
5. The most guilty victim: For this designation, the perpetrator (victim) acts aggressively and is killed by another person who is acting in self-defense.
6. The imaginary victim: This is a person suffering from a mental disorder, such as paranoia, who believes that he or she is a victim.

Many scholars credit Mendelsohn with coining the term *victimology*, and still others consider him the "father of victimology." His typology was one of the first attempts to focus on victims of crimes rather than simply examining the perpetrator. However, Mendelsohn was only one of two early scholars who explored the relationship between victims and offenders. The other noted early researcher in victimology was Hans von Hentig.

Von Hentig's Theory of Victimization

In an early classical text, *The Criminal and His Victim*, von Hentig (1979/1984) explored the relationship between the "doer" or criminal and the "sufferer" or victim. Von Hentig also established a typology of victims. This classification was based on psychological, social, and biological factors. Von Hentig established three classes of victims: the general classes of victims, the psychological types of victims, and the activating sufferer victims. His classification identified victims by examining various risk factors. The typology includes the items discussed next.

The General Classes of Victims

- The young: They are weak and the most likely to be a victim of an attack. Youth is the most dangerous period of life.
- The female: The female sex is another form of weakness recognized by the law since numerous rules of law embody the legal fiction of a weaker (female) and stronger (male) sex.
- The old: The elder generation holds most positions of accumulated wealth and wealth-giving power and, at the same time, is physically weak and mentally feeble.
- The mentally defective: The feebleminded, the insane, the drug addict, and the alcoholic form another large class of victims.
- Immigrants, minorities, and dull normals: Immigration means more than a change in country. It causes a temporary feeling of helplessness in vital human relations. The inexperienced, poor, and sometimes dull immigrant, minority, or other is easy prey to all kinds of swindlers.

Psychological Types of Victims

- The depressed: These victims may suffer from a disturbance of the instinct of self-preservation. Without such an instinct, the individual may be easily overwhelmed or surprised by dangers or enemies.
- The acquisitive: This type of person makes an excellent victim. The excessive desire for gain eclipses intelligence, business experience, and inner impediments.
- The wanton: Often, a sensual or wanton disposition requires other concurrent factors to become activated. Loneliness, alcohol, and certain critical phases are "process accelerators" of this type of victim.
- The lonesome and the heartbroken: Loneliness causes critical mental facilities to be weakened. These individuals become easy prey for criminals. The heartbroken victims are dazed by their loss and therefore become easy targets for a variety of "death rackets" that might, for example, charge a widow an outlandish fee for a picture of her late husband to be included in his biography.
- The tormentor: This victim becomes a perpetrator. This is the psychotic husband/father who may abuse the wife and children for a number of years until one of the children grows up and, under extreme provocation, kills him.
- The blocked, exempted, and fighting: The blocked victim is so enmeshed in a losing situation that defensive moves become impossible. This is a self-imposed form of helplessness and an ideal condition for a victim from the point of view of the criminal.

The Activating Sufferers

- The activating sufferers: This classification occurs when the victim is transformed into a perpetrator. A number of factors operate as activators on the victim, such as certain predispositions, like age, alcohol, and loss of self-confidence.

Von Hentig theorized that a large percentage of victims, because of their acts or behavior, were responsible for their victimization. This concept has since been repudiated by modern studies, which have more closely examined and defined the relationship between the victim and the offender.

Review Questions

1. What historical event had the most impact on victims' rights? Did it involve a change in attitudes? Justify your answer.
2. Can you draft a more complete definition of victimology? Why is it more comprehensive than the one contained in the text?
3. What role does the victim play in being selected as the victim? Justify your response.

References

Gordon, T. F. (1957). *Hammurabi's Code: Quaint or forward looking.* New York: Rinehart.

Maine, H. S. (1905). *Ancient law* (10th ed.). London: Murray.

Masters, R., and Roberson, C. (1985). *Inside criminology.* Englewood Cliffs, NJ: Prentice Hall.

Mendelsohn, B. (1963, June). The origin and doctrine of victimology. *Excerpta Criminologica,* 3, 239–244.

Mueller, G. O., and Cooper, H. H. A. (1974). Society and the victim: Alternative responses. In I. Drapkin and E. Viano (eds.), *Victimology: A new focus* (Vol. 2, pp. 85–102). Lexington, MA: Heath.

Mueller, O. W. (1955). Tort, crime and the primitive. *Journal of Criminal Law, Criminology, and Police Science,* 43, 303.

Schafer, S. (1968). *The victim and his criminal.* New York: Random House.

von Hentig, H. (1984). *The criminal and his victim.* New Haven, CT: Yale University Press. (Original published 1979, Schocken Books, New York.)

Wallace, H. (1997). *History of law: The evolution of victims' rights.* National Victim Assistance Academy Text. Washington, DC: Office for Victims of Crime.

Wallace, H., and Roberson, C. (2010). *Victimology: Legal, psychological, and social perspectives* (4th ed.). Boston: Pearson.

Appendix: Bibliography of Youth Violence Studies

Adams, M. S. (1996). Teacher disapproval, delinquent peers, and self-reported delinquency: a longitudinal test of labeling theory. *Urban Review* 28:199–211.

Adams, M. S. (1997). Labeling and differential association: Towards a general social learning theory of crime and deviance. *American Journal of Criminal Justice* 20:146–164.

Adams, M. S., and Evans, T. D. (1996). Teacher disapproval, delinquent peers, and self-reported delinquency: A longitudinal test of labeling theory. *Urban Review* 28:199–211.

Adams, M. S., Johnson, J. D., and Evans, T. D. (1998). Racial differences in informal labeling effects. *Deviant Behavior* 19:157–171.

Ageton, S. S. (1983a). The changing patterns of female delinquency: 1976–1980. *Criminology* 21(4):555–584.

Ageton, S. S. (1983b). *Sexual assault among adolescents.* Lexington, MA: Lexington Books, and Washington, DC: Health and Company.

Agnew, R. (1990). Adolescent resources and delinquency. *Criminology* 28(4):535–556.

Agnew, R. (1991a). The interactive effects of peer variables on delinquency. *Criminology* 29:47–72.

Agnew, R. (1991b). A longitudinal test of social control theory and delinquency. *Journal of Research in Crime and Delinquency* 28(2):126–156.

Agnew, R. (1994). The techniques of neutralization and violence. *Criminology* 32:555–580.

Agnew, R. (1995). Determinism, indeterminism, and crime: An empirical exploration. *Criminology* 33:83–109.

Bartusch, D. J., and Matsueda, R. L. (1996). Gender, reflected appraisals, and labeling: A cross-group test of an interactionist theory of delinquency. *Social Forces* 75:145–176.

Blackwell, B. S., and Reed, M. D. (2003). Power-control as a between- and within-family model: Reconsidering the unit of analysis. *Journal of Youth and Adolescence* 32:385–399.

Bushway, S. D. (1998). The impact of an arrest on the job stability of young white American men. *Journal of Research in Crime and Delinquency* 34:454–479.

Calvert, W. J. (2002). *Neighborhood disorder, individual, family, and peer behavior protective factors, and the risk of adolescent delinquent behavior.* St. Louis: University of Missouri.

Canter, R. J. (1982a). Family correlates of male and female delinquency. *Criminology* 20(2):149–168.

Canter, R. J. (1982b). Sex differences in self-reported delinquency. *Criminology* 20:373–394.

Canter, R. J., and Ageton, S. S. (1984). The epidemiology of adolescent sex role attitudes. *Journal of Sex Roles* 2(718).

Chien, C. Y. (1994). *Developmental adaptation of social learning theory.* Department of Sociology, University of Colorado, Boulder, CO.

Covey, H. C., Menard, S., and Franzese, R. J. (1992). *Juvenile gangs.* Springfield, IL: Thomas.

Covey, H. C., Menard, S., and Franzese, R. J. (1997). *Juvenile gangs* (2nd ed.). Springfield, IL: Thomas.

Craven, D. (1987). *Criminal careers: The role of the adolescent peer group.* Department of Sociology, University of Colorado, Boulder, CO.

Demuth, S. (2004). Understanding the delinquency and social relationships of loners. *Youth and Society* 35:366–392.

Duncan, T. E., Alpert, A., and Duncan, S. C. (1998). Multilevel covariance structure analysis of sibling antisocial behavior. *Structural Equation Modeling* 5:211–228.

Duncan, S. C., Duncan, T. E., and Strucker, L. A. (2000). Risk and protective factors influencing adolescent problem behavior: A multivariate latent growth curve analysis. *Annals of Behavioral Medicine* 22:103–109.

Duncan, S. C., Duncan, T. E., and Strycker, L. A. (2001). Qualitative and quantitative shifts in adolescent problem behavior development: A cohort-sequential multivariate latent growth modeling approach. *Journal of Psychopathology and Behavioral Assessment* 23:43–50.

Dunford, F. W., and Elliott, D. S. (1984). Identifying career offenders with self-reported data. *Journal of Research in Crime and Delinquency* 21(1):57–86.

Elliott, D. S. (1985). The assumption that theories can be combined with increased explanatory power: Theoretical integrations. In R. F. Meier (ed.), *Theoretical methods in criminology.* Beverly Hills, CA: Sage, 31–44.

Elliott, D. S. (1987). Self-reported driving while under the influence of alcohol/drugs and the risk of alcohol/drug-related accidents. *Alcohol, Drugs, and Driving* 3(3–4):31–44.

Elliott, D. S. (1994a). Longitudinal research in criminology: Promise and practice. In E. G. M. Weitekamp and J. H. Kerner (eds.), *Cross national longitudinal research on human development and criminal behavior* (pp. 189–201). Dordrecht, the Netherlands: Kluwer.

Elliott, D. S. (1994b). An overview of youth violence. *Congressional Program: Children and Violence* 9(2):15–20. Reprinted, New Haven, CT: Center for the Study of Youth Policy (1995); adapted for Youth violence: An overview. In A. Nakaya (ed.), *Juvenile crime: Opposing viewpoints* (pp. 83–89). San Diego, CA: Greenhaven Press, 1996.

Elliott, D. S. (1994c). Serious violent offenders: Onset, developmental course, and termination. *Criminology* 32:1–22. Reprinted (in whole or in part) in the following: Conger, J. J., and Talambus, N. L., eds. (1997). *Adolescence and youth: Psychological development in a changing world.* New York: Harpers; Greenberg, D., ed. (1996). *Criminal careers* (Vol. 2). Hampshire, England: Dartmouth. Dobrin, A., Loftin, C., McDowall, D., and Wiersema, B., eds. (1994). *The statistical handbook of violence in America.* Phoenix, AZ: Oryn, National Institute of Justice, Technical Assistance and Support Program, 1994.

Elliott, D. S. (1998). Life-threatening violence is primarily a crime problem. *University of Colorado Law Review* 69:1081–1098.

Elliott, D. S., and Ageton, S. S. (1980). Reconciling race and class differences in self-reported and official estimates of delinquency. *American Sociological Review* 45(1):95–110.

Elliott, D. S., Ageton, S. S., and Canter, R. J. (1979). An integrated theoretical perspective on delinquent behavior. *Journal of Research in Crime and Delinquency* 16(1):3–27.

Elliott, D. S., and Huizinga, D. (1983). Social class and delinquent behavior in a national youth panel: 1976–1980. *Criminology* 21(2):149–177.

Elliott, D. S., and Huizinga, D. (1989). Improving self-reported measures of delinquency. In M. W. Klein (ed.), *Cross-national research in self-reported crime and delinquency.* Dordrecht, the Netherlands: Kluwer, 136–149.

Elliott, D. S., Huizinga, D., and Ageton, S. S. (1985). *Explaining delinquency and drug use.* Beverly Hills, CA: Sage.

Elliott, D. S., Huizinga, D., and Dunford, F. W. (1987). The identification and prediction of career offenders utilizing self-reported and official data. In J. Burchard and S. Burchard (eds.), *Primary prevention of psychopathology* (pp. 90–121). Beverly Hills, CA: Sage.

Elliott, D. S., Huizinga, D., and Menard, S. (1989). *Multiple problem youth: Delinquency, drugs and mental health problems.* New York: Springer.

Elliott, D. S., Huizinga, D., and Morse, B. J. (1986). Self-reported violent offending: A descriptive analysis of juvenile offenders and their offending careers. *Journal of Interpersonal Violence* 1(4):472–514.

Elliott, D. S., Huizinga, D., and Morse, B. J. (1987). A career analysis of serious violent offenders. In M. Nielson (ed.), *Violent juvenile crime: What do we know about it and what can we do about it?* (pp. 23–34). Minneapolis, MN: Hubert H. Humphrey Institute of Public Affairs, University of Minnesota.

Elliott, D. S., and Menard, S. (1996). Delinquent friends and delinquent behavior: Temporal and developmental patterns. In D. Hawkins (ed.), *Delinquency and crime: Current theories* (pp. 28–67). Cambridge, UK: Cambridge University Press.

Elliott, D. S., and Morse, B. J. (1987). Drug use, delinquency and sexual activity. In C. Jones and E. McAnarney (eds.), *Drug abuse and adolescent sexual activity, pregnancy and parenthood.* National Institute on Drug Abuse. Washington, DC: U.S. Government Printing Office, 321–340.

Elliott, D. S., and Morse, B. J. (1989). Delinquency and drug use as risk factors in teenage sexual activity. *Youth and Society* 21(1):32–60.

Esbensen, F. (1983). Measurement error and self-reported delinquency: An examination of interviewer bias. In G. P. Waldo (ed.), *Measurement issues in criminal justice.* Beverly Hills, CA: Sage, 149–164.

Esbensen, F., and Elliott, D. S. (1994). Continuity and discontinuity in illicit drug use. *Journal of Social Issues* 24:75–97.

Esbensen, F., and Menard, S. (1991). Interviewer-related measurement error in attitudinal research: A non-experimental study. *Quality and Quantity* 25:151–165.

Esbensen, F.-A. (1982). *Measurement error in survey research: An examination of interviewer effects upon adolescent respondents in a national youth survey.* Department of Sociology, University of Colorado, Boulder, CO.

Fagan, A. (2003). The short- and long-term effects of adolescent violent victimization experienced within the family and community. *Violence and Victims* 18:445–458.

Finkel, S. E. (1995). *Causal analysis with panel data.* Thousand Oaks, CA: Sage.

Gelb, K. A. (1993). *The antecedents of depression: Individual and social contextual factors.* Department of Sociology, University of Colorado, Boulder, CO.

Gooden, M. P. (1998). *When juvenile delinquency enhances the self-concept: The role of race and academic performance.* Columbus, OH: The Ohio State University.

Gunnison, E. K. (2002). *Understanding female desistance from crime: Exploring theoretical and empirical relationships.* Cincinnati, OH: University of Cincinnati.

Haas, S. M. (2000). *High school aggression: A social learning analysis.* Cincinnati, OH: University of Cincinnati.

Hannon, L., DeFronzo, J., and Prochnow, J. (2001). Moral commitment and the effects of social influences on violent delinquency. *Violence and Victims* 16:427–439.

Hartjen, C. A., and Kethineni, S. (1993). Culture, gender, and delinquency: a study of youths in the United States and India. *Women and Criminal Justice* 5:27–69.

Hayes, H. D. (1997). Using integrated theory to explain the movement into juvenile delinquency. *Deviant Behavior* 18:161–184.

Heimer, K. (1996). Gender, interaction, and delinquency: testing a theory of differential social control. *Social Psychology Quarterly* 59:39–61.

Heimer, K. (1997). Socioeconomic status, subcultural definitions, and violent delinquency. *Social Forces* 75:799–833.

Heimer, K., and De Coster, S. (1999). The gendering of violent delinquency. *Criminology* 37:275–312.

Hilarski, M. C. (2002). *A secondary analysis of the relationship between victimization and conduct disorder behavior and stability of conduct disorder behavior in a national probability sample.* Buffalo: State University of New York at Buffalo.

Hoffman, J. P. (1994). Investigating the age effects of family structure on adolescent marijuana use. *Journal of Youth and Adolescence* 23:215–235.

Hoffman, J. P. (1995). The effects of family structure and family relations on adolescent marijuana use. *International Journal of the Addictions* 30:1207–1241.

Huizinga, D. (1991). Assessing violent behavior with self-reports. In J. Milner (ed.), *Neuropsychology of aggression.* Dordrecht, the Netherlands: Kluwer Academic, 41–69.

Huizinga, D., and Elliott, D. S. (1986). Reassessing the reliability and validity of self-report delinquency measures. *Journal of Quantitative Criminology* 2(4):293–328.

Huizinga, D., and Elliott, D. S. (1997). Juvenile offenders: Prevalence offenders incidence, and arrest rates by race. *Crime and Delinquency* 33(2):206–223.

Huizinga, D., Esbensen, F., and Weiher, A. (1994). Examining developmental trajectories in delinquency using accelerated longitudinal research designs. In E. G. M. Weitekamp and H. J. Kerner (eds.), *Cross-national longitudinal research on human development and criminal behavior* (pp. 203–216). Dordrecht, the Netherlands: Kluwer.

Huizinga, D., Menard, S., and Elliott, D. S. (1989). Delinquency and drug use: Temporal and developmental patterns. *Justice Quarterly* 6:419–455.

Jang, S. J. (1999). Age-varying effects of family, school, and peers on delinquency: A multilevel modeling test of interactional theory. *Criminology* 37:643–685.

Johnson, B. D., and Wish, E. D. (1991). Concentration of delinquent offending: serious drug involvement and high delinquency rates. *Journal of Drug Issues* 21:205–229.

Johnson, B. R., Jang, S. J., Li, S. D., and Larson, D. (2000). The "invisible institution" and Black youth crime: The church as an agency of local social control. *Journal of Youth and Adolescence* 29:479–498.

Koita, K., and Triplett, R. A. (1998). An examination of gender and race effects on the parental appraisal process: A reanalysis of Matsueda's model of the self. *Criminal Justice and Behavior* 25:382–400.

Lackey, C. (2003). Violent family heritage, the transition to adulthood, and later partner violence. *Journal of Family Issues* 24:74–98.

Lauritsen, J. L. (1993). Sibling resemblance in juvenile delinquency: Findings from the National Youth Survey. *Criminology* 31:387–409.

Lauritsen, J. L. (1994). Explaining race and gender differences in adolescent sexual behavior. *Social Forces* 72:859–883.

Lauritsen, J. L., Laub, J. H., and Sampson, R. J. (1992). Conventional and delinquent activities and implications for the prevention of violent victimization among adolescents. *Violence and Victims* 7(2):91–108.

Lauritsen, J. L., and Quinet, K. F. D. (1995). Repeat victimization among adolescents and young adults. *Journal of Quantitative Criminology* 11:143–166.

Lauritsen, J. L., Sampson, R. J., and Laub, J. H. (1991). The link between offending and victimization among adolescents. *Criminology* 29(2):265–292.

Liu, X. (2000). The conditional effect of peer groups on the relationship between parental labeling and youth delinquency. *Sociological Perspectives* 43:499–514.

Marciniak, L. M. (1998). Adolescent attitudes toward victim precipitation of rape. *Violence and Victims* 13:287–300.

Matsueda, R. L. (1992). Reflected appraisals, parental labeling, and delinquency: Specifying a symbolic interactionist theory. *American Journal of Sociology* 97:1577–1611.

Matsueda, R. L., and Anderson, K. (1998). The dynamics of delinquent peers and delinquent behavior. *Criminology* 36:269–306.

Mazerolle, P. (1998). Gender, strain, and delinquency: An empirical examination. *Justice Quarterly* 15:65–91.

McDermott, S., and Nagin, D. S. (2001). Same or different? Comparing offender groups and covariates over time. *Sociological Methods and Research* 29:282–318.

McMorris, B. J. (1998). Using latent structure analysis to examine the distribution of problem behavior: Discrete types vs. propensity explanations of criminality. Lincoln: University of Nebraska, Lincoln.

Mears, D. P., Ploeger, M., and Warr, M. (1998). Explaining the gender gap in delinquency: peer influence and moral evaluations of behavior. *Journal of Research in Crime and Delinquency* 35:251–266.

Menard, S. (1987). Short-term trends in crime and delinquency: A comparison of UCR, NCS and self-report data. *Justice Quarterly* 4(3):455–474.

Menard, S. (1991). *Longitudinal research*. Thousand Oaks, CA: Sage.

Menard, S. (1992). Demographic and theoretical variables in the age-period-cohort analysis of illegal behavior. *Journal of Research in Crime and Delinquency* 29(2):178–199.

Menard, S. (1995a). *Applied logistic regression analysis*. Thousand Oaks, CA: Sage.

Menard, S. (1995b). A developmental test of Mertonian anomie theory. *Journal of Research in Crime and Delinquency* 32:136–174.

Menard, S. (1997). A developmental test of Cloward's anomie-opportunity theory. In N. Passas and R. Agnew (eds.), *The future of anomie theory*. Boston: Northeastern University Press, 14–27.

Menard, S. (2000a). Coefficients of determination for multiple logistic regression analysis. *The American Statistician* 54(1):17–24.

Menard, S. (2000b). The "normality" of repeat victimization from adolescence through early adulthood. *Justice Quarterly* 17(3):543–574.

Menard, S. (2002a). *Applied logistic regression analysis* (2nd ed.). Thousand Oaks, CA: Sage.

Menard, S. (2002b). *Longitudinal research* (2nd ed.). Thousand Oaks, CA: Sage.

Menard, S. (2002c). *Short- and long-term consequences of adolescent victimization*. Youth Violence Research Bulletin. Washington, DC: U.S. Department of Justice.

Menard, S., and Elliott, D. S. (1990a). Longitudinal and cross-sectional data collection and analysis in the study of crime and delinquency. *Justice Quarterly* 7:11–55.

Menard S., and Elliott, D. S. (1990b). Self reported offending, maturational reform, and the Easterlin hypothesis. *Journal of Quantitative Criminology* 6:237–267.

Menard, S., and Elliott, D. S. (1993). Data set comparability and short-term trends in crime and delinquency. *Journal of Criminal Justice* 21:433–445.

Menard, S., and Elliott, D. S. (1994). Delinquent bonding, moral beliefs, and illegal behavior: A three-wave panel model. *Justice Quarterly* 11:173–188.

Menard, S., Elliott, D. S., and Wofford, S. (1993). Social control theories in developmental perspective. *Studies in Crime and Crime Prevention* 2:69–87.

Menard, S., and Huizinga, D. (1989). Age, period, and cohort size effects on self-reported alcohol, marijuana, and polydrug use. *Social Science Research* 18:174–194.

Menard, S., and Huizinga, D. (1994). Changes in conventional attitudes and delinquent behavior in adolescence. *Youth and Society* 26:23–53.

Menard, S., and Mihalic, S. (2001). The tripartite conceptual framework in adolescence and adulthood: Evidence from a national sample. *Journal of Drug Issues* 31(4):905–938.

Menard, S., Mihalic, S., and Huizinga, D. (2001). Drugs and crime revisited. *Justice Quarterly* 18(2):269–299.

Mihalic, S., Wofford, S., and Elliott, D. S. (1997a). If violence is domestic, does it really count? *Journal of Family Violence* 12(3):293–311.

Mihalic, S., Wofford, S., and Elliott, D. S. (1997b). Short- and long-term consequences of adolescent work. *Youth and Society* 28(4):464–498.

Mihalic, S., Wofford, S., and Elliott, D. S. (1997c). A social learning theory model of marital violence. *Journal of Family Violence* 12(1):21–47.

Mihalic, S., Wofford, S., Elliott, D. S., and Menard, S. (1994). Continuities in marital violence. *Journal of Family Violence* 9:195–225.

Miller, D., and Miller, T. (1997). The relationship between marijuana use and socioeconomic status. *Addictive Behaviors* 22:479–489.

Miller, T. (1994). A test of alternative explanations for the stage-like progression of adolescent substance use in four national samples. *Addictive Behaviors* 19(3):287–293.

Miller, T. (1997). Statistical methods for describing temporal order in longitudinal research. *Journal of Clinical Epidemiology* 50:1055–1068.

Miller, T., and Volk, R. (1996). The relationship between weekly marijuana use and cocaine use: A discrete-time survival analysis. *Journal of Child and Adolescent Substance Abuse* 5(4):55–78.

Miyazaki, Y., and Raudenbush, S. (2000). Tests for linkage of multiple cohorts in an accelerated longitudinal design. *Psychological Methods* 5:44–63.

Morse, B. J. (1986). *Self-reported juvenile violent offenders: A descriptive analysis*. Department of Sociology, University of Colorado, Boulder, CO.

Morse, B. J. (1995). Beyond the conflict tactics scale: Assessing gender differences in partner violence. *Violence and Victims* 10(4):257–272.

Nagin, D. S., and Smith, D. A. (1990). Participation in and frequency of delinquent behavior: A test for structural differences. *Journal of Quantitative Criminology* 6(4):335–356.

Needle, R., Su, S., and Lavee, Y. (1990). A comparison of the empirical utility of three composite measures of adolescent overall drug involvement. *Addictive Behaviors* 14:429–441.

O'Neal, K. K. (2001). *Adolescent risk behaviors and developmental contextualism: A person-oriented approach*. Lubbock, TX: Texas Tech University.

Ousey, G. C., and Maume, M. O. (1997). The grass is always greener: explaining rural and urban differences in marijuana use. *Sociological Focus* 30:295–305.

Paternoster, R., and Brame, R. (1997). Multiple routes to delinquency: A test of developmental and general theories of crime. *Criminology* 35:49–84.

Paternoster, R., and Maxerolle, P. (1994). General strain theory and delinquency: A replication and extension. *Journal of Research in Crime and Delinquency* 31(3):235–263.

Piquero, A. R., MacIntosh, R., and Hickman, M. (2002). The validity of a self-reported delinquency scale: comparisons across gender, age, race, and place of residence. *Sociological Methods and Research* 30:492–529.

Ploeger, M. (1997). Youth employment and delinquency: Reconsidering a problematic relationship. *Criminology* 35:659–675.

Ramsey, T. G. (1997). *A test of social control elements and developmental processes to account for age-related variance in delinquent behavior.* Department of Sociology, University of Colorado, Boulder, CO.

Raudenbush, S. W. (1993). Modeling individual and community effects on deviance over time: Multi-level statistical models. In D. P. Farrington, R. J. Sampson, and P.-O. H. Wikström (eds.), *Integrating individual and ecological aspects of crime* (pp. 205–239). Stockholm: National Council for Crime Prevention.

Raudenbush, S. W. (1995). Hierarchical linear models to study the effects of social context on development. In J. M. Gottman (ed.), *The analysis of change.* Mahwah, NJ: Erlbaum, 39–56.

Raudenbush, S. W., and Chan, W. (1992). Growth curve analysis in accelerated longitudinal designs. *Journal of Research in Crime and Delinquency* 29(4):387–411.

Reed, M. D., and Rose, D. R. (1998). Doing what Simple Simon says? Estimating the underlying causal structures of delinquent associations, attitudes, and serious theft. *Criminal Justice and Behavior* 25:240–274.

Reed, M. D., and Rountree, P. W. (1997). Peer pressure and adolescent substance use. *Journal of Quantitative Criminology* 180(13):143–180.

Roitberg, T., and Menard, S. (1995). Adolescent violence: A test of integrated theory. *Studies on Crime and Crime Prevention* 4:177–196.

Rowe, D., and Britt, C., III. (1991). Developmental explanations of delinquent behavior among siblings: Common factor vs. transmission mechanisms. *Journal of Quantitative Criminology* 7(4):315–331.

Smith, D. A., and Brame, R. (1994). On the initiation and continuation of delinquency. *Criminology* 32(4):607–629.

Smith, D. A., Visher, C. A., and Jarjoura, G. R. (1991). Dimensions of delinquency: Exploring the correlates of participation, frequency and persistence of delinquent behavior. *Journal of Research in Crime and Delinquency* 28:6–32.

Tolan, P. H., and Thomas, P. (1995). The implications of age of onset for delinquency risk. II. Longitudinal data. *Journal of Abnormal Child Psychology* 23(2):157–181.

Triplett, R. A., and Jarjoura, G. R. (1994). Theoretical and empirical specification of a model of informal labeling. *Journal of Quantitative Criminology* 10:241–276.

Triplett, R. A., and Myers, L. B. (1996). Evaluating contextual patterns of delinquency: Gender-based differences. *Justice Quarterly* 12:59–84.

Warr, M. (1998). Life-course transitions and desistance from crime. *Criminology* 36:183–216.

Wells, L. E., and Rankin, J. H. (1996). Juvenile victimization: convergent validation of alternative measurements. *Journal of Research in Crime and Delinquency* 32:287–307.

Zhang, L. (1997). Informal reactions and delinquency. *Criminal Justice and Behavior* 24:129–150.

Zhang, L., and Messner, S. F. (2000). The effects of alternative measures of delinquent peers on self-reported delinquency. *Journal of Research in Crime and Delinquency* 37:324–337.

Index

215